# MOTO GUZZI
## *V-Twins*

## Mick Walker

The Crowood Press

First published in 1998 by
The Crowood Press Ltd
Ramsbury, Marlborough
Wiltshire SN8 2HR

**British Library Cataloguing in Publication Data**

A catalogue record for this book is available from the British
Library.

ISBN 1 86126 180 2

To the memory of my son Gary who died following an accident at
Brands Hatch in September 1994, whilst competing in the sport
he loved so much.

Typeset by Annette Findlay.

Printed in Great Britain by the Bath Press.

# Contents

# Acknowledgements

For the last quarter of a century the Moto Guzzi 90 degree V-twin has built up a loyal and enthusiastic band of owners and admirers right around the world. This has been possible because of its special set of values, including the toughness of its engine, the ease with which the maintenance work can be carried out – and most of all the pure pleasure provided by riding one of these unique machines out on the road. It is surely the most 'practical' of all Italian machines – a motorcycle that can transport its rider, passenger (and luggage if needed) almost anywhere, with the minimum of fuss.

The Guzzi V-twin story is also about people; for example, the Argentinian industrialist Alejandro De Tomaso, engineers such as Giulio Cesare Carcano, Lino Tonti and today, Angelo Ferrari; riders and race teams, and of course the countless Guzzi enthusiasts worldwide. There is also the factory's tremendous historical background, probably unmatched by any other Italian marque. In its time Moto Guzzi has built just about every engine configuration – horizontal singles, vertical singles, parallel twins, wide angle (120 degree) V-twins, three cylinders, four cylinders, V-8 and of course, the main subject of this book, the classical 90 degree V-twins.

*Moto Guzzi V-Twins* has only been possible because a number of key people have provided information, photographs and personal accounts, all given with the usual helpfulness which is so typical of the motorcycling fraternity. In particular, I should like to record a debt of thanks and appreciation to the Moto Guzzi factory and its British importers, Three Cross Motorcycles of Three Legged Cross, Dorset, for their unstinting efforts. I was also lucky to have been not only a Guzzi dealer, but also the official parts distributor for the UK during the 1970s which gave me 'inside information' on the subject. Also, to have ridden virtually every Guzzi V-twin from the 1965 700 V7 through to the latest California EV.

The racing section received the benefit of many entrants, tuners and competitors, including Jim Blomley, Amadeo Castellani, Roy Armstrong, Chris Clarke, John Sear, Paul Lewis and Keith Davies to name but a few. The majority of the photographs either came from Italian sources, the factory, the British importers or from my own files. However, I would also like to acknowledge the work of Vic Bates and Austin Colle. It is now left for me to wish you as much pleasure in reading *Moto Guzzi V-Twins* as I have had researching and writing it.

Mick Walker,
Wisbech,
Cambridgeshire
July 1998

# Foreword

*by Keith Davies*

Mick Walker and Moto Guzzi have been closely linked, in my mind, since March 1975. Back then Mick was a leading Moto Guzzi dealer and the sole official UK distributor for Moto Guzzi parts. I had just made a decision which was to change my life: I'd joined the new UK Moto Guzzi importer, Moto Guzzi Concessionaires (UK) Ltd Coburn & Hughes as the UK Sales Manager, working with the directors to establish Moto Guzzi firmly on the UK market. Since then, like Mick, my life has been inextricably bound up with Italian motorcycles and in particular Moto Guzzi, Ducati and Laverda.

To Italian bike enthusiasts everywhere, Moto Guzzi is very special indeed. Founded in 1921, it has gone on to produce just about every conceivable engine type and configuration, from 50cc two-strokes to V8 racing bikes. However, without doubt, history will forever primarily remember Moto Guzzi for its varied range of transverse V-twins in all their styles and capacities.

If you've never experienced the uniqueness of a Moto Guzzi V-twin, you owe yourself a ride at the earliest opportunity. But take a long test ride: 50 miles may well leave you doubting, 150 miles should help you to understand and by 500 miles you'll think either that it's great or quite the reverse. People are hardly ever neutral about a Moto Guzzi V-twin – you either love them and appreciate their qualities, or you don't.

Fortunately, enough enthusiasts do love them and these *Guzzisti* have enabled Moto Guzzi to survive both market recessions and the continued onslaught of breathtakingly varied and capable competition from Japan, Europe and the USA

Moto Guzzi V-twins are tough and built to last. The company is tough, too, and so is its new management team. As we move into the next millennium, the factory is readying itself for a move to a new and modern production facility in Monza. Their aim – to increase production dramatically and enter production with new high-performance liquid cooled transverse V-twins, which will be sold alongside the ageless and ever improving air-cooled twin.

So after almost thirty years of uninterrupted V-twin production, we can look forward to at least another decade of an engine concept that refuses to die. Moto Guzzi's unique series of V-twins have a past, present and, happily for Mick, myself and all Guzzi enthusiasts, an exciting future!

*Keith Davies, founder and Managing Director of British importers, Three Cross Motorcycles.*

# 1 A Glorious Past

The Great War of 1914–1918 was instrumental in the birth of what was to become over the following decades, Italy's biggest and most famous motorcycle marque, Moto Guzzi.

Before the outbreak of war there had already existed a fledgling Italian motorcycle industry thanks to the efforts of men such as Edoardo Bianchi (1897), the brothers Borg (1906), Giuseppe Gilera (1909) and Adalberto Garelli (1912).

Moto Guzzi's origins lay within the war itself. A young Carlo Guzzi who had been summoned to serve his country at the outbreak of hostilities, initially with the army, but eventually he found himself transferred to the air corps, and it was this move which was to be the key to his unlocking of a true biking legend.

Guzzi, by now a mechanic and driver, came into contact with two flying officers, Giorgio Parodi and Giovanni Ravelli, both young men of means from wealthy and influential families. Parodi's family was an old established dynasty of ship owners from the port of Genoa, while Ravelli, whose home was in Brescia, a large town already well-known in sporting motorcycling spheres, having already successfully competed in a number of pre-war racing events.

The three men soon became close friends, joined as they were by their mutual interest in motorcycling, and planned a business association for when the war ended. Guzzi would design, Parodi organize the finance, and Ravelli ride the machines to fame on the race circuit. But before their dream could become reality fate was to intervene, when a few short days after the end of the conflict in

the autumn of 1918, Ravelli lost his life in a flying accident. The winged-eagle emblem carried by virtually all the subsequent company's motorcycles, even to this day, was to be a constant reminder and a dedication to his memory. The two remaining partners then set about their task with a renewed purpose. First, they needed finance, and Parodi, as good as his word, came up with the necessary funds to enable a prototype to be constructed. The money for the project came from Parodi's father, Emanuele. The now-famous letter dated 3 January 1919, in which he granted approval to the project, is still kept in the Moto Guzzi museum within the factory at Mandello del Lario, on the eastern fringe of Lake Como in northern Italy. Translated, Emanuele Parodi's letter reads: 'So the answer you should give your companions is that on the whole I am in favour of the idea, that 1,500 or 2,000 liras [this being in a time when the lira was of much greater value than it is today!] for the experiment are at your disposal provided this figure is absolutely not exceeded, but

*The winged eagle emblem in Moto Guzzi's badge is in memory of the 'third man' Giovanni Ravelli, killed in a flying accident during 1918, shortly before the marque was founded.*

that I reserve the right to personally examine the design before giving my final support for seriously launching the product, because in the fortunate event that I like the design I am ready to go much further with no limitation on the figure.' As will become apparent the mere fact that Carlo Guzzi and Giorgio Parodi were from different social classes and were quite different personalities was really why the whole project was to be so strongly based. Although Guzzi himself had been brought up within a relatively poor family in the urban sprawl of Milan, both men shared a common bond in wanting the project to succeed. This, together with the stabilizing influence wielded by Parodi Senior, was to see the partnership through those testing early days.

As for personalities, the two men were as different as any two men could be. Carlo Guzzi being a reserved, quiet individual who was entirely bound up in his experiments and theories, and once convinced of the correctness of a design function would not be tempted to exceed what he knew to be prudent and safe. In other words, he was not a man to take unnecessary financial risks.

Giorgio Parodi, on the other hand, was both flamboyant and impulsive. It was a combination of both their respective natures which was to provide just the right ingredients for success. There is no doubt, had Carlo Guzzi been left wholly to his own devices his design genius would never have reached the public's attention. Conversely, had Giorgio Parodi taken total control of the company, it would have risen and fallen in a most spectacular fashion. But the combination of the two men provided what was to emerge as a unique formula for success which was to last 35 years; while the company is still going strong almost 80 years later.

Work on the first prototype machine was not completed until well into 1920. When it was shown to Parodi Senior, it not only got his nod of approval, but also a glowing comment of how much he was impressed by the standard of workmanship! The result was the additional funding as had been promised in the original document. Named simply GP (Guzzi and Parodi), the prototype was, for its day, an extremely advanced machine, full of real technical innovation. It was dominated by its engine, which displayed much that pointed towards aeronautical engineering practices, with its four parallel valves which were operated by a single overhead cam driven by shaft and bevel gears. There was also a dual ignition system with twin sparking plugs fired by a single German Bosch magneto. But perhaps even more interesting was the adoption of the layout which was to characterize the marque for much of its early years – a single cylinder laid horizontally with unit construction of engine and transmission. A prominent characteristic of the design which was also to endure for a long period was the 'bacon slicer' shape of the external flywheel. Yet another feature was Guzzi's adoption of the then unusual oversquare bore and stroke dimensions of 88 × 82mm. Almost all of this was virtually unheard of in its day. Not only

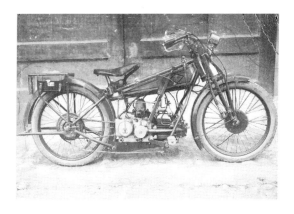

*The great-grandfather of all Moto Guzzis – the original GP prototype featured four valves and overhead cam, circa 1920.*

7

unit construction – with geared primary drive – but also the horizontal cylinder and a bore which was larger than the stroke. The frame was a sturdy affair with duplex front downtubes which passed either side of the cylinder head. Completing the picture came a pair of girder front forks, with dual springs placed centrally just forward of the steering head, square-section mudguards, a sprung single saddle, and a single brake which operated on the rear wheel. The front wheel carried a massive gear (like a sprocket) which drove the speedometer. The three-speed gearbox was operated by a massive hand lever mounted on the offside of the flat, box-like fuel tank.

The first printed word regarding the new machine, now renamed Moto Guzzi, came in the 15 December 1920 issue of *Motociclismo* magazine. The name change come about because Giorgio Parodi had not wanted the 'GP' to be taken as his initials and he suggested instead that it should be named Moto Guzzi, meaning simply Guzzi Motorcycle. For its time, the prototype was simply too advanced. Therefore Guzzi carried out something of a re-design for the production ver-

sion which soon followed. The overhead camshaft was ditched in place of the more simple pushrod operated valves whilst the cylinder head of the 498.4cc single (the bore and stroke measurement remained unchanged) sported two instead of four valves. This first production machine, known as the Tipo Normale (standard model) produced 8bhp at 3200rpm, operating via a three-speed gearbox with chain final drive. The fledgling company's ten employees built seventeen motorcycles in that first year, but the design, with its massive outside flywheel, semi-unit construction gearbox, and magneto ignition mounted centrally atop the engine/gearbox was to remain in production, albeit updated from time to time, until as late as 1976 and still retain its original 88 × 82mm engine dimensions.

Over the years, many variations of this classic format appeared, including the Tipo Sport (1923–1928), GT and GT16 (1928–1934), Tipo Sport 14 (1929–1930), Tipo Sport 15 (1931–1939), V, GTV, GTW and GTC (1934–1948), Tipi S and GTS (1934–1940), Condor (1938–1940) and Dondolino (a little

*Officially incorporated on 15 March 1921, during that first year, seventeen machines were produced from a total workforce of ten people, including the two founders, Giorgio Parodi and Carlo Guzzi.*

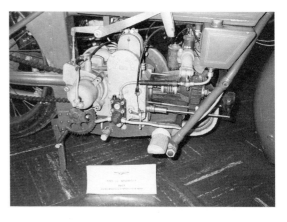

*The first production Guzzi, the horizontal single-cylinder Tipo Normale; built from 1921 through to 1924.*

*The Tipo Sport was produced between 1923 and 1928 and was typical of many early Guzzi's with its 88 × 82mm bore and stroke dimensions.*

rocking horse) (1946–1951) clubman's racers; the Astore (Goshawk) with fully enclosed valve gear (1949–1953) and finally, perhaps the best known of them all – the Falcone. The original Falcone was built from 1950 through to 1967, with a revised version, the Nuova Falcone, being produced from 1970 until 1976. It was also manufactured in military and police variants, as indeed were several of the other Guzzi big singles.

Apart from this vast range of five-hundreds, the horizontal single-cylinder layout was also offered in other capacities. The first came in 1932, with the introduction of the 174cc (59 × 63.7cc) P175, followed by a deriv-

---

**1932–1933 Three Cylinder**

Designed by Carlo Guzzi himself, the Tre Cilindri (Three Cylinder) was a magnificent grand touring motorcycle, which in many ways was far ahead of its time. Built in the period 1932–1933, the machine was powered by a near horizontal across-the-frame 498.8cc (56 × 67mm) ohv engine. Generating 25bhp at 5500rpm, it used a single British-made Amal carburettor, hand operated three-speed gearbox, multi-plate clutch, 3.25 × 19in tyres, girder front forks and an early type of rear springing. Capable of a genuine 100mph (160kph) it ranked alongside the very best machines of its day, includ-

ing the Brough Superior SS100 and original ohc Ariel Square Four. But it was also a time when Europe was struggling to come out of recession, and so there were simply not enough buyers for such a de luxe and expensive piece of machinery. It was nonetheless a triumph in engineering terms and was to signal Guzzi's arrival on the European, if not the world stage. Another three-cylinder Guzzi appeared in 1940. This time it was a pure-breed 491.8cc (59 × 60mm) racing machine with dohc and 65bhp at 8000rpm – thanks to the help of its Cozette supercharger. Making a successful debut on the very eve of Italy's entry into the war in June 1940 at the Circuito del Lido, Genova with Guglielmo Sandri at the controls, it looked set for bigger things. The war and the FIM's subsequent ban on supercharging conspired to seal its fate. So instead of being one of Guzzi's outstanding designs it was relegated to the sidelines of history.

*Designed by Carlo Guzzi, the Tre Cilindri (Three Cylinder) was a magnificent grand touring motorcycle which was an Italian rival to the top British bikes such as the Brough Superior SS100 and Ariel's original ohc Square Four.*

---

*The first of the smaller singles was the 174cc (59 × 63.7mm) P175 which arrived in 1932; it was followed by the P250 a couple of years later.*

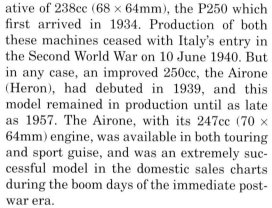

*An improved two-fifty, the Airone (Heron) debuted in 1939, and this model remained in production until as late as 1957. A 1952 Sport version is illustrated.*

ative of 238cc (68 × 64mm), the P250 which first arrived in 1934. Production of both these machines ceased with Italy's entry in the Second World War on 10 June 1940. But in any case, an improved 250cc, the Airone (Heron), had debuted in 1939, and this model remained in production until as late as 1957. The Airone, with its 247cc (70 × 64mm) engine, was available in both touring and sport guise, and was an extremely successful model in the domestic sales charts during the boom days of the immediate post-war era.

Right from the very beginning, Moto Guzzi had realized that there was no better form of publicity than participating in motorcycle sport; road racing in particular. So in 1921, to launch their very first products, the Mandello del Lario marque entered Aldo Finzi and Gino Cavendini for the Milano–Taranti long-distance road race on a pair of Corsa 2V five-hundred Guzzi singles. Both completed the course (an event in itself, in those far-off days) to become the first works' Guzzi riders which, in the future, would see the factory win virtually every race and championship not just in Italy, but eventually around the globe. Finzi and Cavendini took 20th and 22nd placings, and with their efforts not only proved their performance, but reliability too, the combi-

nation of these two features playing such a vital role in the Guzzi success story over the forthcoming years. Moto Guzzi's confidence was proved to be well placed just over a month later, when Finzi's brother Gino won the arduous Targa Florio in Sicily, then open to both automobiles and motorcycles. The following year, 1922, Guzzi garnered yet more racing successes, again using machines based on its standard production range. Racing was also instrumental in the re-adoption of technology from Guzzi's very first prototype, with its single overhead camshaft and 4-valve head. This new machine, coded Corsa 4V had made a winning debut at the local Circuito de Lario. This event is best described as the Italian equivalent of the Isle of Man TT Mountain circuit. Over a 24.8-mile (39.9km) lap around the public roads, the Lario circuit took in, like the Isle of Man, some breathtaking scenery and some extremely difficult going with an array of climbs, descents and hairpin bends around Lake Como, near the factory. Running through the eastern hills bordering the lake, it swept through the difficult bends of the Valbrona Valley, and an added hazard in those early days was a road surface of dirt rather than tarmac! First run in 1921, the Italian Tourist Trophy, as it was widely known, ran until 1939. All that survives today is a large monument which was erected alongside the old course and dedicated to its memory by the FIM (Italy's governing body for motorcycle sport) on 9 December 1961.

The 1924 Corsa 4V winning machine was ridden to victory by Pietro Ghersi who averaged 42.2mph (67.9kph) which, considering the tortuous nature of the course and the loose surface, was quite a feat. Ghersi's performance came a year after Guzzi's first victory in the event. This was achieved by a Corsa 2V ridden by Valentino Gatti, Carlo Guzzi's brother-in-law, who averaged 27.8mph (44.7kph). International recognition came later in 1924, when that September, Moto Guzzi won the European Championship, which that year was being staged as a single event held at Monza Autodrome on the outskirts of Milan. Guido Mentasi averaged 80.6mph (129.7kph) to take a popular victory. Even more publicity resulted, when, two weeks later, Mario Ghersi won the German Grand Prix on a similar machine. By now Moto Guzzi was well and truly on a roll, with the Mandello del Lario factory selling everything it could make, and it was fast becoming obvious that longer established marques such as Bianchi and Garelli had better keep on their toes.

Next, Carlo Guzzi, assisted by his elder brother, Giuseppe, designed a smaller version of their successful racing machine. But unlike its larger counterpart, this featured square 68 × 68mm bore and stroke dimensions, giving 246.8cc. Soon named the TT250, this machine was not only Guzzi's first foray into the quarter-litre category, but also marked the company's debut in the Isle of Man TT series, which came in 1926. Although the new machine was a success, the TT debut was very much a bittersweet affair. With a power output of 15bhp at 6000rpm, this meant a specific figure of 60bph per litre – almost unheard of at that time, and then only in the realms of auto-

mobile Grand Prix racing. This, coupled to a dry weight of only 105kg (231.5lb) meant a very competitive motorcycle. But the TT did not quite pan out as the Guzzi squad had hoped and was instead dogged with controversy. This was because even though Pietro Ghersi finished a brilliant runner up to Cotton-mounted C. W. Johnson – and had set the fastest lap at 63.12mph (101.6kph) drama was to follow. On his entry form, Ghersi had specified one particular make of spark plug, but had used a total of three plugs during the race, all of which were of a different make to that stated on the entry form. Only when the machine was examined by officials of the ACU (Auto Cycle Union) in the post-race *parc ferme* was the discovery made. In a sensational judgement, which *The Motor Cycle* (24 June 1926 issue) reported as 'The Guzzi Incident', Ghersi was deleted from the official results, even though he was still credited with the fastest lap.

The TT was to prove something of a bogey for the luckless Ghersi, for when he returned in 1928 he led the Lightweight (250cc) race only to retire when comfortably in the lead on the final lap. He then rode for Cotton in the 1929 Junior (350cc) and Senior (500cc) races, but with no success there either, he quit bikes for cars in 1930, driving for Alfa Romeo. Ghersi was back on two wheels again in 1931, piloting a two-fifty Guzzi single in the Lightweight TT, but again retired. Three times unlucky, he then gave up motorcycle sport entirely, driving cars for Bugatti and Maserati as well as Alfa Romeo, before finally retiring from competition in 1938. In 1935 however, Moto Guzzi, if not Ghersi, were to have their revenge when Irishman Stanley Woods won the Lightweight TT for the Italian company. The other riders were also contracted by Guzzi: the Italian Omobono Tenni and another Irishman, Wood's brother-in-law, Gordon Burney.

### 1933–1951 120 degree 500 V-twin

The first Guzzi V-twin was actually a racer and it debuted way back in 1933. The idea came as a way of making a competitive machine for the 500cc category by using a pair of 68 × 68mm cylinders from the successful works two-fifty racing design. Doubling up these measurements gave a displacement of 494.8cc. The cylinders were set at a very wide 120 degrees, giving a long wheelbase. Running on a compression ratio of 8.5:1 and breathing through a pair of 28.5mm Dell'Ortos the engine initially produced 44bhp at 7000rpm. Eighteen years later, when it was finally retired, the power output had risen to 47bhp.

Highlights in a career which spanned the war years, included Irishman Stanley Woods' victory in the 1935 Senior TT (he also won the Lightweight event on a Guzzi single that year), and the pairing of Terzo Bandini and Guglielmo Sandri who were victorious in the great Nord–Sud (North–South) road events of the 1930s which included the Milano–Napoli victories coming in both 1934 and 1937 (the latter with a sidecar attached!).

That great Italian legend, Omobono Tenni, gained many of his most famous victories with the Bicilindrica as the V-twin was more commonly known in Italy. Postwar it was also raced by leading British riders, Fergus Anderson and Bob Foster. Perhaps its most famous postwar victory came in the Swiss Grand Prix at Berne in May 1951, when Fergus Anderson won in appalling conditions of heavy rain which forced many more-fancied runners into an early retirement. The V-twin was finally pensioned off at the end of that year.

*(Top left)*
*Pre-war Guzzi 120-degree V-twin of the type used by Stanley Woods to win the 1935 Isle of Man Senior TT. It first appeared in 1933.*

*(Top right)*
*Post-war 494.8cc (68 × 68mm) V-twin engine – virtually identical to the original, but with power output upped from 44 to 47bhp.*

*(Bottom right)*
*Probably the five hundred V-twin racer's most famous victory came when Fergus Anderson won the Swiss Grand Prix at Berne in May 1951. At the end of that year the design was finally retired.*

*Omobono Tenni was without doubt the leading Italian rider of lightweight machinery in the years immediately prior to the outbreak of the Second World War. He was also the first man to score an all-Italian TT victory, a feat he achieved in the 1937 Lightweight (250cc) event. This photograph was taken at Genova in the summer of 1945.*

The combination of an Italian machine and Irish rider might have seemed a strange pairing but was about to make news. As *Motor Cycling* summed it up in their 26 June 1935 issue, 'For the first time in the history of the TT races an Italian machine won the Lightweight.' Stanley Woods put up a stirling performance despite poor weather conditions, to average 71.56mph (115.14kph) for the 264-mile (425km) distance. Woods went on to win the Senior TT a few days later, again on a Guzzi, but this time on a wide-angle V-twin (see page 12). Woods also made history by becoming the first man to win both the 250cc and 500cc classes of the TT in the same year.

More records were set two years later when Omobono Tenni became the first Ital-

---

### Stanley Woods

Many would argue that the greatest rider of the interwar period was Irishman Stanley Woods. He was born in Dublin in 1905 and competed in the TT for the first time in 1922 as a works rider for Cotton in the Junior race. The Gloucester company had been founded two years previously and was eagerly seeking publicity. Woods had gained the ride by writing to Cotton and saying how good he was; the story goes that they were so surprised to receive such a letter they simply caved in and lent him a bike! His Isle of Man debut was in quite spectacular style – not only did his bike catch fire while refuelling in his pit at half distance, but he recovered from this setback to finish a very creditable fifth!. The following year Stanley Woods entered all three TTs, but retired in the Lightweight and Senior. The Junior, like the other two, was over six laps, giving a total race distance of 226.5 miles (364.4km). After an action packed race which saw several favourites retire Woods emerged the winner at an average speed of 55.73mph (89.67kph) to give Cotton its first TT victory. It was also the fastest race average on the island that year.

After two barren years of no finishes, he returned to the TT as a Norton works rider in 1926 and repaid them handsomely by winning the Senior race in convincing fashion. And this really was where his career took off. He stayed with Norton for eight years, from 1926 to 1933, bringing them victory in the TT in 1926, 1932 and 1933. The latter two years he was supreme – winning both Senior and Junior events. He then did the double yet again in 1935, aboard Italian Moto Guzzi machines, winning the Senior on a V-twin and the Lightweight on a horizontal single. Towards the end of his career Woods moved to Velocette and in 1936, finished runner up in the Senior, but set a new outright TT lap record at 86.98mph (139.95kph). His last TT victory came in the 1939 Junior on a Velocette and his final tally was ten TT victories, which even to this day, has only been bettered by two men, Mike Hailwood and Joey Dunlop. Postwar, Stanley became the Guzzi distributor for Southern Ireland. His close contacts meant that in October 1956 he got to ride one of the legendary V-8 models around Monza to celebrate his fifty-first birthday.

ian to win a TT by finishing ahead of the field in the 1937 Lightweight race. Most observers agree that he was the finest rider produced by Italy during the interwar period. An interesting aside is that the 1937 victory had a very special significance for the whole Tenni family, as their newly-born son was named Titono (TT) in recognition of the event. Less successful, but still interesting technically was the 492.2cc (56 × 60mm) horizontal four, with pushrod operated valves, supercharging at three-speed transmission. But for all the modern lines of the engine the four never lived up to its potential and was soon axed for the company's future plans.

On the very eve of war came a supercharged version (actually there were more than one type) of the single-cylinder two-fifty, the first of which appeared in 1938 and a three-cylinder 491.8cc (59 × 60mm) dohc model with steeply inclined cylinder. Again, this latter machine was supercharged; the factory claiming a power output of 65bhp at 8000rpm. Like the rest of Europe, the factory's smooth running was rudely interrupted in June 1940 when Mussolini

*One of the 250cc class supercharged engines used by Guzzi for racing and record breaking just prior to the outbreak of war. It put out 38bhp at 7800rpm.*

plunged Italy into a war it was largely unprepared to fight. In the months leading up to this, and for most of the war, Guzzi were involved in supplying the Italian military authorities with a series of motorcycles (these included the famous Alce and Trialce models), but fortunately, Guzzi's lakeside location in mountainous country protected it during the heavy Allied bombing of northern Italy from 1943 until the end of the conflict. As a result, unlike many of its rivals, Guzzi were in a position to resume production of civilian motorcycles and recommence their race effort almost at soon as the war ended in the spring of 1945. The major difference between the racing scene prewar and postwar, was the decision taken by the sports international body, the FIM, to ban all forms of supercharging. For Guzzi this meant their campaign, except for the wide-angle V-twin five-hundred, rested firmly on the normally aspirated singles. Much of the initial postwar racing development was entrusted to Ing. Antonio Micucci, who had joined Moto Guzzi in the winter of 1942 and who was promoted to managing designer in 1945. It was in September that year that Carlo Guzzi laid out the basic specification for a brand new Bicilindrica Bialbero (twin cylinder, double camshaft). Progress was rapid, for very early in 1946, construction of the first prototype began. Less than a year later, this interesting machine was ready to undertake its initial testing. The original design had been laid down as a supercharged machine, so the cylinder heads of the 247.2cc (54 × 54mm) dohc twin called for a change from 60 to 80 degrees included angle to accommodate larger diameter valves. At an early stage in the development cycle the power output was superior to that being achieved by the existing single-cylinder Albatros racer. These tests were not only carried out on the bench, but also on the autostrada, where the new twin proved itself capable of close to 100mph (160kph) first time out. This equated to a shade over 20bhp at 9100rpm; all this was achieved on low-grade, 73-octane fuel. Ultimately, the power was upped to 25bhp at the lower engine speed of 9000rpm. Correspondingly, maximum speed rose to 105mph (169kph). The original prototype, with which all the test programme was carried out, was joined by a second machine in the spring of 1948. At the end of May, company president, Giorgio Parodi, together with Ing. Micucci, Omobono Tenni, Ing. Moretto (engine specialist), two mechanics and a total of no less than ten various Guzzi motorcycles arrived in the Isle of Man for the forthcoming TT. Included were the pair of dohc parallel twins. Both were for Stanley Woods' protégé, Dubliner Manliff Barrington, to race. After completing a relatively trouble-free practice period, Barrington's twin led the Lightweight race for the first two laps, but on lap three, the Irishman's luck ran out when the machine expired about half-way into the circuit. Before his retirement, Barrington had averaged around 75mph (120kph). *The Motor Cycle* race report commented, 'It [the 250 twin] is too new for immediate triumph, but it will be hard to lick in 1949.' But this was not to be, instead Guzzi taking the decision to update, yet again, its venerable quarter-litre horizontal single. The twin was shelved, which in the light of subsequent events was to prove a short-sighted move, as the appearance of the twin cylinder NSU Rennmax in 1952 effectively ended Moto Guzzi's dominance of the 250cc class.

Even though the introduction of the World Championship series for the 1949 season meant increased publicity for whoever won the individual classes (125, 250, 350, 500cc and sidecar), Guzzi still viewed the TT as the year's premier single event. The factory's support was rewarded by them gaining several post-war TT victories. Manliff Barrington won the Lightweight in 1947, Maurice Cann (after Barrington had retired

on the twin) repeated the performance in 1948, Barrington won again in 1949, Tommy Woods did it in 1951, while Fergus Anderson won in 1952 and again in 1953. These victories were followed by Bill Lomas and Ken Kavanagh who became Junior TT winners in 1955 and 1956 respectively.

Only a year later, the long connection with Grand Prix road racing came to an end when Guzzi joined Gilera and FB Mondial in withdrawing from the sport. For many, this was to mark the end of an era, viewed now as the golden days of the European racing effort. By then, Moto Guzzi had scored more than 3,000 international racing victories throughout the world, and no fewer than eight world championships: Bruno Ruffo, 1949 and 1951 250cc; Enrico Lorenzetti, 1952 250cc; Fergus Anderson, 1953 and 1954 350cc; Bill Lomas, 1955 and 1956 350cc; and finally, Keith Campbell, 1957 350cc. So Guzzi's record up to the end of 1957 was a magnificent 3,329 international racing victories, 47 Italian championships, 55 national championships, 11 Isle of Man TT wins, and 14 world championships for the machines' riders and manufacturers.

Hidden amongst this myriad of facts and figures are a maze of star riders and machines and their development histories. Added to this is the fact that the company built and raced motorcycles with virtually every conceivable configuration, with single, twin, three, four and even eight cylinders.

Against this glamorous backcloth, Guzzi's standard production motorcycles might seem rather tame. But the fact is that following the end of the Second World War the factory had reinforced its position as the largest of all Italian bike builders, with a range that included several top selling models, including the Airone and Falcone. The traditional flat singles were soon joined by a number of new designs including the 64cc (42 × 46cc) Motoleggera 65 and Cardellino (goldfinch) two-strokes, and the Galletto

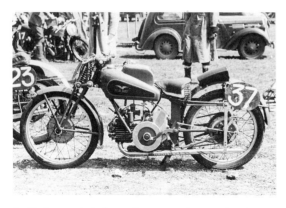

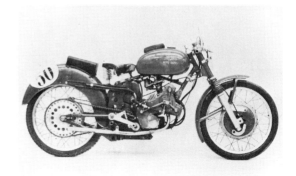

*Built from 1939 through to 1949 (except for the war years) the 246.8cc (68 × 68mm) Albatros was Guzzi's racer for privateers. Maximum power was 20bhp at 7000rpm – tuned versions gave higher figures.*

*Designed by Ing. Antonio Micucci, the 247.2cc (54 × 54mm) dohc racing twin first appeared in 1947. The original prototype was joined by a second machine (seen here) in the spring of 1948. Although it led the TT that year before retiring, Guzzi axed it in favour of its long running single.*

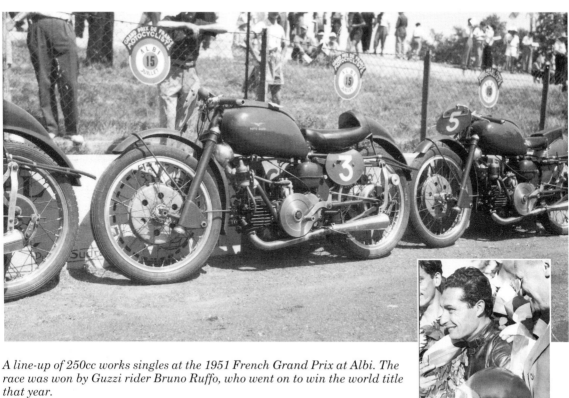

*A line-up of 250cc works singles at the 1951 French Grand Prix at Albi. The race was won by Guzzi rider Bruno Ruffo, who went on to win the world title that year.*

*The 1951 250c world champion Bruno Ruffo. He had also won the crown for Guzzi in 1949, the first ever year of the championship series.*

### Amazing Sidecar Records

On 26 August 1952, Luigi Cavanna, using one of the prewar 248cc supercharged single-cylinder Moto Guzzi engines broke no fewer than twenty world sidecar speed records in a single day on the Munich–Ingoldstadt autobahn in Germany. Cavanna not only captured eight standing-start and flying-start records up to ten miles in the 350cc class (the smallest class in Category B), but he also broke the existing records in all the other Category B classes (500, 750 and 1200cc) for the five kilometres and five miles flying start, and ten kilometres and ten miles standing start. Cavanna's machine was extensively streamlined and was one of the earlier beneficiaries of Guzzi's recently opened wind tunnel facilities. At the rear, the streamlining blended into a massive, vertical stabilizing fin. Ballast was carried instead of a passenger.

The newly created records were as follows:

*Standing start*
One km (350cc) 73mph (117kph)
One mile (350cc) 84mph (136kph)
Ten km (all classes) 117mph (188kph)
Ten miles (all classes) 108mph (175kph)

*Flying start*
One km (350cc) 137.5mph (221kph)
One mile (350cc) 137mph (220kph)
Five km (all classes) 128mph 206kph)
Five mile (all classes) 126mph (203kph)

As a matter of further interest, Cavanna's speeds for the flying kilometre and flying mile were higher than the 250cc solo records for those distances (the latter then standing at 132.5mph (213.2kph) and 131.5mph (211.6kph) respectively), and his speeds for the five kilometres and five miles beat the existing 250cc and 350cc solo times too!

*Luigi Cavanna set no less than twenty new world speed records with this supercharged two-fifty Guzzi single and sidecar over the Munich–Ingoldstadt autobahn, 26 August 1952.*

*Scot Fergus Anderson, later to become Guzzi race manager, with a four-valve, dohc two-fifty single during testing at the Osidaletti circuit, February 1953. This was the first appearance of the distinctive 'bird beak' streamlining used that year.*

*The fully streamlined 349.2cc (80 × 69.5mm) dohc single used by Bill Lomas to win the 1955 350cc world title; the same rider repeated the performance for Guzzi the following year.*

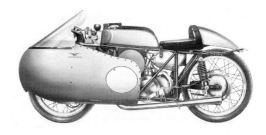

*Italian National Championships, Monza 6 May 1956. Enrico Lorenzetti's Guzzi (21) battles for the lead with MV's Carlo Ubbiali (23).*

*Guzzi production 1947. The machines are top selling Motoleggera two-strokes. Using a 64cc (42×46mm) rotary valve two-stroke engine, these tiny machines provided cheap, reliable transport for thousands in postwar Italy.*

span of sixteen years from 1950 through to 1966. Similarly long-lived was the 98cc (50 × 50mm) and 110.3cc (52 × 52mm) rotary valve two-stroke Zigolo (bunting). The sporting Lodola (hobby) introduced in 1956 was another single, but this was a four-stroke with a vertical cylinder and chain-driven single overhead camshaft. Up to 1958, the Lodola had a capacity of 174.5cc (62 × 57.8mm), but for 1959 this was increased to 235cc (68 × 64mm) but with ohc replaced by ohv. Besides its standard and sportster versions, it was also a gold medal winner on several occasions in the ISDT (International Six Days Trial) with Italian team riders using 175, 235 and a special version of 247cc (69 × 64mm). The Lodola also had the distinction of being Carlo Guzzi's final design.

Another four-stroke single produced in more than one engine size was the Stornello (starling). This was available from 1960 as first a 123.1cc (52 × 58mm), before being joined by 153.24cc (58 × 58mm) version in 1968. It was built in both round engine cases and square style cases in the smaller version, but only in the latter with the larger

(rooster). This was a successful cross between a scooter and a conventional motorcycle; at first, in prototype form only a 150cc (61 × 53mm) was built, followed by versions with 159.5cc (62 × 53mm) before being finally offered in 192cc (65 × 58mm) form. All these engines were horizontal ohv, with three- or four-speed gearboxes. In its various forms, the Galletto had a production life

*Built from 1950 through to 1966 (in capacities ranging from 150 to 192cc), the Galletto (rooster) was neither scooter nor motor cycle, but a successful marriage featuring the best of both worlds. It used a four-stroke ohv engine.*

*Another popular Guzzi lightweight of the immediate postwar era was the Zigolo. Making its debut as a 98cc in 1953, it was then upped to 110cc in 1960. Production finally ceased in 1966. All versions used a horizontal rotary valve two-stroke engine.*

## The Incredible V-8

Sitting quietly on the grass near the famous Parabolica bend of the Monza autodrome, Ing. Giulio Cesare Carcano, the brilliant chief of Guzzi's experimental and racing department, was watching the 500cc class practising for the 1954 Italian GP. That year had not been a good one for the factory in the 500cc category. The four-cylinder inline machine with fuel injection and shaft drive, designed in 1952 by Ing. Carlo Giannini (responsible with Pietro Remor and others for the prewar Rondine which became the Gilera four) had proved a costly failure. Not only did the inline four prove less than reliable, but on winding circuits the torque reaction from its shaft drive made it almost impossible to ride. On the other hand, the second racing model fielded by Guzzi, the horizontal single, developed by Carcano and his team, although excellent through the bends, lacked steam down the straights, and thus was unable to challenge the MV and Gilera fours on the faster circuits.

From his trackside vantage, Carcano was watching a rider of one of his rival fours making a major riding error while negotiating the bend and, even worse, showing no sign of any improvement on succeeding laps. Yet, on consulting his stop watch, Carcano discovered that the rider's lap times were far better than those of his Guzzi riders who negotiated that bend with perfect technique, flat out on their singles. 'This is too much!' he exclaimed. 'We'll have to start with a clean sheet of paper and design a new multi-cylinder job.'

*Over forty years on and the Guzzi V-8 is still the world's only eight-cylinder Grand Prix motorcycle.*

And so it was. The inline four was abandoned at the end of the season (the single, meanwhile, was refined with some good results on appropriate circuits), and work put in hand on what was to become the most glamorous racing motorcycle of all time, the Moto Guzzi V-8. It featured eight cylinders arranged in two blocks of four, at an angle of 90 degrees. The axis of the engine was transverse to the frame – to simplify the employment of the chain final drive – which Carcano rated as more practical than shaft for the race track. Other features included dohc and water cooling.

The reason for such a complex design? The cubic capacity of each cylinder could be reduced to a minimum, for very high rpm and consequent high power output. There was the added attraction that the originality of the design gave great

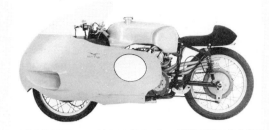

*The 1956/57 version of the V-8. Highlights included being timed at over 180mph (290kph) in the 1957 Belgian GP and finishing fourth in the seven-lap Senior TT the same year on only seven cylinders. Development was not fully complete before Guzzi quit racing a few months later.*

possibilities of development in a new field (nobody had attempted such an arrangement for a motorcycle four-stroke engine before) and the overall dimensions, both longitudinal and transversal, could still be quite reasonable, so enabling the engine unit to be housed in a conventional double-cradle frame. The linear speed of the tiny pistons was actually lower than those of a single-cylinder 500cc racing engine such as a Manx Norton operating at around half the engine revolutions! The project crystallized during the winter of 1954–1955 in an atmosphere of the greatest secrecy. However, Carcano was not only a brilliant designer, and a champion yachtsman, but also had a great sense of humour. As vivid proof of this, without adding any written explanation, he sent his friends in the press, who were clamouring for information, a drawing of his latest project seen from the right-hand (offside) and invited them to guess what it was. Not a correct answer was published – in fact one journal went as far as to suggest it was a jet turbine powered engine! The prototype first appeared midway through 1955 at an Italian national event at Senigallia. The newcomer was a sensation, even though it was not exactly raced. The same thing happened during practice for the Italian GP later that year. The main teething

*The 498.48cc (44 × 42mm) dohc water-cooled engine. Each cylinder was fed by its own 20mm Dell'Orto SS1 carburettor.*

troubles encountered were with the ignition, carburation and mechanically, with crankshaft lubrication. With bore and stroke dimensions of 44 × 42mm, giving each cylinder a swept volume of 62.31cc, the 498.48cc engine was oversquare, with a 0.932:1 bore to stroke ratio. During the early stages of development, power output of the V-8 was 65bhp at 12,000rpm, but gradually this figure was increased. By the end of 1957, when Guzzi decided to withdraw from Grand Prix racing, it had been boosted to almost 80bhp at 14,000rpm – almost ten horsepower more than the best of its four-cylinder rivals and unsurpassed until the 1970s. There is little doubt, that had the factory not quit, the V-8 would most likely have dominated Grand Prix racing for many years. Instead, as the history books reveal, this honour went to MV Agusta – but with three and four cylinder models.

*The 174.4cc (62×57.8cc) ohc Lodola (Lark) was Carlo Guzzi's final design. Debuting at the Milan Fair in April 1956, a Sport version (seen here) arrived in 1958. The final version, a 235cc (68×64mm), used pushrods and ran through to 1966.*

*A big cheer from race fans at the 1963 Italian GP was reserved for members of Italy's victorious ISDT Silver Vase team; all rode Guzzi singles.*

engine size. Production of both ended in the mid-1970s. The Dingo and Trotter were both small-capacity two-strokes. The Dingo was available from 1973 through to 1976. It had a 48.9cc (38.5×42mm) engine and was built in just about every conceivable version from the Turismo commuter moped, right through to the Dingo Super Sport and Cross models for the young enthusiast. The Trotter was a 40.8cc (37 × 38mm) two-speed automatic commuter moped. Another top selling Guzzi was the Motocarri series. Essentially a cross

between a motorcycle (the front half), and a lightweight truck (the rear section), the first version, the Tipo 107, was initially offered way back in 1928. Powered by the familiar 498.4cc (88 × 82mm) horizontal single, the Motocarri in 500cc class size was listed until as late as 1980 (except for the war years), making it Guzzi's longest running model of all time. During that period, the basic concept was unchanged, and after fifty-two years the final variant could be seen to have much in common with the first. The reason

*One of Guzzi's top selling models down the years was the Motocarri series. Essentially a cross between a motorcycle and a lightweight truck, it ran from 1928 until as late as 1980. It was also the Mandello del Lario factory's longest running model, spanning an incredible fifty-two years with hardly any changes.*

for the machine's incredible life span was the practical use to which the three-wheel vehicle could be put. At minimum running cost, it could cope with almost every urban task from goods delivery to sewage collection, plus everything in between. The same concept was also offered in other engine sizes as the 192cc Galletto-powered Motocarri Ercolino (Little Hercules) built during 1956–1970 and the much shorter-lived 110 Zigolo-based Motocarri Alce of 1962–1963. There were also a number of moped-based three-wheelers, named Ciclocarros. The first of these was the Ciclocarro Dingotre (Dingo three) (1965–1968), followed by the Ciclocarro Furghino (small van) of 1968–1971. In addition, several interesting Motocarri prototypes were built including a 238cc (68 × 64mm) horizontal single in 1934 and finally a twin cylinder diesel-powered three-wheeler in 1960. But it was to be an even less obvious source which ultimately played such a key role in producing the engine configuration which forms the main content of this book – the 90 degree V-twin. This was spawned by a lineage of military vehicles.

It all began with the Mototriciclo 32, which utilized the standard 498.4cc, horizontal single-cylinder engine. The '32' had the front section of a 1933 Sport 15 grafted on to a twin wheel chassis similar to that found on the civilian Motocarri. However, for military use, the Moto Guzzi three-wheeler did not achieve the same level of success enjoyed by its civilian counterpart and only managed to remain in production until 1936. Just prior to the war, and during its course, Guzzi built a three-wheel armoured machine-gun carrier, and an experimental miniature tank which was designed to operate on steep hillsides by extending one track below the other. The factory even built a military truck with two wheels at the front and one at the rear, powered by a rear-mounted five-hundred flat-single. After supplying a series of both military and police motorcycles including versions of the well-known Falcone in the 1950s, Guzzi's management were asked to build an entirely new military vehicle by the Italian government. Called the 3 × 3, this first appeared in prototype form in 1960 and was the brainchild of General Garbari. The engine which was ultimately to play such a vital role in Guzzi's motorcycle future was designed specially for the 3 × 3 by none other than Ing. Guilio Cesare Carcano (who had carried out much of the design work for both the 350 dohc single and 500 V8 racers of the 1950s). According to Mario Columbo in his book *Moto Guzzi*, the V7 engine project originally started life as a souped-up version for the Fiat Toplino. First, a 500, then a 650cc

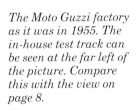
*The Moto Guzzi factory as it was in 1955. The in-house test track can be seen at the far left of the picture. Compare this with the view on page 8.*

*Powered by a 90-degree 754cc (80 × 75mm) ohv V-twin engine, the 3 ×3 military tractor led directly to the first of the V-twin motorcycles. This strange looking device was built for the Italian army between 1960 and 1963.*

*Carlo Guzzi pictured here (right) during the early 1960s. He died in November 1964, aged 75.*

engine was built which mated perfectly to the Fiat's transmission. The larger version developed some 34bhp and was capable of propelling the vehicle to 87mph (140kph). A lack of agreement with Fiat finally killed off the project but the basic engine design was then used in the 3 × 3, albeit in detuned form.

Weird is the only way of describing the 3 × 3, certainly it was one of the most bizarre vehicles ever to be constructed. During the late 1950s, the Italian Defence Ministry in Rome first conceived the requirement for a go-anywhere, lightweight tractor to operate under virtually any condition, over any terrain including deep mud, sand or snow. The final result of this complex specification was a three-wheel vehicle which plainly owed much to the Guzzi Motocarri principle, and the 3 × 3 was most certainly able to achieve almost impossible tasks – it could even climb almost vertical surfaces! The driver sat out in the open, and unlike the conventional Motocarri, the 3 × 3 had a steering wheel and car-type steering column. Behind him was a 53 litre (11.7 imp gal) fuel tank and a spare wheel. The single front and twin rear wheels all carried heavy-duty 6.00 × 15

tyres, and for heavy going, the rear wheel could be fitted with tracks after lowering retractable bogie wheels. But it was the engine layout which attracted much of the interest and was to deliver so much more in the future, in a role which is doubtful that its creator could ever have imagined. It was a 90 degree V-twin of 745cc (80 × 75mm). Although the 'paper' power figure was only 20bhp at 4000rpm, this hid the massive amounts of engine torque available, making it ideal for its intended role. The compression ratio of 6.5:1 was obviously intended for torque rather than outright power as were other details such as camshaft profile and valve sizes. At the rear of the engine was a single plate dry clutch, and behind this was a six-speed gearbox which drove the rear wheels by Cardan shaft. Although only produced in limited quantities between 1960 and 1963, the 3 × 3 was of equal significance to the future of Moto Guzzi, as had been the original G&P prototype back in 1920. For from this unlikely source was to be born a range of motorcycles which would still be very much in evidence as the twenty-first century beckons.

# 2  V7 *Arrivo*

On either side of Lake Como stands towering mountainous terrain. The town of Lecco is at the southernmost tip of the lake and to the traveller arriving from the urban and industrial flatlands of Milan, the shock to the system is breathtaking. The road into Lecco leads over a long bridge into the streets of the town, many of them still wearing the cobbles of antiquity. A casual visitor might never notice the sign to the left which takes the initiated northward, along a series of tree-lined streets at the edge of the lake. As the town is left behind, the road ahead can be seen clinging perilously to the foot of a steep mountainside ensuring that the highway itself twists and turns around the contours of the water. Quite often, it suffers from the dangers of landslides and rockfalls for a stretch of some seven miles, when all of a sudden, around yet another bend, the cliff-face retreats, a road sign leaps forward with 'Mandello del Lario' emblazoned upon it and

the visitor finds himself within a sizeable township, housing not only the population, but Italy's most famous motorcycle factory also.

It was against such a setting that the first prototype of what was ultimately to emerge as the V7 was begun in 1964. As related in the previous chapter, the V-twin's power unit had begun life motovating a small military tractor whilst the V7 motorcycle was created with military and police work very much in mind, rather than the civilian market. Early the following year, the first of the pre-production models went for governmental inspection, the full story of this being related in Chapter 5. But even before these official tests had begun, the factory had realized that the machine was also entirely suitable for the field of everyday use. Soon, a civilian prototype was built and tested. This machine was given its public debut in December 1965 at the 39th International

*The original civilian 703.717cc (80 × 70mm) V7 made its public début at the Milan Show in December 1965. It had been developed from the prototypes funded for police and military useage by the Italian government.*

Milan Show at which no less than 599 firms from eight countries attended. It was immediately proclaimed as the star exhibit. *Motor Cycle News* in their issue of 8 December 1965 said, 'There was the monumental Moto Guzzi 700cc V7, with a layout that was dictated by army and police designers rather than by the factory. It weighs in at a colossal 470lb (213.2kg), is a four-stroke pushrod ohv transverse V-twin, with a four-speed box and a top speed in excess of 110mph.' A feature of the show in general was that faced with a falling home market, the Italian motorcycle industry was following much the same pattern as the British at that time, and placing greater emphasis on exports. The background was a serious sales crisis, with the domestic bike builders in Italy attempting to stem a crash in demand of some 30 per cent since the previous year – which had itself seen declining sales. But unlike their British brothers at that time, who simply seemed to be giving up despondently, the leading Italian marques were not prepared to take this lying down. Instead, they made a real bid to revive flagging interest in a trade that only a few short years earlier had enjoyed the enthusiastic support of more than two million of their fellow countrymen. So the Milan exhibition of 1965 witnessed a whole new crop of models from the majority of Italy's most famous names, including MV Agusta, Benelli, Laverda, Moto Morini, Gilera and Ducati; but the new Guzzi heavyweight V-twin was the most significant of the new arrivals.

The V-7 was a big, big bike by any standard. It was also the biggest and fastest roadster to have ever graced the famous production line at the Mandello del Lario plant. But like many a famous machine before it, there was a touch of genius – this time the gifted hand of perhaps the greatest designer Italy has ever seen – Ing. Giulio Cesare Carcano. Less than a decade earlier, his innovative mind had brought the world what is still

today regarded as the most famous racing motorcycle of all time, the legendary 498.58cc (44 × 42mm) V8 Grand Prix racer. The tremendous speed and the awesome technical specification of his engineering masterpiece are still held in awe over forty years after it was last raced. During the 1957 Belgian GP, the watercooled dohc 'dustbin'-faired V8 had been timed at over 178mph (286kph), and, without a doubt, if Guzzi had not quit the GP scene at the end of that year, Carcano's masterpiece would have ruled the racing world for a good many years, and Guzzi, not MV, would have dominated the blue riband 500cc racing category.

So why you ask, had Moto Guzzi (together with FB Mondial and Gilera) quit racing at all? The simple answer was money, or lack of it. Even during the late 1950s the sellers' market of the immediate postwar period in Italy was rapidly becoming a buyer's one – fuelled by over production and falling demand, Guzzi simply could not afford to fund the vast sums needed to go on racing at the highest level. But a continued decline in sales throughout the 1960s saw Guzzi slip deeper and deeper into a financial quagmire. In truth, had not the government largely funded the development costs of the V7 project, even this would not have been possible. Shortly after the launch of the V7 at the Milan Show at the end of 1965, things got even worse and by mid 1966 the situation was critical.

Bankruptcy was only avoided by expending the entire Parodi family fortune, and later that year Moto Guzzi was forced into compulsory court administration (the Italian equivalent of receivership). On 1 February 1967 a trusteeship company called SEIMM (Societe Esercizio Moto Meccaniche SpA.) set up by the creditor banks and the IMI (state financing agency), effectively took over the financial control of the company to enable Guzzi to continue trading. The president of this controlling body was Prof.

Arnaldo Marcartinio. Besides a falling market Guzzi had suffered from another problem – that of the men at the top of the management structure. The 'founding fathers' had by then all left the scene, a process which had started during the Second World War, when Emanuele Parodi had died at almost the same time as his nephew Angelo. His son Giorgio died suddenly in 1955, and to complete the gloomy picture, Carlo Guzzi by now old and ill, died in 1964 at the age of 75, shortly after finally retiring from the company he had helped create some forty-five years earlier.

By 1966, the only remaining link was Giorgio Parodi's brother Enrico, who had himself joined Guzzi in 1942. Although in many ways a gifted man, he was not, unfortunately, a prudent one, being responsible for a series of unfortunate speculations, many outside the motorcycle industry, which caused the entire Parodi empire to crumble just when Moto Guzzi had to cope with its biggest-ever crisis. This meant that not only were a large number of workers made redundant, but a severe pruning of the model range (which at that time, except for the V7, was entirely comprised of single-cylinder machines of various capacities, both two- and four-stroke). But the one ray of hope amidst a horizon of gloom was the V7 project. Thanks to its police/military heritage, the V7 was designed with a priority given over to simplicity, ease of maintenance and reliability in service. In many ways, in fact, for a motorcycle it was surprisingly 'agricultural', especially when one compares it to the vast majority of designs which began to appear with the dawning of the Superbike age.

The V7 name was drawn from the engine's transverse 90-degree V-twin layout, and its original capacity of 703.717cc (80 × 70mm). Running on a compression ratio of 9:1, the oversquare pushrod motor pumped out 50bhp at a relatively leisurely 6000rpm. The engine layout provided superb accessi-

bility and its simplicity and relatively 'soft' state of tune made for a long, maintenance-free life. These characteristics were to prove the design's strongest and most enduring assets over the years. There were, however, one or two features which seemed at odds with the designer's priorities as evidenced elsewhere. One such feature was the use of chrome-plated cylinder bores. This might have been a technically superior solution, offering as it did closer running tolerances and potentially longer life (under ideal operating conditions), but it has the disadvantage that if the bore becomes worn or scored, only a complete new cylinder and piston assembly will suffice; whereas a cast-iron liner can be rebored several times, or have a replacement sleeve pressed in when its largest oversize has been exhausted. It was therefore of the utmost importance that the pistons were ideally matched to the cylinder on manufacture, and Moto Guzzi cylinder/piston assemblies were given three individual sizes to ensure that they were within tolerance. Class 'A' represented 80.00 to 80.006mm, class 'B' from 80.006 to 80.012mm, and class 'C' between 80.012 and 80.018mm. The pistons were of Borgo manufacture and featured a high dome, although

*The early V7 engine had several differences compared with the models which followed, including carburettors, starter motor and valve covers.*

without the usual valve pockets. They carried three compression rings above the 22mm diameter gudgeon pin, and a single scraper ring at the base of the skirt, which was solid.

The one-piece steel crankshaft had steel con-rods with bolt-up big-end eyes running on thin wall split-end big-end shells. Like the main bearings, these were manufactured in AL-TIN alloy and were available in various oversizes. The original thickness of the standard big-end bearings was from 1.534 to 1.543mm, and underside half bearings were available in 0.254mm, 0.508mm, 0.762mm and 1.016mm. Mains were originally from 37.995 to 37.959mm in diameter for the front mainshaft (flywheel) bearing, and 53.970 to 53.931mm for the rear (timing) bearing. Undersizes were made in 0.2, 0.4, 0.6 and 0.8mm thicknesses. Both the crankpin area and the main bearing surfaces were constructed so that if very slight seizing marks were detected, these could be eliminated using fine carborundum – but if the surfaces were deeply scored or worn oval, regrinding had to take place before the next bearing size could be used. After a regrind, it was necessary to restore the shoulder relief radiuses, 1.5mm for the crankpin and 3mm for the mainshaft at the flywheel end.

Like the crankcase and cylinder barrels, the cylinder heads were constructed in light alloy, and they were each retained by four long and two short studs passing through the cylinders and screwing into the crank cases. Oil tightness was ensured by a paper cylinder base gasket and six cylinder head bolt O-rings per cylinder. The cylinder head gasket was a thick car-type sandwich. Each exhaust port was threaded in the alloy to receive a matching screwed nut retaining the exhaust pipe, while the inlet had separate stubs. These were bolted in place with a heat-resistant gasket and three large Allen screws, ready to receive one of the pair of

*A 1967 production V7 under test in Germany; very much a luxury grand touring motorcycle for transporting one or two people in supreme comfort.*

Dell'Orto SSI 29 carburettors. Easy access to the valve gear on either side was provided by a large aluminium rocker cover, inscribed with the 'Moto Guzzi' legend and fixed to the head with eight Allen screws and a one-piece gasket. Underneath this cover, a cast-iron one-piece detachable support held each pair of rockers in place. The tappets were of the simple adjuster screw and locknut variety. The valves themselves were inclined at 70 degrees, and a 34.6mm exhaust and 38.6 inlet were used. These were fitted with single coil springs and seated on special cast-iron inserts. The camshaft was centrally located between the cylinders, and the base of each pushrod located on a tappet which ran on the appropriate camshaft lobe. The front of the camshaft was connected to the large upper timing gear, part of a matched train of three helical-cut steel gears for the timing and oil-pump drive, housed in the timing chest at the front of the engine. The other end of the camshaft incorporated a worm gear to drive the Marelli car-type distributor located at the rear base of the offside cylinder.

Engine lubrication was taken care of by way of a 3-litre (5½-pint) heavily-finned, detachable wet sump which acted as an oil tank, and the gear-type oil-pump housed in the base of the timing chest on the nearside and driven by the lowest of the three gears which connected to the central crankshaft timing pinion. The pump itself consisted of a pair of gears with a serviceable width of between 15.983 and 15.994mm, housed in an alloy pump body. The only other component was a Woodruff key locating the pump gear shaft in the taper of the timing case gear, where it was retained by a nut and washer. Pressure in the system was maintained at a constant level by the oil pressure relief valve fitted inside the crankcase on the section which supported the sump. This valve was pre-set at the factory, to a delivery pressure in the circuit of 2.5 to 3kg/cm²

(35.6–42.7lb/sq in). If the pressure rose above the prescribed rating, the valve would open and restore the correct level. The crankcase itself breathed through a pipe situated on top of the engine, into a metal breather box and then by hose into the atmosphere. An oil pressure switch was fitted externally on top of the crankcase, which activated a red oil-pressure light on the instrument console. The oil pump drew a steady supply from the sump and, after passing it through a wire gauze strainer, delivered the oil through ducts in the crankcase. These directly supplied the oil under pressure to the main bearings, the camshaft housings and the crankshaft, through which it passed to lubricate the big-end bearings. Oil passing out around the big-ends was flung out to lubricate the cylinder walls and the remainder of the engine by splash. The cylinder heads received their own, separate supply through external oil feed pipes.

The big Moto Guzzi's transmission system was closer to car, rather than motorcycle, practice. Securely bolted to the rear of the crankshaft with six screws was a large-diameter flywheel which also formed the housing for the dry clutch. This consisted of two friction and two plain plates, and eight springs. The clutch assembly was retained inside the flywheel by the electric starter ring gear, but was held in place by eight bolts and spring washers. Passing through the centre of the clutch shaft was a single long clutch pushrod, this in turn passed through the input shaft of the gearbox to finally exit behind the clutch operating lever on the rear of the gearbox.

The gearbox housing itself was bolted on to the back of the crankcase. It had four speeds and was of the constant mesh, frontal engagement variety. The mainshaft was driven by the driving gear on the clutch shaft. All four gears were fixed to the mainshaft – in other words – a one-piece assem-

# TECHNICAL SPECIFICATIONS
## V7 700 (1966)

**Engine**

| | |
|---|---|
| Cycle | 4 strokes |
| Number of cylinders | 2 |
| Cylinder disposition | 'V' – 90° |
| Bore | 80mm (3.149in) |
| Stroke | 70mm (2.755in) |
| Displacement | 703.717cc (42.93cu.in) |
| Compression ratio | 9 to 1 |
| Revs at max engine speed | 6000rpm |
| Output at max engine speed | 50HP SAE |
| Crankcase | light alloy |
| Cylinders | light alloy barrels with hard chrome linings |
| Cylinder heads | light alloy, hemispherical, with special cast iron inserted valve seats |
| Crankshaft | steel construction |
| Crankshaft supports | of anti-friction material pressed in suitable housings (as used in all F1 race cars) |
| Connecting rods | steel construction with AL-TIN alloy thin wall bearings |
| Pistons | light alloy |

Valve gear

ohv, pushrod-operated via the camshaft in the crankcase and gear-driven by the crankshaft

| | |
|---|---|
| Inlet | opens 24° before TDC closes 58° after BDC |
| Exhaust | open 58° after BDC closes 22° before TDC |
| Rocker clearance for valve timing | 0.5mm (.0196in) |

Normal rocker clearance (cold engine)
inlet 0.15mm (0.058in)
exhaust 0.25mm (0.098in)

Carburation

Both carburettors are gravity fed from the tank.

Carburettor Make
type Dell'Orto S.S.I. (right and left)

Lubrication

Pressure, by gear pump, driven by the crankshaft.

Oil strainer in crankcase.

Normal lubricating pressure 2.5 – 3kg/sq cm (35.6 – 42.7lb/sq in) (Controlled by relief valve)

Electrically controlled oil pressure gauge.

Cooling by air. Cylinder and cylinder heads deeply finned.

Starter motor

Marelli starter MT 40 H (12V – .7hp) with electromagnetic ratchet control. Ring gear bolted on flywheel.

Ignition

By battery with automatic advance Marelli distributor type S123A.

Initial advance 10°. Automatic advance 28°

Ignition timing 38° full advance

Contact breaker gap: 0.42–0.48mm (.016–.018in)

Spark plug: n. 225 in Bosch-Marelli scale or equivalent.

Plugs point gap: 0.6mm (.023).

Ignition coil Marelli BE 220 D.

Exhaust system

Dual exhaust pipes and mufflers.

## Transmission

### Clutch

Twin driven plates, dry type, located on the flywheel. Controlled by lever on left handlebar.

### Gear box

Four speeds, frontal engagement. Constant mesh gears.

Cush drive spring incorporated.

Separate case bolted on crankcase, operated by rocker pedal on the right hand side of the machine.

Engine-gearbox ratio  1 to 1.375 (16-22)

Internal gear ratios

| | | | |
|---|---|---|---|
| Low gear | 1 to 2.230 | (13:29) |
| Second gear | 1 to 1.333 | (18:24) |
| Third gear | 1 to 0.954 | (22:21) |
| High gear | 1 to 0.750 | (24:18) |

### Secondary drive at rear wheel

By constant speed homokinetic double joint cardan shaft. Bevel layshaft gear-wheel ratio 4.625 (8:37)

Overall gear ratios

| | |
|---|---|
| Low gear | 1 to 14.180 |
| Second gear | 1 to  8.473 |
| Third gear | 1 to  6.063 |
| High gear | 1 to  4.768 |

## Frame

Duplex cradle, tubular structure.

### Suspension

Rear swinging fork with external adjustable springs.

Telescopic front fork incorporating hydraulic dampers and with external adjustable spring.

Wheels $18 \times 3$ spoked steel rims, front and rear.

### Tyres

$4.00 \times 18$ front and rear, block type 'high speed'

### Front tyre pressure

| | |
|---|---|
| Solo rider | 1.5 kg/sq cm = 21 psi |
| | With pillion Rear tyre |
| | Solo rider    1.8 kg/sq cm = 25 psi. |
| | With pillion 2.0 kg/sq cm = 28 psi |

Note The above recommendation is for normal riding (cruising speed). If using the machine at constant high speed or on motorways the above pressures should be increased by 0.2 kg/sq cm 2.8psi

Brakes Twin leading shoes expanding type front brake, operated by hand lever on the right handlebar. Large rear brake operated by pedal on left hand side of machine.

## Overall dimensions and weight

| | |
|---|---|
| Wheelbase | 1.445m (56.9in) |
| Length | 2.230m (87.5in) |
| Width | 0.795m (31.2in) |
| Height (dry) | 1.050m (42.2in) |
| Minimum ground clearance | 0.150m (5.9in) |
| Curb weight | 243kg (536 lb) |

### Performance

Maximum permissible speed and gradients climbable in each gear, solo riding.

Low gear 66kph (41mph)
Climbing ability 60%

Second gear 96kph (59.6mph)
Climbing ability 34%

Third gear 120kph (97.5mph)
Climbing ability 23%

High gear 170kph (106mph)
Climbing ability 14%

### Capacities

| | |
|---|---|
| Fuel tank | 20ltr (4.4gal) |
| Sump | 3ltr (0.66gal) |

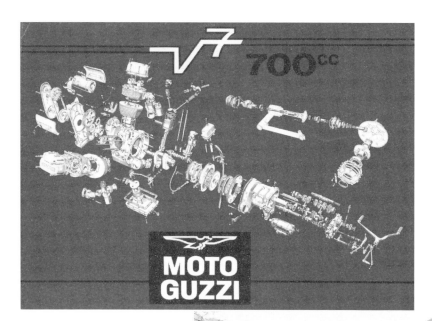

*Exploded view showing the engine, transmission and final drive details.*

*The caption reads 'Powerful, fast, smooth, and quiet the Moto Guzzi V7 is the machine for the most discriminating enthusiast and for unlimited touring'.*

Powerful, fast, smooth, and quiet the Moto Guzzi V7 twin is the machine
Puissante, rapide, souple et silencieuse, la V7 c'est la deux-cylindre du
Kraftvoll, Schnell, Geräuschlos, die V7 ist ein Zweizylinder für echte

bly. The layshaft was provided with four separate engagement gears, two sliding sleeves and also carried the speedometer drive gear. The gears were selected directly by the gear lever – a traditionally Italian heel-and-toe job on the offside. This pedal controlled the selector shaft which had a toothed sector in mesh with a gear on the selector drum. The drum carried a series of grooves in which the selector mechanism ran, so that its position, and the position of

the gears which it selected on the layshaft, was governed by the rotation of the selector. In the drum were five holes, one for each gear, plus neutral, and a spring-loaded pawl ensured that it was positively located in each of the positions in turn as the gear lever was operated. This pawl was drilled and worked additionally as a gearbox breather. The gearbox was also provided with a neutral indicator switch which had an orange warning light on the console to remind the rider not to attempt to start whilst in gear.

Rear drive was by Cardan shaft and bevel gears, again a feature which displayed its police and military background. This took the drive from the rear of the gearbox, via splines on the end of the gearbox layshaft which connected to a universal joint running in a $28 \times 58 \times 16$mm ball race housed in the end of the swinging arm. The exposed section between the swinging arm and the rear of the gearbox was protected by a rubber gaiter to accommodate the suspension movement. Inside the swinging arm, the universal joint mated up with the drive shaft which ran in a pair of $25 \times 52 \times 16.25$mm ball races, one at each end. At the rear, this was splined to the bevel drive pinion inside the rear drive box, an aluminium casting filled with EP90 oil to lubricate the drive. The crown wheel was meshed directly with the pinion, and mated up with the rear wheel through an internally-toothed sleeve in the rear hub. The rear wheel could be removed without the need to disturb the drive, simply by removing the wheel spindle and spacer which kept the wheel centred and in mesh.

The V7 was blessed with a powerful 12-volt electrical system, based around a 300-watt Marelli DN62N generator located on top of the engine between the vee of the cylinders and driven from the crankshaft by two pulleys and a rubber belt. The belt ran down in front of the timing cover, and a large alloy outer casing between the two cylinders down to the base of the timing cover was fitted over the belt, pulleys and the front of the generator to protect them from road filth and the elements. The generator was held in position by a sturdy split metal band and was covered from either side by separate steel pressings. The generator charged a massive 32-amp hour battery, needed mainly because no kick-starter was fitted and, unusually for the time, the bike relied entirely upon its electric starter. This was

operated by a Marelli MT40H motor, a four-pole design with an output of 0.7hp and rotating clockwise. It was mounted on the nearside of the crankcase, engaging with the flywheel ring gear via a Marelli IE13DA solenoid fitted directly below the starter motor.

Ignition was also taken care of by the Marelli company, who provided the S123A distributor, housing a single set of contact breakers and a single condenser. The distributor was driven by a worm on the camshaft and provided sparks via a single Marelli or Bosch ignition coil. Illumination was provided by a CEV headlamp with a 168mm lens and a 45/45 watt bulb. The rear light was an oblong alloy-bodied affair housing a single 20/5 bulb. There were also 3-watt bulbs for the warning lights indicating main and dip beam, neutral, oil pressure, and charging, plus another to illuminate the speedometer. The handlebar switch fitted on the nearside of the handlebar was a typical spartan CEV device, with an oblong chrome cover retained by a pair of screws. Its simple task was to control the lights, dip and horn – a Marelli type T12DE/F with screw terminals. There was also a four-way ignition switch mounted in the centre of the instrument console. This selected 0, for off; 1, for stationary parking lights; 2, the running position, when the handlebar switch could also be used to activate the lights; and 3, for starting only so that the key returned to position 2 automatically when released. The electrical system was protected by four 25-amp ceramic fuses.

As with the remainder of the specification, the chassis also clearly displayed its government origin with its massive (and heavy!) duplex cradle tubular frame and equally robust swinging arm. One side of the latter contained the drive shaft and carried a mounting for the rear bevel drive box. Because of the drive shaft, a conventional swinging arm pin could not be employed, so

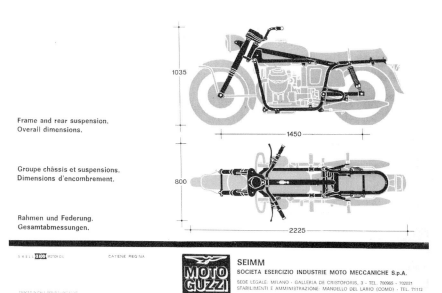

1035

Frame and rear suspension.
Overall dimensions.

Groupe châssis et suspensions.
Dimensions d'encombrement.

Rahmen und Federung.
Gesamtabmessungen.

1450

800

2225

SEIMM
SOCIETA ESERCIZIO INDUSTRIE MOTO MECCANICHE S.p.A.
SEDE LEGALE: MILANO - GALLERIA DE CRISTOFORIS, 3 - TEL. 700965 - 702021
STABILIMENTI E AMMINISTRAZIONE: MANDELLO DEL LARIO (COMO) - TEL. 71112

two separate, part-threaded stub spindles were fitted on either side of the swinging arm pivot. These ran on $17 \times 40 \times 12$mm taper roller bearings sealed from the outside by $30 \times 40 \times 7$mm oil seals. Side play could easily be taken up by screwing the stub spindles in to tension the bearings.

The 35mm (1.4in) front fork stanchions were completely enclosed by top covers which also acted as headlamp brackets. These covers extended halfway down the length of the Marzocchi-made forks, and were much longer than the chrome-plated bottom spring covers. Each fork leg carried a single $35 \times 50 \times 10$mm oil seal, as with full enclosure, no more were deemed necessary. The steering head pivoted on a pair of $25 \times 52 \times 16.25$mm taper roller bearings.

In the braking department, on paper at least, the massive full-width 220mm drums appeared impressive, with a twin-leading shoe version at the front. Unfortunately, the brakes were to prove the Achilles heel in the machine's make-up – being hard-pressed to retard the progress of this 220kg plus (500lb) heavyweight. The hubs were laced to 18in WM3 Borrani alloy rims, which carried large-section Pirelli $4.00 \times 18$ MTs with a block tread, front and rear.

The remainder of the cycle parts were entirely conventional. One feature was the usefully large, 20 litre (4½ imp gal) fuel tank, which had chrome-plated knee recesses. Twin taps gave a quarter of the capacity in reserve, and there was a quick-action hand lever filler cap. Impressive the V7 may have looked, but out on the street there was none of the sporting performance of the most famous Guzzis of yesteryear. Having ridden an original example, I can say with total confidence that the machine was at heart and in aspiration a tourer in the grand tradition, with a performance inferior to almost every six-fifty British vertical twin and had a maximum speed of 100mph (160kph). What it did offer was a far higher level of comfort and flexibility, plus an air of quality unmatched by almost anything of the era save BMW. When cruising sedately at around 50mph (80kph), fuel consumption was in the mid-sixties, dropping down to around the mid-thirties when the wick was turned up fully. Mechanical noise was distinctly muted – in fact, induction noise was louder than the engine or exhaust once on the move! But the gearbox was noisy, and with the rear drive layout and the four-speed gearbox, had to be treated with respect. Changing down in anything approaching a sporting manner felt very much as if the rear wheel was locking as though the machine was decelerating too rapidly through the lower gears. But while it was true that the customer who thought that 'Moto Guzzi' on the tank automatically meant the bike was a sportster would be sadly disappointed, in its element the V7 could be one of the most pleasant motorcycles to ride for those who were lucky enough to experience one of the original models. It was to be a long wait for most people. Although the first civilian prototype had been shown to the public at the end of 1965, the earliest production machines that customers could actually purchase did not begin to appear in dealers' showrooms until the spring of 1967. There was very little change from the prototype, other than minor alterations to cosmetic details – the saddle, with twin grab rails replacing the single one at the rear of the seat, different silencers and rear suspension units, a round rear light, and a headlamp rim with no peak. The prototype had been in silver and black, but this had been changed, with the tank now in a rich claret although still with chrome recesses, and lined in white rather than black.

The following year, 1968, saw the 700cc V7 continue, but now with a new starter motor and the carburettors changed to square slide Del'Orto VHBs, although these were still the 29mm (1.1in) size. The saddle had again been redesigned, and now had a hump at the rear to prevent passengers from sliding backwards under acceleration. An oblong rear light like the prototype's, replaced the round CEV unit of the previous year. And finally, the colour scheme was changed to white with red lining replacing the silver and red.

A bigger change occurred in 1969 when an enlarged version called the V7 Special was introduced. This had grown in size to 757.486cc, achieved by increasing the bore to 83mm while the stroke was unaltered at 70mm as before. A new type of piston was used – although there were still four rings, the oil scraper was moved to join the other three above the gudgeon pin and the skirt was relieved to give an almost semi-slipper type appearance. There were still three sizes of piston assembly, but with new measurements. Class 'A' now went from 83.000mm to 83.006mm, class 'B' from 83.006mm to 83.012mm, and class 'C' from 83.012mm to 83.018mm. The remainder of the power unit displayed very little change except for a few

*A 1968 American advertisement from the importers – the Premier Motor Corporation (a part of the Berliner empire), proclaiming the virtues of the 700 V7.*

*A 700 V7 with touring accessories including screen, legshields, panniers and extra chroming seen in Verona, Italy during March 1969.*

*The larger capacity 757.487cc (83 × 70mm) V7 Special entered production during 1969.*

minor alterations and improvements. The valves were increased slightly in size to a 36mm exhaust and 41mm inlet. They also gained smaller internal valve springs fitted inside the main coils. The clutch springs were changed too, for a slightly stronger type. The gearbox was the original four-speeder, with identical ratios, but the bevel drive ratios were changed to 8/35 giving a new gearing of 4.375:1. Engine oil pressure was increased from 3.8 to 4.2kg/cm sq (54 to 60lb/sq in).

Despite the limited nature of these changes, the performance was quite substantially increased, with the maximum power up to 60bhp at 6500rpm. Aided by a fall in kerb weight from 243kg (536lb) to 228kg (502lb), this resulted in an increase in maximum speed to 115mph (185kph), with proportionately snappier acceleration. Two models of the new V7 were manufactured between 1969 and 1971, when production ceased. As well as the 'basic' Special, there was a version named the Ambassador and intended for the Stateside customer, where

puissante,
rapide,
sûre,
la V7 bondit désormais
sur les routes
du monde entier

powerful,
safe,
fast,
the V7 known
the world over

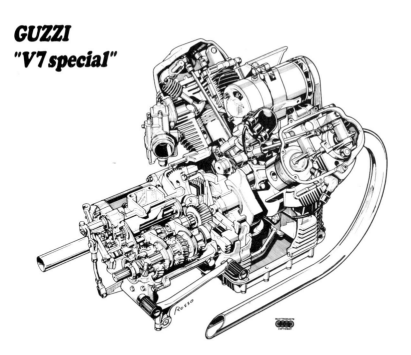

# GUZZI "V7 special"

*Cutaway view of the V7 Special engine, clutch and gearbox assembly. Note massive 300-watt generator located on top of engine between the vee of the cylinders.*

*A characteristic of the original V7 range was the much taller timing cover at the front of the engine, shown here on a V7 Special.*

Moto Guzzi imports were handled by the Premier Motor Corporation, an offshoot of the Berliner Motor Corporation who over the years handled several top European brands, notably Ducati, Norton, Matchless and Zündapp. The Ambassador was largely the V7 Special with American-market accessories and modifications. These included side reflectors on the mudguards, the round rear light from the 1967 V7 and a cherry red metallic paint job for the tank, side panels and tool boxes. The decals were also changed and there was an 'Ambassador V750' artwork on the side panels. Another American-market modification was the adoption of a sealed beam front light unit.

So the V7 moved into the new decade, much as it had been when first conceived; enlarged, updated, but still at heart a soft touring machine. Now, from these somewhat humble beginnings, was to emerge a whole new generation of Guzzi V-twins, based on the original, but in many differing guises and engine sizes.

*The Ambassador was the American version of the V7 Special. The same machine except for sealed-beam headlamp and side reflectors.*

## The First 850

It was a fact that neither the 703 nor the 757cc engine size of Guzzi's 90-degree V-twin had really proved sufficiently powerful to make the various V7 touring models anything other than willing, reliable performers. This was certainly the main criticism levelled at them by factory testers and the biking press alike. To counter this perceived lack of zest, the Guzzi engineering team again enlarged the engine size, but this time by resorting to a lengthening of the stroke, rather than the bore as had been done to transform the original 700cc V7 into the V7 Special/Ambassador. The result was to be the first of the 850s; actual dimensions being the same bore of 83mm with a new stroke of 78mm – adding up to 844.057cc. There were other changes. The pistons had three rings instead of the four-ring type used previously, and with a 9.2:1 compression ratio, the power output was upped to 51bhp at 6000rpm. The rest of the engine remained virtually unchanged, with only very minor improvements, but the really big news was the introduction of a five-speed transmission.

The new, larger engined Guzzi was first displayed in public at the Milan Show in November 1971 – appearing in two versions, the V850GT and the GT California. The latter machine (described in Chapter 8), was an update of a model which had first appeared on sale earlier that year, in Europe only, powered by the earlier 757cc engine with four-speed gearbox. And, in fact, both the 850GT and the GT California shared much with their predecessors. The only changes to the 850GT apart from the engine and transmission were extremely superficial. It gained Aprilia direction indicators, chrome-plated mudguards and new cosmetics. The latter amounted to fresh tank and side panel decals. These were now in white and consisted of '850' above a 'GT' logo, plus a large 'V' flanked by horizontal lines. The small toolboxes to the rear of the large side panels carried simple, matching horizontal double lines. The main colour scheme amounted to metallic cherry red (tank, panels and toolboxes) and black (frame, suspension and ancillaries).

Both 850s first went on sale in early 1972, and instantly gave a new impetus to sales; their extra reserves of power being very much appreciated. Not just at home, but in several foreign countries, including the USA, Germany, France, Scandinavia and Great Britain. It was of course in 1972 that the first supplies of Guzzi V-twins reached Britain. In earlier years Guzzis had been sold, but only the various singles; at first through racer Bob Foster, then through Motor Imports (the trade arm of London dealers Pride & Clarke). Rivetts of Leytonstone, North London brought in a very limited number of both the V7 Sport (see Chapter 3) and 850GT, selling the latter for £1,145, including purchase tax. But soon, in 1973, a new importer was appointed. This was Barretts of Redhill, Surrey, headed by Don Barrett, who had been involved during the early 1960s with importing the Capriolo range of Italian lightweights into Britain. During 1973 and 1974, Barretts imported several different Guzzi models, including the 850GT.

The final year that the 850GT (Eldorado in North America) was available was 1974 and in its final form was sold with a single 300mm diameter cast-iron disc at the front which replaced the former massive drum brake. This was operated by a twin piston Brembo caliper mounted at the front of the offside fork slider. Another change was the fitment of British Lucas direction indicators on some machines. Later that year, the last of the original heavyweight V7-style tourers was replaced by the all-new 850T (see Chapter 4), a machine which was to transform Guzzi's non-sporting Vees perhaps more than any other before or since.

*First Guzzi V-twin to use the 844.057cc (83 × 78mm) engine was the 850GT. Making its debut at the 1971 Milan Show it entered production early in 1972, running through to 1974. The final year saw the drum front stopper replaced by a single Brembo disc.*

## TECHNICAL SPECIFICATIONS
### V850GT (1972)

| | | | |
|---|---|---|---|
| Engine | 4-stroke 90° V-twin | Brakes | Front, double drum 200mm 2LS; Rear, drum 200mm |
| Bore | 83mm | | |
| Stroke | 78mm | | |
| Displacement | 844.057cc | Tyres | 4.00 × 18 front and rear |
| Maximum power | 51bhp at 6000rpm | Front suspension | telescopic oil-damped forks. |
| Valve type | ohv | | |
| Final drive | cardan shaft | Rear suspension | twin rear shock, swinging arm. |
| Clutch | dry | | |
| Starting | electric | Fuel capacity | 22.5ltr (4.9gal) |
| Ignition | coil | Dry weight | 230kg (506lb) |
| Gearbox | 5-speed | Maximum speed | 118mph (190kph) |

# 3 V7 Sport

Probably the most important Guzzi motorcycle of its era, the V7 Sport made its public debut at the Milan Show in November 1971. Previously, the Mandello V-twins had been a decidedly touring package but with its slim, low and aggressive stance, the V7 Sport outlined the path which all the large capacity Guzzi twins would follow in the future. Earlier, 1967 had been a bad year for the famous old factory. Founder Carlo Guzzi had died, the firm's finances were at rock bottom and the chief designer, Ing. Cesare Carcano, retired. There was one major asset however, the V7 engine; and with the appointment of Ing. Lino Tonti, a new man who was at last able to design the company out of trouble.

It was to be Lino Tonti, albeit with the help of Alejandro de Tomaso, who would be largely responsible for steering Guzzi away from the abyss. The V7 Sport was, without doubt, the motorcycle which in retrospect was not only its designer's finest creation (in terms of its place in history) but the machine which spawned the rebirth of the factory itself. Before joining Moto Guzzi towards the end of 1967, Ing. Tonti had held design posts at a number of leading Italian manufacturers including Aermacchi, Bianchi and Gilera. He had also played a major role in the birth of Paton, and had even found time to pen the Linto racer. This was essentially a pair of Aermacchi pushrod Ala d'Oro singles on a single crankcase to create a five-hundred twin for the top privateers in international racing events. In fact the Linto was his last brief before joining Guzzi.

*Ing. Lino Tonti was responsible for many famous motorcycles from a large number of factories, but the Guzzi V7 Sport was probably his finest creation. It made its début at the Milan Show in late 1971.*

Tonti's first task for his new employers was the fairly straightforward job of enlarging the V7 engine from 703 to 757cc (later upping it again, this time to 844cc). His personal view was that the increases in engine capacity were secondary because he realized that it was the chassis which was where his efforts should really be concentrated. As the creator of several of the sleekest racing designs of the previous decade, Tonti was frankly less than enthusiastic with the distinctly touring, heavyweight character of the V7 as it was when he joined the company. It was certainly at odds with his own views of what a motorcycle should be – both in terms of rider appeal and road behaviour.

During 1970, after a series of successful record breaking visits to Monza in June and October the previous year (see Chapter 9), Ing. Tonti turned his attention to creating the Guzzi V-twin of his dreams; something lower, leaner, sleeker, faster and better handling than the predecessors. The first problem Tonti encountered was the height of the engine between the vee of the cylinders, This was due to the position taken by the belt-driven generator atop the crankcase, reflected in the tall timing cover casting at the front. This particular problem was solved when Tonti substituted the top-mounted generator with a Bosch GI (R) 14V 13A 19 alternator carried directly at the front of the crankshaft. With a suitably redesigned timing cover, this substantially reduced the overall height along the centre line of the engine, allowing the whole machine to be reconstructed in a lower, lighter, and obviously much more sporting, manner. The result was to be a true classic, one of the most beautifully efficient motorcycles constructed up to that time – at least for road use. It had to be good, for it embodied Tonti's own personal commitment, belief and effort, best illustrated by the tale of the man himself testing a prototype and coming off – breaking a leg in the process! One can but wonder

just how many other designers of the modern era actually get out there and ride, let alone carry out their own testing? The phrase sweat, blood and tears springs to mind to describe Lino Tonti's own efforts in this direction.

As well as employing an alternator for the first time, the other significant engine alteration was a change in displacement. The new engine size was 748.388cc, achieved by reducing the bore from the 83mm of the 757cc size down to 82.5mm, while the stroke remained unchanged at 70mm. The main reason for doing this was to take advantage of new Formula 750/Superbike regulations, which at that time had a maximum allowed cubic capacity of 750cc, irrespective of the number of cylinders. To achieve the level of performance to match the new frame there were higher compression, four-ring, pistons with a ratio of 9.8:1, lumpier cam profiles, paired coil valve springs, and 30mm Dell'Orto square slide VHB carburettors. These resulted in the new engine producing 52bhp at 6300rpm (measured at the rear wheel). As with other V7 series machines, the aluminium cylinder bores were chrome plated, and as before, this meant that pistons were offered in three matched sizes (relevant to cylinder bore measurement). For the V7 Sport, there were class 'A' from 82.500 to 82.506mm, class 'B' between 82.506 and 82.512mm, and class 'C' from 82.512 to 82.516mm. Tonti selected the best features of the various models to provide an option drive package. As with the recently announced '850', the V7 Sport benefited from a five-speed gearbox. But this had been created with the sportster in mind, rather than the other way round. As with the earlier versions of the V7, the gears themselves were helically cut, mainly it was claimed in the interests of quietness.

If the engine formed an integral part of Tonti's strategy, then it was the remainder of the machine which really set the V7 Sport apart from its touring brothers. It was the stunning lines which really created the headlines, allied to the way it went out on the street. Lean, low, racy – it was a style that is as much loved today as when the original V7 sport first made its bow in public at the Milan Show in November 1971. It was not only the flagship of the Moto Guzzi range, but the pride of the entire Italian bike industry. Over a quarter of a century later its brilliance has not dimmed, such was its impact. Matching the stunning looks was an equally breathtaking finish of metallic lime green for the handsomely-sculpted 22.5 litre (4.95 gal) fuel tank, and the equally catching angular side panels. The V7 Sport's double cradle frame was in an equally eye-catching bright Italian racing red, contrasting sharply (and successfully) with the green.

The motorcycle's length contributed to the low, sleek looks, but it really was low as evidenced by the seat height of a mere 750mm (29.5in) – exceptional for a machine of its size. The frame and swinging arm consisted of near-straight steel tubes and the layout was masterful, with the result that it was to last, largely unchanged until the early 1990s and the arrival of the Daytona. Also new were the front forks, which were of Guzzi's

*Lean, low, racy – these words sum up the V7 Sport best of all. A classic amongst early 1970s Italian motorcycles.*

own manufacture and incorporated internal sealed damper assemblies – again a feature which was to endure over the years. With such an abundantly low frame, accessibility might have been expected to have been compromised, but this was not to be the case. Tonti aided maintenance by providing fully-detachable bottom rails, a feature for which countless mechanics have thanked the designer, providing as it does great freedom of access. At the rear, the mudguard, in polished stainless steel to match the front was hinged, allowing the rear wheel to be removed without resorting to leaning the machine over. Although the 220mm drum brakes were retained from the earlier models, the front was now double-sided, each having twin leading shoe operation. This effectively removed one of the major criticisms of the V7 series, that of below par braking performance, since not only was the front friction area doubled, but the all-up weight had been reduced by a significant margin (down from 234kg (516lb) of the original 700V7, to 206kg (454lb) for the V7 Sport – both dry figures).

One feature of the V7 Sport which was universally praised was the swan-neck clip-on handlebars. These allowed adjustment both fore and aft and up and down – one of the few sports machines ever to provide a stance to suit every size of rider. It also allowed either a touring sit-up-and-beg or racing crouch to be adopted, without being uncomfortable in either position. Except for the moped-like handlebar switches, the balance of the electrics was of a much higher standard than was usually found on Italian motorcycles of the period. This was probably because Guzzi employed the most suitable regardless of the country of manufacture. This saw German-made Bosch equipment in the shape of the alternator, regulator, rectifier of starter motor, allied to locally sourced products such as the Marelli S311A distributor with twin contact breakers and con-

*Although the 220mm (8.6614in) drum front stopper was retained from the touring V7 range, it was now doubled-sided, each having twin leading shoe operation.*

*The much-loved swan neck clip-on handlebars. These allowed adjustment both fore and aft and up and down. The V7 Sport was one of the few sports machines ever to provide a stance to suit every size of rider.*

densers, dual ignition coils from the same company, powerful Belli high and low tone horns, and a 170mm CEV 12-volt headlamp, which had a chrome-plated shell as well as rim. The first examples of the V7 Sport, for general sale, began to roll off the production lines in early 1972, although in truth, mass-production is hardly a suitable word as they were truly hand-made. Demand was so high in relation to numbers built that virtually no machines were exported in those early months of the model's life. However, some did escape Italian borders including a few which were purchased by Rivetts of Leytonstone High Road, London (who also brought in the same number of 850GTs) from February 1972 onwards at a price of £1,350. Although only a handful were ever imported, customers who were lucky enough to buy one were full of praise. This was typified by a particular gentleman who wrote affectionately about his V7 Sport in an article published in *Motorcycle Sport*.

For 1973, the factory made one change – to the colour scheme. The striking metallic lime green and Italian racing red gave way to a much more conservative finish consisting of a red tank and panels with the remainder in black; some machines had an all-black finish. Other schemes included green/black and metallic burgundy/black. The original polished stainless steel mudguards were retained, and detail relief was provided as earlier by the silver-painted fork sliders and chrome-plated headlamp, handlebars, grab rail, rear suspension springs, mudguard stays and minor fittings. The complete exhaust system was also in bright chrome-plate, with the rear section of each Lafranconi-made muffler cut back diagonally and slashed with three angled slots akin to a shark's gills.

All European-specification models had right-hand gearchange. American-market machines came with left-hand change and electric, instead of manually operated fuel taps as standard equipment. Another difference between European and American markets was that the V7 Sport was available in the latter throughout 1974, whereas in Europe it was superseded by a new machine. The American magazine *Cycle* carried out a 'Cafe racer shoot out' in its July 1974 issue. In this they pitted the V7 Sport against a BMW R90S, Ducati 750SS Desmo and a Rickman Triumph. The Guzzi came out well 'as the thinking man's motorcycle'. The longer staff rode the Mandello vee, the more they liked it, summing it up as a 'time drug'.

## 750S

The newcomer, the 750S, was clearly based on the original, but there were several engineering and styling changes. The only alteration to the basic engine of any real importance saw the factory replace the timing gears with a chain and sprockets. The major reason was one of cost, and the 750S introduced a system which was to become standard practice throughout the entire V-twin range. The major change to the cycle parts was the replacement of the massive 220mm double-sided 2LS drum front stop-

*Introduced for the 1974 model year (except in the USA), the 750S had a number of changes over the V7 Sport. Notably chain and sprockets in place of timing gears, twin front Brembo discs instead of the massive 4LS drum, and revised styling.*

per with a pair of hydraulically-operated 300mm cast-iron Brembo brake discs. Situated next to the front brake lever up on the offside of the handlebars was a master cylinder with a metal screw cap, and hydraulic hoses connected this to the calipers carried at the front of each fork slider.

Another change, at least for non-Americans, was that the gear lever was now on the left. The seat was exchanged for a new, more racy style featuring a bum-stop, and with room for exactly 1½ people in comfort! So in effect you either had to find a very, very petite partner – or go alone. But the style was great. Provision was made for mounting a set of Aprilia-made turn signals, later to become standard equipment. Matt black was now used instead of bright chrome on the Lafranconi silencers, although the balance pipe (H-section) under the engine and exhaust header pipes remained in chrome. Having a matt black paint finish on the silencers was a bad move, certainly in coun-

tries likely to have rain, snow and ice, dampness and road salt soon turning these into rusty components.

For Europe an ignition-activated electric fuel tap was fitted on the offside, with a conventional lever operated manual tap on the nearside, which also acted as a useful reserve. Another alteration was the fitment of a hydraulic steering damper, which it must be said, was largely redundant on such a fine handling bike, at least for the normal road rider. It only serving to make the steering heavier than it need have been. Except for the questionable features mentioned above, the *Motorcyclist Illustrated* Road Test Annual was pretty accurate when they summed up the 750S in the following way: 'that unlike other, or at least the majority of sports classics, the 750S is also highly practical'. Although the factory claimed a maximum speed of 130mph (209kph), neither the 750S nor the V7 Sport were actually capable of this in standard 'as sold' state of tune. The

---

### TECHNICAL SPECIFICATIONS
### 750S (1974)

| | | | |
|---|---|---|---|
| Engine | 4-stroke 90° V-twin | Tyres | Front 3.25 × 18, Rear 3.50 × 18 |
| Bore | 82.5mm | | |
| Stroke | 70mm | Frame | duplex cradle, removable bottom members. |
| Displacement | 748.388cc | | |
| Maximum power output | 53bhp at 6300rpm | Suspension | Front, telescopic forks; Rear, twin shock with swinging arm. |
| Compression ratio | 9.8:1 | | |
| Valve type | ohv | | |
| Transmission | primary by gears, secondary by cardan shaft. | Fuel capacity | 22.5ltr (4.9gal) |
| | | Fuel consumption | 6ltr × 100km. |
| Starter | electric | Dry weight | 206kg (453lb) |
| Gearbox | 5-speed | Maximum speed | 119mph (191kph) standard; 129mph (206kph) with race kit. |
| Brakes | Front, twin 300mm cast iron Brembo discs; rear, drum 220mm 2LS | | |

true figures being a shade over 10mph (16kph) slower. Owners might have thought the factory's claims accurate, simply because of the optimistic Veglia-made speedometer. But if you needed more 'go' for road or track, help was at hand in the shape of an official factory-produced race kit. The full kit, originally intended for Formula 750 racing, was made up of a full race camshaft, 36mm carbs, straight-cut close-ratio gears and an open unrestricted exhaust system. To achieve the full benefits of these components it was also necessary to have the cylinder head ported and gas-flowed, the crank dynamically balanced and the remainder of the engine blueprinted. With a full fairing fitted, maximum speed then rose to between 132 and 134mph (212.4 and 215.6kph). Customers buying the 750S had a choice of three colour schemes. All were basically an overall black, but there were diagonal thick and thin stripes slashing down the tank and panels, with these being in orange, green or red. The side panels themselves were the same pressings as those on the 850T tourer of the same vintage, and were likewise lockable, but they carried a pair of '750S' badges.

## 750S3

The final version of the classic 1970s seven-fifty sportster was the 750S3, launched together with the 850T3 in spring 1975. The S3 looked much the same as the machine it replaced, and was even finished in the same colours. There were in fact many differences between the two models. Several of the cosmetic components were off the 750S, including the front and rear suspension, silencers and balance pipe, mudguards (hinged at rear), seat and grab rail, hydraulic steering damper and adjuster – but sadly, the popular, but expensive to produce, swan-neck clip-ons had gone to be replaced by cheaper non-adjustable components. Virtually everything else including the main part of the engine, the electrics and wheels (complete with their patented linked brake system and three brake discs) came straight from the T3 parts bin.

Mechanically, in fact, the S3 owed more to the touring 850 (albeit one with the Tonti-designed chassis). In the engine department, the S3 was much more T3, than either the V7 Sport or 750S. Because of this fact

*Virtually a combination of two machines, the 750S and 850T3, the 750S3 was launched in early 1975. Together with the T3 tourer it used the then revolutionary linked braking system.*

the reader is advised to consult the 850T/T3 development story in Chapter 4 in conjunction with the S3 data contained herewith. Except for cylinder barrels, piston assemblies, carburettors/manifolds, crankshaft, and clutch flywheel, the remainder of the entire power drive train was pure T3. The cylinder heads were T3 castings which retained the exhaust pipes with bolt-up clamps rather than the threaded ring nuts of the earlier seven-fifty vees, this meant that fresh exhaust header pipes (shaped as per V7 Sport/750S) were required. This was actually a positive move, because the old nuts had a nasty habit (as with a similar arrangement in Ducati bevel V-twins) of working loose. Left unchecked this can mean a damaged thread in the head casting itself. Owners are advised to always make sure that the nuts on the earlier models are both secured correctly and wire locked. As with the 850T (and unlike the T3), there was no replaceable air filter element, simply a massive section of rubber tubing connecting the carburettors but not the breather box.

This was to cause more than one press road test to slate both the 750S3 and 850T, for 'loud induction noise, which is higher than the level of mechanical noise'.

Attending the official dealer launch of new importers, Coburn & Hughes in Luton, Bedfordshire during May 1975 (my company, Mick Walker Motorcycles, was to act as the spares importer in a joint agreement) I was able to appreciate at first hand the merits of the entire Guzzi V-twin range. The two models which impressed me most as a keen motorcyclist myself were the 850T3 (of which I was subsequently to own two examples over the next three and a half years) and the 750S3. The sportster struck me straight away as being so low. It was truly amazing: almost anyone would, I thought, be able to place both feet firmly on the ground – which with the Guzzi V-twin's lurch to the right when the throttle was blipped at a standstill was a good idea!

I well remember borrowing a 750S3 which had belonged to a Rolls Royce engineer for a week-long test. This particular

*Except for the cylinder barrels, piston assemblies, carburettors/manifolds, crankshaft and clutch flywheel, the remainder of the drive train was pure T3.*

*The 750S3 was one of the original Guzzi models imported by the Luton-based Coburn & Hughes organization when it began to act as the factory's British distributors in May 1975.*

machine stands, even today, as probably the most complete Guzzi riding experience I have ever sampled. I do not know quite what the previous owner had done to the machine, time dims (this was in 1976), but it was much smoother, had a superb gearchange, and cornered as if on rails. Believe it or not, I even got to ride the thing in a motorcycle

police display at a country park – on wet grass at speeds of up to 80mph (125kph). Even with its combination of clip-ons and shaft final drive I actually felt entirely safe and secure (well, as much as I would have done on a much more suitable type of machine!). Somehow other S3s never quite matched up to this special bike.

When it first went on sale, it was the most expensive Guzzi imported into Britain up to that time, at £1,749, but this price remained unaltered during the eighteen months in which the model was offered to British enthusiasts. Around 200 examples were imported up to October 1976, when supplies finally dried up, due to the launch of the new 850 Le Mans model. When *Motor Cycle* tested an S3 in 1975, they expressed disappointment with a maximum speed (one-way) of 115.8mph (186.3kph), and a mean (two-way) figure of 114.2mph (183.7kph). Tester John Nutting did however laud certain of the machine's other features, notably its stopping power, for 'any bike that can pull up in 24½ft (7.5m) from 30mph (50kph) has

*When* Motor Cycle *tested an S3 in 1975, they achieved an electronically timed maximum speed of 115.8mph.*

---

### 1000S — Guzzi's Retro Bike

In the late 1980s, Moto Guzzi played the nostalgia card and introduced the world's first 'true' retro, the 1000S. This aped the long-gone but much-loved 750S3 of the mid-1970s. But as Kawasaki were to do with the Zephyr series, Guzzi provided its customers with the advantages of progress since the original model had bowed out. In the 1000S' case these changes were limited to the engine improvements on the Le Mans III, a larger 948cc (88.78mm) capacity, revised lighting and electrical equipment, quieter silencers and very little else. Colour schemes included Red/Black and Green/Black. In reality, the 1000S as a far closer imitation of the original than were later retros such as the Zephyr, Honda's CB1000 Big One, Suzuki's Bandit range or Kawasaki's ZRX1100.

Besides the standard 1000S, the factory also offered the SE. This model can be distinguished by the Le Mans Mark I-type fairing. Both versions were offered with a choice of spoked or cast alloy wheels, the latter at extra cost. The specification included a compression ratio of 10:1; twin Dell'Orto PHM carbs with accelerator pumps; triple Brembo 270mm disk brakes; a 24ltr (5.3gal) fuel tank and a dry weight of 215kg (473lb) for the S and 218kg (480lb) for the SE. Guzzi sources claimed a maximum speed of 137mph (220km/h).

The final batch of 1000SE models rolled off the production line in 1993.

*In the late 1980s Guzzi played the nostalgia card and introduced the world's first 'true' retro, the 1000S. It was also made available with cast alloy wheels, at extra cost.*

---

to have good brakes', and its handling was to match, for 'the bike is rock steady at speed with plenty of ground clearance'. Several owners chose to cough up and buy the fully adjustable swan-neck clip-ons from the 750S. This went a long way to solving what was otherwise a largely uncomfortable stance for anyone under 6ft, as the standard fixed S3 clip-ons were too far forward and too low for most requirements. And a new position for the footrest did not help either. Even though it was eclipsed by its replacement in Guzzi's sporting line by the Le Mans, the S3 was still a fine machine in its own right. Although the basics owed much to its touring counterpart the 850T3, the 750S3 still managed to retain the low, lean, aggressive looks of an uncompromising sports bike, shouting 'performance' from every angle. One magazine went as far as to say 'the S3 looks as though it's travelling at 100mph even when it's standing still'. It was a style at which the factory showed themselves to be masters, and one which was carried on into the highly successful Le Mans series. But above all, the S3 and the 750S which preceded it proved the viability in both sales and production terms of creating a sportster relatively cheaply and simply by utilizing an engine and a large number of component parts from less glamorous and exciting touring mounts. It was a principle that Guzzi would use to great effect again and again down through the years.

# 4  T for *Turismo*

## 850T

If 1972 and the V7 Sport marked out Guzzi's sporting future, 1974 and the 850T did the same thing for the large capacity touring V-twin lineage. The 850T, although in production for only a few months, was a machine which was to transform both the image and the actual on-road ability of what had, up until then, been a large-capacity motorcycle of strictly limited appeal. Previously, buyers of Guzzi's (except the Sport) had been usually touring-oriented riders, those who were content to travel at a leisurely gait and who had little or no interest in exploring their machines' potential by pressing on hard. The arrival of the 850T altered all this at a stroke. Here was a motorcycle which, although managing to largely retain all the softer attributes of the original V7 series, also offered its owner many of the advantages conferred by the highly-acclaimed V7 Sport.

Going on sale during the early summer of 1974, the 850T introduced a number of subtle features which provided it with a much wider appeal. In effect, its arrival ushered in a new era for Moto Guzzi, one in which, for the first time it could challenge market leaders BMW in the quality sports/touring category. It would be accurate to state that the newcomer owed far more to the V7 Sport than it did to the V7 touring range. Not only did it utilize the Sport chassis, but it also incorporated much of the engine redesign which Tonti had carried out when he created the sportster and its subsequent update the 750S, which had also entered production in 1974. One innovation which was shared by both the 850T and the 750S (and it should be

*Going on sale during the early summer of 1974, the 850T introduced a number of improvements which gave it a much wider appeal than previous Guzzi V-twins.*

pointed out, by the final GT850) was the adoption of hydraulic disc front brakes. The new brakes were manufactured for Guzzi by Brembo, with the 750S having twin front discs, the 850T a single one. At the rear, both models retained the 220mm drum of earlier models, but now with a finned brake plate and twin-leading shoe operation. It must be mentioned straight away that its brakes, or the lack of them, was the 850T's main weakness compared with both the 750S and the 850T's successor, the T3. Simply put, the performance provided by the single 300mm cast-iron disc and forward-mounted twin-piston caliper on the offside fork slider is best described as wooden; lacking both feel and finesse – also calling for too much lever pressure. The factory obviously soon realized this weakness as an additional brake disc and caliper conversion kit was made available (Part number 17.92.30.00) to convert the 850T to twin front discs. A very useful and necessary modification, but one which today may be difficult or impossible to source.

The balance of the 850T closely followed the route taken in the specification of the V7 Sport and 750S model detailed in Chapter 3, with only relatively minor differences to both engine and chassis. The main area of difference was that although the 850T's engine was built around that of the 750's, it utilized the larger 844.057cc (83 × 78mm) dimensions of the 850GT and GT California models. But even here, the 850T could prove its more serious sporting intentions, with the hard chrome-plated cylinder bores carrying the higher compression 9.5:1 pistons, and the same cam profile as used in the 750S (and for that matter retained by the Le Mans, when it entered production a couple of years later!). As was the traditional Guzzi V-twin practice at the time, the piston assemblies were matched to the cylinders in 'A', 'B', or 'C' coding sizes, whilst crankshafts and connecting rods were colour-coded in

either blue or white. Compared to the original 850s, the T received larger carburettors – 30mm (against 29mm) square slide VHB instruments. Thus modified there was not only more power – 53bhp at 6000rpm (rear wheel measurement) – but also a much more lively throttle response thanks to not only the high state of tune, but the much improved power-to-weight ratio provided by the lighter chassis. The 850T (and for that matter the 750) engines were the last of the Guzzi vees to use the wire-mesh oil filtration system introduced on the original 700V7, so were not built to carry the car-type canister oil filter found on later machines. Just prior to the 850T being taken out of production in 1975, the final batch constructed were fitted with the improved system designed for the T3 and 750S3 engines. This required a new sump.

Externally, the most noticeable difference between the 850T's engine and the earlier V7 touring and GT850 series was the replacement of the belt-driven Marelli generator. Previously, the position of this in the vee of the cylinders above the crankcase had seen the front of the engine dominated by a massive elongated alloy outer casing. Now, like the V7 Sport, the 850T came equipped

*The 850T utilised the larger 844.057cc (83 × 78mm) dimensions of the 850GT, but with the hard chrome-plated cylinder bores carrying higher compression 9.5:1 pistons.*

with not only a much more effective Bosch 180-watt alternator, but the added advantage of this being mounted at the end of the crankshaft and encased in a much smaller, circular, polished alloy cover held in position by four Allen bolts. The majority of the remaining electrical equipment was also changed to bring the 850 into line with 750 sports series. Many of the new components were also of Bosch origin, with the exceptions being the lighting and switchgear, the Marelli S3IIA distributor (now with twin contact breakers and condensers), and the twin external Marelli HT coils, located out of view underneath the fuel tank.

The 170mm headlamp with its separate Bosch 40/45 watt bulb, was the product of that infamous Italian 'Prince of Darkness' Aprilia (no relation to the motorcycle manufacturer of the same name) electrical concern. The organization closed a couple of years later, but for years after, dissatisfied press and riders were bemoaning their prod-ucts. If one company did more to harm the Italian motorcycle industry of the era it was Aprilia – its products being of a particularly low standard. Its switchgear was poorly designed and flimsy in the extreme, the silver plating on headlamp reflectors soon tarnished, while chrome-plating on shells and rims peeled off. All in all it was a sad tale indeed.

For the American market, machines were fitted with sealed-beam headlamp units. Both the headlamp rim and shell were chrome-plated, as were the turn signals (also an Aprilia-made item). Together with a larger, almost square CEV rear light, all these components were essentially the same as those fitted to the then current Guzzi's 250TS two-stroke twin (itself a badge engineered Benelli – as the two companies were by now both owned by de Tomaso). Except for the previously mentioned Aprilia content, the electrical system was generally well received, at least compared with other

---

**TECHNICAL SPECIFICATIONS**
**850T (1974)**

| | | | |
|---|---|---|---|
| Engine | 4-stroke 90° V-twin | Brakes | Single front disc, 300mm |
| Bore | 83mm | | Rear drum, 220mm |
| Stroke | 78mm | Tyres | 3.50 × 18 front; |
| Displacement | 844.057cc | | 4.10 × 18 rear |
| Max. power | 53bph at 6000rpm | Frame | duplex cradle, with |
| Compression ratio | 9.5:1 | | detachable bottom rails |
| Valve type | ohv | Suspension | Front, Moto Guzzi |
| Lubrication | by pressure pump | | telescopic, oil damped. |
| Transmission | primary by gears; secondary by cardan shaft with cush-drive in rear wheel. | | Rear, twin shock with swinging arm. |
| | | Fuel tank capacity | 25ltr (5.5gal) |
| Clutch | dry with double disc | Fuel consumption | 6.2ltr × 100km |
| Starter | electric | Dry weight | 216kg (477lb) |
| Gearbox | 5-speed | Maximum speed | 122mph (195kph) |

motorcycles, with the exception of Laverda, who like Guzzi had been sensible enough to use foreign-made items as necessary. The switchgear was entirely new and offered a considerable advancement over the earlier moped-style chrome 'snuffbox' variety. This was also more reliable and controllable; the four-position ignition switch was similar to that of the V7 Sport (which had five-positions) and was a type used on many Italian cars of the period. There was also a set of four idiot lights for neutral (orange), ignition (orange), charging (red), and lights (green). These were mounted on a black-painted cast aluminium plate bolted to the top fork yoke and which also carried the instruments on either side of the warning lights. A Veglia mechanical tachometer replaced the earlier electronic type, and a matching speedometer, both of which were suitably inscribed with the winged eagle Moto Guzzi emblem. Powerful 12-volt Vox Bell horns ensured a most powerful alarm in an emergency. The majority of the cycle

parts were from the 750S, but with a rather more comprehensive specification. Both stainless steel mudguards were redesigned to provide increased protection, and although the front assembly appeared similar to that of the 750S, the 850T's rear guard did not feature the hinged section found on the sportster. Front and rear wheels carried WM3 Borrani welled alloy rims, shod with 3.50 × 18 front and 4.10 × 18 rear tyres. There was a pair of chrome-plated front crashbars, plus centre and side stands, and lockable tool boxes behind the side panels; unlike the later T3 model which held only decorative panels and no carrying capacity. A large, 25-litre (5.5gal) fuel tank added to excellent economy (it was possible, from my own experiences, to top 55mpg (5.1l/100km), whilst maintaining a steady 75mph (121kph)). A comfortable riding position was provided by the near ideal relationship of foot and hand controls, which combined with a low, almost flat handbar bend and an extremely spacious and well-

*A pair of powerful Vox Bell 12-volt horns ensured others were informed by the 850T's riders in an emergency.*

padded dual saddle equipped with a sensible grab rail for passenger security, meant that many hours of comfort could be enjoyed by both rider and pillion alike. Buyers had the choice of three colour options, although except for the fuel tank and side panels the motorcycle was always finished in black with balance of the various metal finishes in chrome, cadium or simply polished or as cast aluminium. As for the trio of colours these were brown, red or metallic green. A unique feature of the 850T was the use of metallic gold tape to provide striping for the tank and panels, but this tended to distract from the overall quality of the machine – and is why it was not used later. The tank also carried metal 'Moto Guzzi' badges (as did the V7 Sport and 750S/S3) rather than transfers, and there were matching metal '850T' badges for the side panels. Even though it only had a short production life span, the 850T sold well both at home and abroad. It was particularly well advertised in the USA, where the importers, the Premier Motor Corporation (a division of the Berliner Group who also imported Ducati at that time), took a series of full-page advertisements in the top selling *Cycle* and *Cycle World* magazines to promote the new sports/tourer in the range. Premier promoted the 850T as 'The machine built exclusively for unlimited touring, in style – a masterpiece of elegance and craftsmanship.'

Another country to take quite large numbers was West Germany. In fact Germany has always been a strong market for Guzzi V-twins. This might seem strange, given that it is the home of BMW, Guzzi's nearest rivals in many ways. But many Germans chose to buy one of the Italian vees instead of the home-grown Boxer twin. Then there was Great Britain, where the 850T was almost unique in having not one, but two, importers. The first was Barretts of Redhill, Surrey, who brought in a small number during August 1974. However, this was nothing

compared to the numbers seen once the factory appointed Coburn & Hughes, who already held the Ducati concession. Coburn & Hughes unveiled five Moto Guzzi models at a ceremony held in a Luton hotel on Thursday, 8 May 1975.

## 850T3

This line-up not only included the 850T, which had been increased in price from Barrett's 1974 figure of £1,346 to £1,479, but also the brand new 850T3 and T3 California, neither of which had previously been seen in Britain having only just been launched in Italy, and the 250TS and 750S3. The T3 was marked up at £1,599. Its major claim over the T was in the much improved braking power it offered, this being thanks to Guzzi's new, exclusive integral triple hydraulically operated disc system. There were however many other, but less significant, changes. At the top of this list came an improvement in the oil and air filtration for the engine. The disposable car-type canister oil filter which had been fitted on the latest 850T was housed in the sump, so that both this casting and its gasket were revised. For the first time, the Dell'Orto carbs breathed through a disposable paper filter element – vitally important for an engine employing chrome-plated cylinder bores. It also greatly reduced the previous induction roar.

Output of the Bosch alternator had been increased to 280-watt (formally 180-watt); important to anyone wishing to use additional electrical equipment, or for extended night-time riding. Although the headlamp was still one of the dreaded Aprilia components, it now came with a black painted shell. The Stateside (coded 850T/3FB) version with its sealed-beam featured a rim twice as deep as its European type, and with a thick rubber gasket between the rim and the shell. The warning lights and Veglia

*For 1975 Guzzi uprated the T into the T3. A major improvement was in the increased braking power provided by the triple Brembo brake discs and its integral hydraulically operated system.*

instruments now had a plastic console in place of the alloy original, and the ignition switch was revised from four to three positions. The clutch cable had been given an integral cut-out switch, which ensured that the rider could not start the engine unless the clutch lever was pulled in. Other alterations included a revised handlebar – some 100mm (4in) higher than before. (Several riders, including myself, preferred to retrofit a pair from the T model.) The rear shock came with either three or five pre-load adjustment positions – the three-position variety having built-in operating handles. The side panels were retained by rubber grommets and were no longer lockable. The exhaust header pipes were altered as regards their shape, which was more angular; the design of the H-piece balance pipe under the engine was also changed. The T3 was offered in a range of colours: salmon red, dark green, metallic ice blue and black (the latter with a choice of either gold or white pin-striping). Other colours, such as dark brown and silver, were also made available very shortly afterward.

Several 850T3s imported by Coburn & Hughes during 1975 and 1976 for British customers were in fact USA spec models. But this was no real problem, except for having a headlamp which dipped the wrong way – and not having the luxury of simply replacing a bulb if the dip or main beam element failed. Having owned a couple of 850T3s myself during the 1970s, and having ridden many thousands of miles on them I feel well qualified to be able to accurately describe the good and bad points of the machine both from the riding and service viewpoint. As the spares importer and a Guzzi dealer at the time I could have chosen any of the other models, both Guzzi and others which I stocked at the time. (This list included, by the way, not only Italian bikes such as Ducati, Benelli and MV Agusta, but also Harley-Davidson and Suzuki too.) First of all I needed a bike which was just as good two up as solo, the reason being that my wife enjoyed (and still does) motorcycling. Secondly I simply did not have the time to be messing around greasing and adjusting the final drive chain, and thirdly, I not only needed something which was comfortable and could eat up the miles, but also gave riding pleasure too. A pretty tall order, but one which the T3 filled pretty well. Nowadays I would miss having a fairing, but twenty years ago virtually no bikes had them anyway. The first T3 I owned was entirely stock except for having the lower T-model handlebars. On the second one I left the higher bars, but exchanged the saddle for the plusher example off a V1000 Convert automatic. I liked the easy nature of the bike, its safe handling (I could put both feet firmly on the ground whilst stationary), relatively smooth power delivery and torquey nature of the engine. I cannot say I was ever a real

---

### V1000 Convert Auto

The V1000 Convert which made its debut at the end of 1975 was a technically interesting motorcycle which was to prove a dismal sales failure. The V1000's combination of a large engine capacity, shaft final drive and automatic transmission make it unique amongst European machines; subsequently, only mighty Honda have followed the same path, with special versions of their 400 twin and 750 four-cylinder models. It also has to be noted that the Japanese giant was no more successful in attracting customers to the concept than was Guzzi.

Like most automatic cars, the 'auto' Guzzi was closely based on an existing model, in this case the 850T3. As is often the case in the car world, the V1000 was provided with a larger displacement than its manual equivalent.

The engine was essentially the same 90-degree V-twin as the T3, but with the cylinder bores increased from 83 to 88mm, giving a new capacity of 948.90cc. Running on a 9.2:1 compression ratio, Guzzi quoted 71bhp at the crank. But this amounted to a lot less by the time it reached the rear wheels, thanks in no small part to the bought-in German-made Sachs torque converter.

Strictly speaking, the system Guzzi used was not a true automatic gearbox at all, but a form of semi-automatic transmission, based on a type of hydrokinetic torque converter (hence I-Convert or Idro-Convert). This was equipped with a two-speed gearbox on which the ratios could be selected with a heel-and-toe lever operated by the left foot. To complicate matters, there was also a clutch, but its sole purpose was to swap between the two ratios, unlike a conventional gearbox where it is necessary for the clutch to be used to allow the engine to take up the drive. On the V1000, this function was taken up completely by the torque converter and since, in practice, changing ratio was virtually redundant, the machine was to most people as nearly automatic as makes no difference.

Riding the 108mph (174km/h) Convert was more akin to straddling a giant automatic moped than a conventional motorcycle, the transmission robbing the machine of any real performance. Even Guzzi realized this and later offered the V1000 in manual form as the G5 from 1978.

*Except for a couple of hydraulic pipes (below the carb) the V1000 was almost indistinguishable from other big Guzzi V-twins of the mid-1970s*

fan of the linked brakes, although they functioned well enough, whilst the gearchange was all right once I got used to it. My only real gripe was the finish, which unless you kept on top of it would rapidly go downhill in certain areas – certain chromework, all that exposed alloy and the cast iron brake discs being the worst offenders. The performance and economy for an '850' touring machine were excellent. Probably the T3's biggest problem was how ordinary it looked compared to niche models such as the California or Le Mans. It never drew crowds, but nonetheless both my wife and I have fond memories including travelling down to the Isle of Wight and covering the Two-day Trial in 1976, the entry of which included the great Sammy Miller (Bultaco).

Having also ridden its predecessor the 850T, the T3 offered similar performance (around 117mph/188kph), but was a better machine – certainly in braking terms. A feature of the linked braking system was that it was possible to remove both hands from the bar, and just by applying the foot pedal slow down comfortably from high speed to virtually zero in a straight line! Not something I recommend on a regular basis, but entirely possible. When *Motor Cycle* tested a T3 in their 26 July 1975 issue, the tester was full of praise for what was obviously a very fine motorcycle. Here are just a few of John Nutting's comments. 'The bike was strong, quiet and clean as ever, even though it had covered the previous thousand miles without opening the tool kit or wielding a rag. In addition I felt as fresh as when I started out earlier that afternoon. That sort of performance puts the £1,600 Moto Guzzi right out at the pinnacle of the world's best tourers. Of its handling, Nutting went on to say, 'Most un-Italian, they [Guzzi] haven't opted for ultra-taut steering. Helped by the low centre of gravity of the in-line (in reference to the crank/gearbox/clutch assembly) engine, Guzzi have given the bike a pleasing

ability to be flicked through bends. The steering's light and almost telepathic – you're almost through a corner before you think about it!' At the very end of the test John Nutting summed up by saying, 'With its price tag, the Moto Guzzi is a high class, long term proposition, a practical machine built for a purpose. It is different, but this is one of its very charms. In all a classic motorcycle, worthy of the name Moto Guzzi.'

What a road test report of a few hundred miles at best cannot uncover is what a bike is like to own and ride over a long period. Generally the engine itself was the model of reliability, but, as with virtually every mechanical thing, there were weak points. Besides the less than satisfactory standard of finish, came leaking front fork and rear gearbox oil seals, an occasional rectifier failure, and flimsy switchgear. Another of the most common faults was the relatively short life of some rubber components. This was not helped by the factory themselves, who insisted during most of my period as a Guzzi dealer (1975–1981), of spraying a preservative mixture on to the bikes before they left the plant. Whatever this might have achieved with metal items was undone by the damage it did to the rubber it contacted, literally rotting such items as handlebar grips and footrest rubbers. Talking of problems, the long through-bolt at the front of the engine which secures the assembly to the frame can often become seized and extremely difficult to remove.

In keeping with the sports/touring role Guzzi offered a range of accessories, many of these being supplied as standard equipment on the California version (see Chapter 8). Beginning with the T3 series, the factory recognized how popular the V-twins had become with the three-wheel brigade, by offering optional heavy-duty front fork springs with special rod end caps to locate the bottom of the spring. There was also a factory-made kit to lower the final drive gearing, consisting of a pair of 6/32 ratio bevel gears for the rear hub, a special universal joint, and a matching sleeve to connect this to the bevel shaft.

The first real update to the T3 came for the 1979 model year when a number of cosmetic changes occurred. The most notable of these was the introduction of cast alloy wheels of the type already in service on other models such as the SP1000 (Spada in UK) and the Le Mans. The latest, oblong rear lamp used on both these machines was now fitted to the T3, along with the SP1000 seat, a lockable fuel filler cap, SP switchgear, a CEV headlamp (with chrome-plated rim and a black shell) and turn signals, a redesigned centre stand, and a black plastic (instead of polished aluminium) alternator cover at the front of the engine. A tribute to the soundness of the original design was that mechanically it remained unchanged.

## 850T4

The following year, 1980, the T3 was joined by the T4. Joined, rather than replaced, as confusingly, the T3 remained in production, albeit on a reduced scale, mainly for police sales. The T4 was very much a budget version of the SP1000NT, with a smaller engine. The power unit was virtually identical to the T3, but a major departure was the use of the much sturdier Nickasil plating process instead of the former chrome finish for the cylinder bores. The silencers too were SP components, whilst the T4 was fitted with the SP handlebar fairing (without the side panels) as standard, and also as the final version of the T3 had been, the SP saddle (but in the improved, deeper SPNT mode). The centre stand, another SP item, was much easier to operate, and SP rear indicators were specified to match those in the fairing. The front

*The first real update of the T3 came for the 1979 model year. The most notable of these changes included cast alloy wheels and CEV lighting equipment.*

brake calipers were located behind the fork sliders. There is no doubt that with its weather protection and SPNT saddle the T4 offered potential buyers a superior machine for long distance touring than the bike it was trying to replace. But in sales terms it was something of a flop, never getting anywhere near even the poorest T3 sales year figure. Obviously a major reason for this lack of showroom success was the SP1000, which was not only able to offer a full, instead of a half fairing, but an extra 104cc into the bargain. Still, if one rode the two bikes you soon realized that the T4 had a lot going for it, such as a smoother power delivery and a lower purchase price for starters.

Although only one colour scheme was offered it was an attractive choice; a deep wine-red shade for the fairing, tank and side panels, with gold lining. To mark its close relationship to its predecessor, the tank and panel logos remained unchanged except for a number '4' supplanting the '3'.

## 850T5

The final development of the 850T series was the '5'. Launched in the spring of 1983, it was largely the work of the recently-created de Tomaso-inspired styling syndicate in Modena, rather than Guzzi's in-house team back in Mandello del Lario. Sadly for every-

*Weather protection was the main difference between the T4 and its forerunner, the T3.*

*Launched in the spring of 1983, the 850T5 was largely the work of the recently-created De Tomaso styling centre in Modena. There were 16in wheels front and rear.*

one, this body of styling experts was from the four-wheel world, and while they might have been able to transform a tin box into a thing of beauty, the same certainly could not be said of their attempts on two wheels. The 850T5 was to prove one of the least popular of all Guzzi's V-twins. The machine was a mixture of components, some from the T3/4, some from the Le Mans III, some from the new V75 (see Chapter 7), some from the SPII although in fact the SPII arrived after the launch of the T5) and others, only applicable to the T5 itself. The basic mechanics came from the T3/4; the 'square' cylinders, heads, and rocker covers (but not the carbs) from the Le Mans III; the fairing from the

V75; controls, instruments, seat, side panels, tank, front mudguard, and front wheel assembly from the SPII. As with the V35 Imola II, V50 Monza II and V65 Lario, the original T5 had 16-inch front and rear wheels. This, was without any shadow of doubt, a crass attempt to follow a fashion introduced hurriedly by the Japanese industry. In Guzzi's case it was a particularly ill-conceived attempt to modernize, as little thought seems to have been given to the effect of such a move on the ground clearance of items such as silencers, footrests, and pedals; as these were insufficient. Because of these failings Guzzi were forced into bringing out a modified version for the

1985 model year, with an 18-inch rear wheel. This at least solved the matter of ground clearance, although handling, road holding and general on-road characteristics were never to match those of the earlier T series. This was a great pity, because in several other areas the T5 was a competent motorcycle. Certainly the choice of 16in wheels did not affect the handling so much as it did with the Le Mans or the SP II; the two latter machines having greater performance potential were really unsettling under certain conditions. The 'Mk 2' T5NT of 1985 not only sported an 18in rear wheel, but also the frame from the recently

*Poor ground clearance led to the introduction of a 'Mark 2' T5NT with an 18 inch rear wheel*

## TECHNICAL SPECIFICATIONS
### 850 T5 NT (1985)

| | | | |
|---|---|---|---|
| Engine | 4-stroke 90° V-twin | Brakes | twin front disc, single rear disc; integral brake system device. |
| Bore | 83mm | | |
| Stroke | 78 mm | Wheels | light alloy casting. |
| Displacement | 844.05 cc | Tyres | Front 110/90 H 16 or V18 Rear 120/90 H 18 or V18. |
| Max power | 67hp at 7000rpm | | |
| Max torque | 7.5kg at 5800rpm | Frame | duplex cradle, with detachable bottom rods |
| Compression ratio | 9.5:1 | | |
| Timing | ohv | Suspension | Front, Moto Guzzi telescopic air fork with pressure equalizer. Rear, swinging fork with equalized oil/air damper. |
| Lubrication | by pressure pump | | |
| Transmission | primary by gears; secondary by cardan shaft with cush-drive in the wheel | | |
| Clutch | dry with double disc | Instrument panel | speedometer, rev-counter, voltmeter, quartz clock on panel complete with warning lights |
| Fuel delivery | two carburettors 30, with air filtering and inlet silencer | | |
| | | Fuel tank capacity | 26ltr approx. (5.73gal) |
| Electrical system | 12V, alternator 14V-20A, battery 24 Ah | Fuel consumption | 5.4ltr × 100km (1.19mpg) |
| Starting | electric | Dry weight | 220kg (485lb) |
| Ignition | current distributor | Max speed | 200kph approx. (124mph) |
| Gearbox | 5-speed | | |

announced Spada II, a screen for the miniature fairing and several smaller modifications.

Testing both the original and the modified versions of the T5 in May 1985, I was pleasantly surprised – impressed even – and questioned just how good the bike would have been with 17 or 18in rims. But all this could only be speculation; as the factory themselves, no doubt influenced by continuing poor sales, axed the T5 at the end of the year.

## SP1000

With the SP, known as the *Spada* (Sword) in Great Britain, Moto Guzzi set themselves on a path to offer its customers a viable alternative which could break BMW's stranglehold on the long-haul, luxury touring market. The model was in fact a very serious attempt by the Italians to steal the clothes from that Teutonic flagship, the R100RS Boxer twin. One look at the SP's fairing

gives the game away. At Mandello del Lario, in mid-1976, the factory's management had realized that it was necessary to embark on a major expansion, underpinned by backing from the de Tomaso empire, with the expressed goal of doubling production figures by the end of 1978. To achieve this would not only require a new range of middleweight twins, but also a need to attract more customers to its existing larger engine range. A logical move would be to attract some of these extra buyers from the ranks of the current or prospective BMW owners. Thus the plans were laid for what was to finally emerge as the 1-litre SP model. It was an entirely logical move to make, as the luxury sports/tourer project was able to draw heavily on existing technology and could therefore not only reach production after a relatively short development period, but costs would be lower too. In fact, so far as the main chassis and engine components were concerned, the SP was largely a marriage of convenience between the 850T3 and V1000 models. The increased engine capac-

*The SP1000, known as the Spada (Sword) on the British market was Italy's answer to the BMW R100RS sports/tourer.*

ity was necessary to give Guzzi a competitive motorcycle in the by-now vital 1-litre category made full use of the work already carried out on the 948.813cc (88 × 78mm) unit originally devised for the largely unsuccessful V1000 Convert automatic which had been launched as far back as 1975. This was simply given a conventional clutch and gearbox, courtesy of the T3, and housed in a frame and suspension package that was again taken from the existing components of the T3.

But if these measures smacked of pure convenience engineering in order to boost the otherwise by-now ageing T3 into a larger (and more popular) capacity arena, this was not entirely true, as a considerable chunk of the R&D budget allocated to the project had been set aside to confront BMW head on – and in areas which the German giant had so far easily led the field. Guzzi's management targeted two areas which needed special attention – rider protection and a high level of standard equipment. They also set their

first priority to equip the new machine with an efficient, factory-developed fairing as BMW had done with its RS model. In many respects it was surprising that Moto Guzzi had not done this earlier, instead of taking its lead from BMW. For it was Guzzi who had led the world during the 1950s in the development of motorcycle streamlining, becoming the first factory to construct its own wind tunnel facilities, albeit for testing racing, rather than street bikes. It is sad to realize that the company which had most of all realized the importance of aerodynamics in racing had not followed this through into roadster production, instead allowing their test facility to stand idle for some two decades, with its massive Piaggio aero engine, rated at 2,000hp, gathering dust. But with the arrival of the SP1000 project, this was no longer to remain simply a monument to a golden era now past. The mighty piston engine was pressed into service once more and its roaring slipstream was unleashed on to the task of finding the most

*A line-up of twenty SP 1000s outside the factory's wind tunnel. It was this facility which was instrumental in the design of the model's fairing.*

suitable compromise between style and projection for the marque's new flagship. Besides the aviation engine, a marine engine from a torpedo boat was also tested, but this proved unsuccessful. For the majority of the SP project and thereafter, the factory took the decision to modernize its wind tunnel facilities, and this included the installation of a new 300hp electric motor, which is still in use today.

Many ideas were tested before a final decision was taken on the definitive designs for the SP's streamlining. It was certainly not conceived with aerodynamics winning over function, but very much the other way around. By the standard of the late 1970s, Guzzi's solution was both elegant and somewhat unconventional. Even though the streamlining gave the protection of a full fairing, it was actually closer to the traditional combination of a separate handlebar fairing and legshields. But whereas these fittings have normally meant utilitarian ugliness that is the very antithesis of style, Guzzi's version managed to capture something entirely different combining a modern style with aerodynamic efficiency. The reasoning behind the definitive layout was spot on. The separate top section could turn with the handlebars, thus allowing it to be mounted much closer to the rider than a conventional full fairing, which needs to be mounted far enough away to allow clearance for the handlebars on full lock. As a result, the SP fairing offered a much superior level of protection for the extremities of head and hands – areas which often tend to be sacrificed for reason of design or style compromise. There was also an added bonus in that the lower side panels (leg shields), which were firmly fixed to the frame, could be removed individually with little effort and without the need to disturb the main top fairing section. This was a real boon for owners wishing to carry out engine maintenance.

All of these main moulding structures were manufactured in fibreglass. The lower sections mounted closely on to the frame, thus doing away with the need for the bulky bracing tubes so often needed to support large, full fairings. Recessed cut-outs in their flanks allowed the cylinders to protrude into the cooling airstream and also allowed virtually unrestricted access for top-end work on the engine, such as routine valve adjustment. Just above the cylinders were protruding, angled aerofoil sections, found necessary during the wind tunnel testing to increase the downforce on the front wheel at speed, thus enhancing stabil-

*The SP's fairing – actually a handlebar type with separate side panels. It was nonetheless extremely effective.*

ity. The handlebar-mounted section overlapped the lower panels with a minimum clearance, giving the appearance from some views as being a one-piece full fairing assembly. The 170mm CEV headlight was fitted into the top section so that unlike a full fairing it turned with the steering, a particular advantage in low speed manoeuvres. Twin mirror (and oblong built-in turn signals) were also fitted to the top fairing which housed many of the special standard fitment features which set the SP1000 apart from its more mundane brothers in the Moto Guzzi family. Besides the usual speedometers and tachometers, there was also an analogue clock, mounted on the nearside, and a matching voltmeter on the offside. These instruments were all carried in a large, moulded rubber dash with the 'SP' logo, which also supported an array of hazard lights and the centrally-placed ignition switch. The warning light cluster was split into two groups of four. The nearside display

consisted of a green light (left turn signal), another green (neutral), a red (left turn signal) and a second, red (oil pressure). The offside display comprised a red (oil level), a blue (high beam), a green (parking light) and a second green (right turn signal). The dash also had more facilities: a switch for emergency flashes, and a trip meter which could be zeroed to record a chosen mileage.

The handlebar switchgear had also been updated. The new design was characterized by an assortment of brightly coloured buttons which one journalist aptly described as having 'escaped from a Monopoly set'. The switches on the clutch lever side were arranged in two separate assemblies, and operated the lights and dip, the horn, headlamp flash and turn signals. The brake side carried just the starter and engine cut-out buttons. One control that was not handlebar-mounted was the choke. This was to be found in the traditional Guzzi location, with a trigger mounted next to the nearside carb,

*Besides the usual speedometer and tachometer, there were also an analogue clock (left) and voltmeter (right), plus an array of warning lights. Note centrally placed ignition switch.*

with a separate cable for each. In the engine department a pair of 9.2:1 compression pistons ran in steel bores. Power output at the crankshaft was an impressive sounding 71bhp at 6500rpm, with a useful torque figure of 8.6kg/m at 5100rpm. But the real output measured at the rear wheel was only 54.91bhp at 6250rpm. This was not just an increase over the T3, but also the V1000; the latter suffering as it did from the energy-sapping disadvantages of the plate-like torque converter. A modification adapted for the SP in the transmission was the use of a larger rubber bellows which covered a new sturdier universal joint and linked the gearbox casing with the swinging arm.

The SP's silencers were modelled on those used on the Le Mans, with their upswept style, rather than the other touring models' flat variety. But, unlike the Le Mans, they now came with bright chrome-plate. More Le Mans influence by way of component parts were to be found in the silver-painted cast alloy wheels. The braking followed the by now familiar patented Moto Guzzi linked system with twin 300mm front discs and a single 242mm unit at the rear, but with two changes. At the front, the brake calipers were mounted behind the fork sliders, while at the rear, a large P9 caliper (still of the twin piston type) with a pressure relief valve were specified in an attempt to cut down the rather excessive wear rate which the linked system placed on the rear disc. The actual rear brake pads were also a different part number to the standard Guzzi pair found on other models such as the T3 and Le Mans. A friction-type steering damper was also provided.

The frame was left virtually unchanged, but both stands had been modified to make their operation easier. The main priority in both cases was to provide more effective operating arms, both less than satisfactory on earlier V-twins. The 24-litre tank design obviously owed much to the T3; there being

a pair of manually operated taps and a fuel filler cap concealed under a steel, hinged cover which could be released by inserting the ignition key. The seat was new, and was in many ways one of the machine's poorest features; certainly it nowhere matched the comfort of either the T3 or V1000 type. Its only advantage was a slightly reduced seat height. To the rear of the seat came a Le Mans tail lamp, whilst the front mudguard was an extended copy of the Le Mans component. Launched in late 1977 at the Milan Show, where a record 150,000 people swamped the exhibition on the opening day, Guzzi's new luxury fully-faired sports/tourer was one of the stars of the show. Motorcycle journalists from around the world were impressed enough by the new Guzzi to generally report in a favourable fashion typified by the British weekly, *Motor Cycle News* in their 23 November issue: 'A more immediately available challenge [in reference to Laverda's new V6 which was also making its public debut] to BMW comes from Guzzi with foot change versions of their 1000 automatic. Sporting a normal five-speed box, instead of a torque converter, the new 1000SP has mag [aluminium actually] wheels and a nose fairing which gave Guzzi a splendid excuse to start up their old racing wind tunnel.' The factory's model brochure indicated a sense of achievement in the launch of the SP: 'Moto Guzzi are proud to present a new standard of safety in motorcycle fairings. The new SP fairing was designed in the factory's famous wind tunnel, not just to be correct for the machine, but to be correct for the machine with the rider mounted. This new design concept offers the rider not only protection from weather and outstanding streamlining, but with integral front spoilers the machine's front and is held more firmly on the road at high speeds. This new safer fairing combined with the Moto Guzzi unique integral brake system helps to make this new

*Journalists were generally impressed by the SP's road behaviour. However, there were a few criticisms (outlined in the text), plus a less than satisfactory finish (at least on the Mk I).*

machine the world's safest, most beautiful and exciting motorcycle.' Having a backlog of orders on the home market, exports of the SP did not begin until well into 1978; the first batch reaching British dealers in July, at a cost to the customer of £2,399. Colour choices were limited to metallic silver or gold. Sales were well up to expectations and remained so for the balance of the year.

Despite this initial euphoria there were some off-putting faults on the original SP – headed by a combination of spartan comfort and an abysmal finish. To start with many of the fairings were negated in their usefulness by poor finish and fitment of the component parts; but most of all by the louvers (at the rear of the cylinder heads), which crushed the kneecaps of taller riders. The seat on the SP 'Mark I' was painfully uncomfortable (especially for the pillion passenger) after 60–70 miles (95–110km), while the general paint work and chrome plate were simply not up to an acceptable standard. The metallic finishes did not help as they were difficult to match once paint damage/wear occurred.

Because of these factors and intense competition from BMW, importers and distributors found as they entered 1979 stocks beginning to build up. In Britain by the spring of 1979 sales had nosedived to such an extent that importers Coburn & Hughes were being faced by something of a crisis of stockpiled SPs. Faced with this expensive and potentially damaging situation, they came up with a brilliant plan. Enter the Spada Royale. This was a limited edition created by the importers themselves purely for the British market. Cleverly created to confer an aura of exclusivity that would attract discerning buyers, the most noticeable Royale treatment consisted of a special paint finish in metallic cherry red and silver. This was carried out by the well-respected custom paint specialists, Dream Machine of Long Eaton, Nottingham. A practical addition to the package was a pair of excellent quality lockable hard panniers manufactured by the Birmingham company Sigma. When the Royale was introduced, the standard SP (Spada) had been reduced to £2,299. But in typical marketing fashion C&H were able to justify a premium of an

extra £500 for the Royale. The exclusivity ticket worked so well that by August 1979 the initial batch of 100 Royales was virtually all sold – and sales of the basic model were sufficient to stand an increase in price of £255!

The success of the Royale exercise had convinced Coburn & Hughes that the exclusive model ploy was worth playing again. The result was another 'limited edition', introduced towards the end of that year. Known as the Black Prince, and as the name implied, it was finished in black throughout relieved only by tastefully applied gold pin striping of the tank, side panels and fairing and offset by the silver-finished wheels, alloy cylinders and chrome exhaust system. The Black Prince (a name borrowed from the HRD Vincent V-twin of the 1950s) once again proved a profitable sales venture, and one which greatly assisted in the importers task of running down their stock of SPs in

*British importers Coburn & Hughes scored a success out of an overstock problem, by creating the 'limited edition' Spada Royale. It cost £2,799 – an increase of £500 over the standard SP.*

readiness for the launch in early 1980 of an updated model.

## SP NT

Officially coded SP NT80, the newcomer was soon marketed simply as the SP NT (or Spada NT in Great Britain). NT stood for 'New Type'. Although in truth, the NT80 was not anything other than how the original SP should have been in the first place, it was a much superior motorcycle. Reworked, the NT had been given new more restrictive silencers (but in keeping with the machine's image), Nickasil finished cylinder bores in place of the old V1000-originated steel liners of the Mark I SP, the seat was now the same as the deliciously comfortable V1000 type whilst the screen was heightened to compensate for the increase in seat height. Gone were the knee crunching louvers, replaced by much saner, more practical (and most of all comfortable) components. Another improvement was that the footrests were relocated, providing a less cramped position for rider and pillion alike. Other differences

*Officially coded SP NT80 (the NT was for New Type, the 80 in reference to its launch year); the Mark II largely consigned the problems of the Mark I to history.*

included chromed rear shock springs and silver-painted fork sliders (both formerly black), whilst the rocker covers had been polished on their flat top section. A flat, lockable cover hid the filling orifice on the fuel tank, and the exhaust header pipes were now double-skinned in an attempt to rid the 'bluing' experienced on the Series I machines. The frame, originally blighted with the same 'peel-off' matt black as the Le Mans I, was now gloss-painted, albeit still not to BMW standards. Generally, although still not perfect, the paint and chrome was more durable.

Technically, except for the Nikasil cylinder coating process, the NT was unchanged. The real improvements came by way of the superior attention to detail and better ancillary equipment. In other words the NT was a better overall package than the original. Once again, the British concessionaires, Coburn & Hughes came up with a masterful sales promotion – or more correctly dealer promotion, because after all it was the agents who would have to stock and sell the bikes to the paying customer. Code-named 'Operation NT', this was not only a clever way of gaining the dealers' own personal enthusiasm, but also at the same time of ensuring each of the participating dealers would have a demonstration model for the official UK launch. Operation NT saw twenty-five British dealers, two of the importer's staff and two journalists, arriving at Mandello del Lario to collect the first twenty-nine NTs off the production line. The idea was that they would then make a first trans-European crossing together as a demonstration of the revised machine's capabilities. The members of the press, it was hoped, would report favourably, while the dealers would retain their machines as demonstrators. But the best laid plans do not always work out as everyone expects. Reaching the factory the British party was staggered to find the works on strike and the bikes not ready! Fortunately, due to a skeleton of key personnel, the problem was solved twenty-four hours later and the following morning twenty-nine identical pale green SP NTs and their British riders assembled at the factory gates for the long ride home. The biggest problem encountered on the journey was that many of the machines were ridden hard from the very start. This resulted in a few engines suffering partial seizures. None was forced out, but in retrospect a bit more patience would have solved the problem. In their favour the new Guzzis recorded truly excellent fuel economy figures. Bearing in mind the stick many received – often cruising at high speeds on the autostrada, and full bore up steep mountain climbs, figures of 45–60mpg (6.3–8.4l/100km) was better than could have been expected. Certainly higher than the majority of modern motorcycles.

Operation NT had taken place in April 1980, and the new model went on sale in the UK during the following month at £2,709. The NT was to continue with no changes except to price and paint finish until late 1983. Although Coburn & Hughes did try their limited edition, get-rich-quick concept with a model called the Mistral it was to prove a resounding failure. The Mistral, like its forerunners the Royale and Black Prince, was fitted with panniers, but lack of demand saw very few machines sold between the time it first went on sale in February 1982 and when it was discontinued four months later in May that year. In any case, the whole Mistral idea was not helped by the fact that Guzzi themselves had launched a model in striking red and white livery, which did much to improve its appearance – but ultimately, there was by then a falling sales demand. This was not helped by continued price rises and a market in deep recession. In Britain a new imposition of an 8 per cent 'car tax' (levied on motorcycles it should be noticed!) introduced on new motorcycles

*To counter falling demand the factory brought out a version in a striking red and white livery during Spring 1982. But with a world motorcycle market still deeply in recession sales never matched earlier figures.*

from March 1981 by the 'money-grabbing' Tory (Conservative) chancellor Geoffrey Howe and helped kill sales in a further depressed market. By the spring of 1983, what UK dealers who were left, were being asked by Coburn & Hughes to extract £3,459 from their loyal customers. All this showed in C&H's sales figures – over 2,000 Guzzis in 1980, down to less than 200 in 1983 – a fall of over 90 per cent! Guzzi too were feeling the pinch and thus another variation of the SP theme was readied for a launch later that year at the Italian industry's usual venue, the Milan Show.

## SP II

The early 1980s was a bad time to be selling motorcycles; the two-wheeled industry being hit as hard as any in the world-wide recession which had seen manufacturing companies around the globe fold one after the other. As for Moto Guzzi themselves they were faced with a need for new models, but no cash to do so. The result was to be decisions based on marketing rather than on-road performance. Coded SP II, and first displayed to the public at the Milan Show in November 1983, this was a substantially altered motorcycle. It should have been a better one, but for reasons which will become apparent it was anything but. The II's engine now sported the angular cylinder head and barrel finning already found on the Le Mans III, California II, and 850T models. The revised cylinder heads brought maximum power up to 67bhp at 6700rpm – although effective torque figures were actually slightly reduced. But it was to the cycle parts that the main changes occurred. Major amongst these was the decision taken to fit a 16in front wheel. In addition, both cast alloy wheels now featured ten straight-section spokes rather than the original twelve cranked ones. Wider section tyres, a 100/90 H16 front and 130/80 H18 rear provided increased levels of road grip. The brake disc diameter had now been standardized to 270mm all round, and these were drilled and plated, which provided them with a new style. The basic chassis remained largely unchanged as it had been when the original SP had been launched some six years earlier, but it was now dressed in a virtually new set of clothes. One component which had not been altered during the update from NT to II, was the fairing assembly. But behind it lurked a totally new tank shape with an increased 24-litre capacity.

Also fresh were the seat and passenger grab rail, the mudguards (now plastic both front and rear), and the side panels. One additional change that broke with Guzzi tradition was that twin wind-tone horns replaced the former type that had been a feature of the Guzzi vees for almost twenty years. The paint job consisted of red for the tank, side panels and fairing. Black was employed for the frame (including the swinging arm, fork sliders, yokes, stands, cylinder recesses in the fairing rocker covers) and several smaller components.

Unfortunately the machine's great virtues, of general performance, weather protection and fuel economy were more than offset by the truly dreadful handling and roadholding. In fact it was so bad that whilst testing one of the early SP IIs in 1984 I actually felt uneasy. The culprit of course was that 16in front wheel. On the lighter and smaller V65 Lario for example (see Chapter 7) the effect was nothing like it was on the relatively heavy and bulky SP II. How could Guzzi have made such a monumental mistake? As explained elsewhere, it was unfortunately the direct result of a combination comprising four-wheel engineers and marketing men, rather than motorcyclists. It took the factory a little under two years to start rectifying the situation. After no doubt a real, concentrated ear bashing from its ownership, dealers and importers Guzzi were forced into seeing sense and, together with the Le Mans, were given back their 18in front wheels. This solved the stability problems and also meant that customers could buy the product with renewed confi-

*The new SP II was first displayed to the public at the Milan Show in November 1983. Substantially altered, it should have been a better motorcycle, but as the text reveals, it was just the reverse; not helped by the infamous 16in front wheel saga.*

dence. The balance of the technical specification remained unaltered, and in this guise the SP II soldiered on until it was, itself, superseded by the considerably improved III for the 1988 model year.

## SP III

This motorcycle was the one in which the mistakes of the unloved (and largely unbought!) SP II were finally put right in a total package. Besides starting out with having 18in wheels both fore and aft, the newcomer also had the benefit of entirely new bodywork, including a totally new four-section fairing. Other major changes were, for the first time on one of the heavyweight Guzzi V-twins, electronic ignition and large-capacity Givi-made hard panniers.

Other features included a folding handle to ease the task of getting the 230kg (506lb) machine on to its centre stand, a totally new and very comfortable dual-seat, a rear light which blended in with the bodywork, and a large grab handle for the passenger. A revised front end featured an integral fork brace and the same 300mm semi-floating

---

**TECHNICAL SPECIFICATIONS**
**1000 SP III**

| | | | |
|---|---|---|---|
| Engine | 4-stroke 90° V-twin | Brakes | twin front 300mm and one rear 270mm, floating discs. |
| Bore | 88mm | | |
| Stroke | 78mm | Wheels | light alloy casting. |
| Displacement | 948.8 cc | | |
| Max power | 71bhp | Tyres | Front, 100/90 V 18in Rear, 120/90 V 18in |
| Max torque | 7.9kg | Frame | tubular duplex cradle. |
| Carburation | two 36mm carburettors with air filtering and inlet silencer. | Suspension | Front, Moto Guzzi telescopic fork with adjustable spring pre-loads and dampening. Rear, swinging fork with hydraulic Koni shock-absorbers. |
| Compression ratio | 9.5:1 | | |
| Timing | ohv | | |
| Lubrication | by pressure pump | | |
| Transmisson | primary by helical gears; secondary by Cardan shaft and bevel gears. | Instrument panel | includes speedometer, rev-counter, voltmeter and warning lights. |
| Clutch | double plate, dry type | Fuel tank capacity | 22.5ltr (4.9gal) |
| Electrical system | 12V, alternator 14V-20A. Battery 24Ah | Fuel consumption | 5.6ltr × 100km (51mpg Imp) (CUNA Norms) |
| Starting | electric | Dry weight | 230kg (506lb) |
| Ignition | electronic | Max speed | 195kph approx. (122mph) |
| Gearbox | 5-speed | | |

*Guzzi finally came to their senses and the SP III was the result. Besides a new style it had several worthwhile improvements. These included 18in wheels, electronic ignition and large-capacity Givi-made hard luggage.*

brake discs as used on the California III. The SP III was to be the final development of the Spada series, but although it continued to be popular in certain countries, including Britain, it ceased production in late 1990, although stock ensured its continued availability until 1992. Colours were usually white or gun-metal grey metallic.

## MILLE GT

The Mille GT appeared at the same time as the SP1000 III and California III, at the 1987 Milan Show. If it was not for the fact that Guzzi already produced what one might term traditional motorcycles, the Mille GT could be said to have been the world's first retro model – for that is what it really was. Offered in a choice of bright Italian racing red with gold pinstriping or classic black and gold, the paintwork contrasted most effectively with the abundance of bright chrome plate and polished aluminium. It came on to the market long before the Kawasaki Zephyr range or even Guzzi's own

1000S (see Chapter 3) and was proof that after too many years of listening to the wrong people, the Mandello del Lario factory was at last prepared to build bikes their long suffering customers wanted. The electrics (together with the other 1988 model year machines mentioned above) benefited from a complete revamp with new 'user friendly' switchgear replacing the lurid Lego blocks of the previous generation. There were also entirely new, rubber-mounted turn signals, together with anti-dazzle mirrors, the latter mounted on T3-style handlebars. The Veglia instruments were basic, clear, twin round clocks with a warning light console mounted between them.

Riding a Mille GT in the summer of 1988 I well remember the feeling of satisfaction which I had earlier felt whilst owning a couple of T3s in the 1970s. The Mille GT was very much like the T3, but with more power and a number of useful improvements in both build quality and overall finish. However, with the masses of bright chrome and polished alloy I remember thinking that the machine would need not just an enthusias-

*The Mille GT appeared at the same time as the SP III and California III at the 1987 Milan Show. It was very much a machine for traditionalists and would now be referred to as a 'retro'.*

*Moto Guzzi's production line building Mille GT's in November 1988. The machine found considerable favour with a certain section of Guzzi fans.*

*The Mille GT was available both with cast alloy wheels (illustrated) or welled-alloy rims laced to the hubs with spokes.*

tic owner, but one who got as much enjoyment from cleaning as riding! Many buyers opted for the more traditional wire, rather than cast wheels. I also felt that the solid cast iron discs did not provide as much stopping power as the semi-floating type found on the other 1988 model heavyweight Guzzi V-twins. A definite improvement over the previous T series models was the axing of the old flat slide VHB carbs in favour of PHF 30s, fitted with accelerator pumps to assist mid-range power. All-in-all, the Mille GT can be said to have been the true successor to the much loved T3 of the 1970s. Production ceased in 1991.

## 1000 STRADA

The Mille GT's replacement was the Strada, which first entered production in 1992. But, one can best judge what a poor impact it made by realizing that British importers, Three Cross Motorcycles of Dorset, waited a full two years before deciding to import the model, and then in only very limited numbers. With no frills (read no thrills!) the Strada was intended as a 850T3/Mille GT roadster, and was offered with a choice of either wire or cast wheels. Unlike the then current 1100 California, the Strada did not enjoy the benefit of either the extra 115cc or the choice for the owner to specify the superb Weber/Marelli fuel injection/electronic ignition systems. The changes, together with a better styling job, could well have transformed the model's sales prospects. As it was it had hardly anything to recommend it to the 1990's motorcyclist – even the most enthusiastic Guzzi type, let alone Joe Public. It lacked the retro style of the Mille GT, the weather protection of the SP, the charisma of the California or any other attributes which would have meant someone actually wanting to buy one. My own comments made in *Moto Guzzi Buyers Guide* 2nd Edition (Motor-

*Entering production in 1992, the Strada model was supposed to be the Mille GT's replacement. However, it was never to match the earlier machine's appeal. Sales never reached target and it was finally discontinued in 1994. The last machines were sold in 1995, bringing to an end the T-series saga.*

books) really says it all: 'A poor effort to bring the T3/Mille GT concept into the 1990s. Outdated and largely unexciting.'

By 1995 the Strada was no more, Guzzi had moved on; it was now in the process of being reorganized by a new, more aggressive management. Quite simply the bad old days in which machines such as the Strada were allowed to exist side-by-side with far better-planned models was over – this time the author hopes, for good. But let us not forget that for many years Moto Guzzi built affordable, basic roadsters. Classics such as the 850T3, Spada NT and Mille GT stand out as bikes which any owner could be truly proud to own and excited to ride.

# 5  Military and Police Service

As with leading manufacturers in other countries, including Triumph (Great Britain), Harley-Davidson (USA) and BMW (Germany), Moto Guzzi have always maintained strong connections with their government, with both the military and police authorities ordering motorcycles from the Mandello del Lario marque over the years. This pattern of events was very much a reflection of the machines each of the four respective manufacturers have consistently produced – practical, robust and relatively simple in design, making them ideal for the tasks such service demands.

Length of service, ease of maintenance and interchangeability of component parts are all vital ingredients for government usage. This of course is not always the lot of other marques which are often renowned for being more sporting, over-complicated or just plain fragile. The very first Moto Guzzi to enter either government service – in a civil or military role – was the Tipo (type) GT17, a development of the standard production GT and GT16 models manufactured between 1938 through to 1934. Like these, the GT17, which was built from 1932 until 1939 for military use, was an overhead valve flat single employing the classic Guzzi format of 498.73cc (88 × 82mm). In common with its civilian brothers, this was equipped with the Italian factory's early 'spring in box' form the rear suspension, crude, but effective for the time. Besides service in Italy

*Moto Guzzi's GT17, a 498.4cc (88 × 82mm) horizontal ohv single, the definitive prewar Italian military motorcycle. It ran from 1932 through to 1939, seeing service at home and abroad – some fitted with a Breda- or Fiat-made light machine gun.*

itself, the '17' was liberally used in the Italian African colonies, which at that time included Libya and much of East Africa. Many variants were built, one of them even being equipped with a Breda or Fiat-made light machine-gun.

During early 1939 the GT17 was superseded by the generally similar GT20, before production commenced later that year of the motorcycle with which most Italians went to war, the Alce (elk). This machine was a development of both the earlier military models, and was manufactured in huge numbers during the war years in both solo and three-wheel (Trialces) versions. Development continued even after hostilities had ceased, and in 1946 an updated

version, the Superalce, made its bow. This motorcycle was to remain in service for over a decade, before eventually being retired from service in 1957, although in reality it had already been largely phased out in favour of the new Falcone Militaire (the service version of the popular civilian five-hundred Falcone model). From the mid-1950s, this was built for police duties as well as was a near identical two-fifty version, the Airone. As recounted in Chapters 1 and 2, the background to the complete V-twin series was the bizarre 3 × 3 three-wheel military tractor project, from which sprang the first 90-degree V-twin motorcycle, the V7. Although the V7 was ultimately destined to be a massive civilian success

*Well over fifty policemen on Moto Guzzi Falcone singles demonstrate their skills before a gathering of civil dignitaries in Rome during September 1958.*

story, it was itself originally conceived as a military and police motorcycle – as a replacement for the long-in-the-tooth Falcone single-cylinder machine. By 1936, both the military and police authorities in Italy had realized that with traffic becoming ever denser and faster, their two-wheeled fleet had to be modernized in line with the evolving conditions. With similar needs in both fields of duty, it was deemed necessary for both authorities to co-operate in the design and funding of a new motorcycle. This was not a simple matter of looking for a machine already in production and hoping it would meet service needs, or for that matter asking Moto Guzzi to build an updated single. Instead, virtually the whole Italian industry was requested to tender, for what after all would be an extremely lucrative contract. Finally the bids to tender for the new project were whittled down to four companies – Benelli, Ducati, Gilera – and Guzzi.

The first three marques all chose to offer parallel twins. Benelli's design was an ohv creation, which in the fullness of time would eventually be sold in the late 1960s and early 1970s as the 642.8cc (84 × 58mm) Tornado with five speeds and electric start. Gilera's effort was an overhead cam 483.02cc (71 × 61mm), also with five speeds and electric thumb. But although a high quality effort, it suffered from a lack of performance. Even though it was eventually built (it made its debut at the 1967 Milan Show in police guise with single seat and radio carrier), Gilera's gathering financial problems meant that development was slower than would have been hoped for. With Piaggio's buy-out in 1969 the project was soon axed. Ducati meanwhile emerged as the V7's main challenger. It was envisaged as being constructed with two types of engine. The first (for civilian use) was a dohc, the other an ohv for police (and possible military tasks).

During the development of the two designs, Ducati's designer, Ing. Fabio Taglioni, made several experiments in an attempt to reduce the level of vibration that is normally associated with the parallel twin format. Unfortunately, Taglioni's work was largely wasted, as despite trying both 180 and 360-degree configurations, the Guzzi entry proved the most suitable choice for several reasons: development cost and price, delivery schedule, maintenance, shaft final drive and the promise of a longer service life. Where Guzzi scored over its rivals was that they already had the basis for the power unit, whereas the rest had to start from scratch. The original V7 design was the work of Ing. Giulio Carcano, who by then was in the twilight of a truly outstanding career (which had included the legendary V8 and world championship winning three-fifty

*The V7 was first conceived with military and police sales in mind. A fully fitted police version is seen here with fairing, radio, panniers and siren, circa 1967.*

flat singles). Soon the development work for future V-twins would pass from Carcano to another highly respected engineer, Ing. Lino Tonti (formerly with the likes of Aermacchi Bianchi and Gilera). Tonti had also designed the Linto five-hundred racing twin (basically a pair of two-fifty Aermacchi Ala d'Oro top ends on a common crankcase). Finally, the same man had worked with Giuseppe Patoni during the early days of the Paton racing team. The first serious studies of what were

to emerge as the V7 began in late 1963, and by early 1964, a working prototype had made an appearance of what was by now a project receiving top priority by Moto Guzzi. It should be remembered that, like the rest of the Italian bike industry, the Mandello del Lario marque had seen sales fall drastically during the late 1950s and into the early 1960s. It badly needed a degree of stability in production that the government would bring. Later in the same year, both the mili-

*Italy's presidential guard, the Corazzieri, pictured with V7s in 1969. In modern times the motorcycle replaced the horse for many of their escort duties.*

tary and police test riders were reporting back with enthusiastic satisfaction on the basic design. During December 1964, the first details of the newcomer, which was soon dubbed V7, were to appear in the Italian motorcycling press. That the V7 was to spawn such exciting sportsters as the V7 Sport, 750S/S3, Le Mans and ultimately the 4-valve Daytona of the 1990s is all the more amazing when one recalls what leading Italian journalist Carlo Perelli said in March 1965, 'A civilian version of the V7 will follow as soon as expedient. But it should be remembered that the machine has been designed with police and service use in mind – and not just in Italy – and that it is not intended to have any scintillating sporting characteristics.' The initial production batch of V7s was supplied to the Italian police during Spring 1967, at a cost of 725,000 lire each. These original 703.718cc (80 × 70mm) machines were to prove an instant hit with the police patrolmen (and later military despatch riders), whose only criticism was

that the bikes were not powerful enough! But this latter comment did not deter future orders, or for that matter interest from police forces outside Italy itself. Amongst the foreign orders came an unusual request from Holland. The Dutch Guzzis were to be fitted with a single-seat sidecar, and this combination proved so popular that when, in 1969, the larger 757.487cc (83 × 70mm) version was announced, there was instantly a repeat order from the same source. Even more interesting was a trial purchase of ten V7s for the Los Angeles Police Department (LAPD). These were delivered in March 1969, followed by another batch of eighty-five, and many more once the 844.057cc (83 × 78mm) appeared in early 1972. Negotiations for the American deals were carried out between the north American distributors – the Berliner Corporation (Premier Motor Corp.) – and Guzzi's veteran export manager Giuseppe 'Joe' Ermellini. All three engine sizes of the original V7 design were used by the Italian police, split into the three

*Police V7 Ambassador model, Cologne Show, Germany 1970. In essence, the forerunner of the original California model.*

divisions of the Polizia Stradale (traffic police), Polizia Urbana (city police) and Carabinari (local police). There was also Italy's presidency guard (the Corazzieri).

Italian police machines were usually finished in either military drab green or dark royal blue and white, although later bikes sometimes had a black and white livery. For military use, the motorcycle was normally painted in an overall dark green, with only the exhausts and a few minor components in black. The introduction of the 850T (1974) and 850T3 (1975) meant that even more Guzzi V-twins were sold to both military and police forces around the world. By now, many VIP escorts were Guzzi-equipped, performing in a role which had previously been the exclusive domain of BMW, Harley-Davidson and Triumph – except on the home market of course. Among the large numbers of overseas countries which regularly did business with Moto Guzzi, a noteworthy customer was President Fidel Castro of Cuba, on whose orders a fleet of 948.813cc (88 × 78mm) 1000G5 models was supplied in 1982 for VIP duties. The G5 was the manual (five-speed) version of the V1000 Convert Auto-

matic. By the end of the 1970s, virtually every Guzzi V-twin model had been sold to either police or military specification, including the V7 700, V7 750 Special, V7 Ambassador, 850GT, 850 Eldorado, 850T, 850T3, T3 California, 1000G5, and even the V1000 Convert. This latter model had been delivered to customers with such diverse requirements as the Sudan State Police in East Africa, and the Municipal Police Department in Louisiana, USA. The V1000 auto (torque converter) transmission was seen by many as ideal for escort duties. When the first of the new breed of middleweight vees – the V35 and V50 – made their debut in 1978, it was quite obvious that police and military models would soon follow. And follow they did, proving popular because they were not only suitable, but cost-effective too. In fact the smaller vees were to see service with several of NATO's armies for road escort duties. By the end of the decade, Guzzi police and military motorcycles were in operation in every continent except Australasia. Meanwhile in Britain, I had supervised the construction and supply of the very first police Moto Guzzi. This con-

*V1000 Convert automatic LAPD (Los Angeles Police Department) model.*

*British police Guzzi – the 1977 850T3 Pursuit, operated first by the Norfolk Constabulary later also by the Sussex force.*

*Italian Vigili Urbani police 850T3 model on display at the Milan Show, circa 1985, with its female police rider.*

*California II police model; mid-1980s. Operated by a large number of forces around the world.*

verted 'civilian' 850T3 California, was supplied to the Norfolk police in the summer of 1977, and I well remember feeling a special pride in delivering the machine personally to Kings Lynn police headquarters. That the Norfolk constabulary was well satisfied was confirmed when they took the decision to replace their fleet with special, factory-built versions of the police-specified model. Later the larger Sussex force also changed over to Guzzi, now named the Pursuit. During the early 1980s there was a marked recession in the motorcycle market on a worldwide basis. This acted as a spur for Moto Guzzi to take a renewed interest in the police and military field. They took the bold step in 1985, of

---

### TECHNICAL SPECIFICATIONS
### 850T5 Police (1985)

| | | | |
|---|---|---|---|
| Engine | 4-stroke 90° V-twin | Wheels | light alloy castings with rims WM 3.00/2.15 × 18in front and rear. |
| Bore | 83mm | | |
| Stroke | 78mm | | |
| Displacement | 844.05cc | Tyres | front and rear Pirelli Gordon MT 48 110 × 90. |
| Compression ratio | 9.5:1 | | |
| Max torque | 7.5kg at 5800rpm | Frame | duplex cradle, tubular structure. |
| Max power | 67bhp at 7200rpm | | |
| Timing | ohv | Stand | central stand and side stand Italian Police type. |
| Lubrication | by pressure pump | | |
| Transmission | primary by gears; secondary by cardan shaft with cush-drive in the wheel. | Suspension | Front, Moto Guzzi telescopic air fork with pressure equalizer. Rear, swinging fork with hydraulic adjustable 'Koni' dampers. |
| Clutch | dry with double disc. | | |
| Fuel delivery | two carburettors, Dell'Orto PHF30 CS and CD type with air filtering and inlet silencers. | | |
| | | Fuel tank capacity | 22.5ltr (5gal) |
| | | Fuel consumption | 5.4ltr × 100km (52mpg) (CUNA Standards) |
| Generator/alternator | front, on crankshaft (14V – 20A) | | |
| Battery | 12V – 28 Amp hour | Dimensions | wheelbase (loaded) 1.505m (4ft 11in) max length 2.26m (7ft 3in) max width 0.760m (2ft 6in) max height with fairing 1.5m (4ft 11in) |
| Starting | electric starter (12V – 0.7Kw) with electromagnetic ratchet control. | | |
| Ignition | coil-battery with double contact breaker and automatic advance. | Weight | with optionals and gasoline 270kg approx. (595lb) |
| Gearbox | 5-speed | | |
| Brakes | two front discs, one rear disc, integral braking system. | Max speed | 126mph (200kph) without fairing; 105mph (170kph) with fairing. |

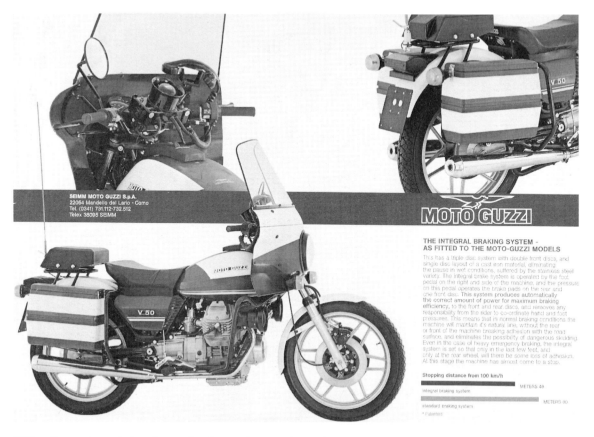

*V50 police motorcycle brochure, showing various equipment.*

issuing a special catalogue and model range for these two roles. There were four purpose-built models, comprising the 948cc California Polizia, the 844cc 850 Carabinieri, and a pair of 490cc V50s, the Polizia and Nato. The California Polizia came the nearest to being a series production model – very similar to the California II. In fact, with the exception of additional blue lights and sirens, it appeared totally stock. The Carabinieri was a much more specialized model. Not only was the T3, on which it was based, no longer in production, but it came equipped with many features, including a handlebar fairing, one-off instrumentation, a single seat, radio and carrier, legshields, front and rear crashbar, panniers and sirens.

The trend of creating specialist police and military motorcycles continued into the 1990s, Guzzi obviously realizing that its standard machines formed the basis for such work, so it was able to generate additional turnover and profit with only a small amount of development. This contrasts with most bike builders who are simply not able to take advantage of such orders because of a lack of suitable bikes to offer. With the arrival of the 1064cc 1100 California in 1994 Guzzi had a much improved model, not only for civilian, but also police use. Then, in 1997 the California EV made its debut. The police version of this latter machine was the California P.A. This was a fully equipped police force model, which had not only bene-

*Radio fitment on police 850T5 model, 1989.*

*The 1990 police and military model range; comprising from top to bottom, 125 Custom Police (a two-stroke single), V35 NT Police, V50 Military, V50 NT Police, V65 NT Police, 850 T5 Police (note 18in wheels front and rear!) and V1000 California III Police.*

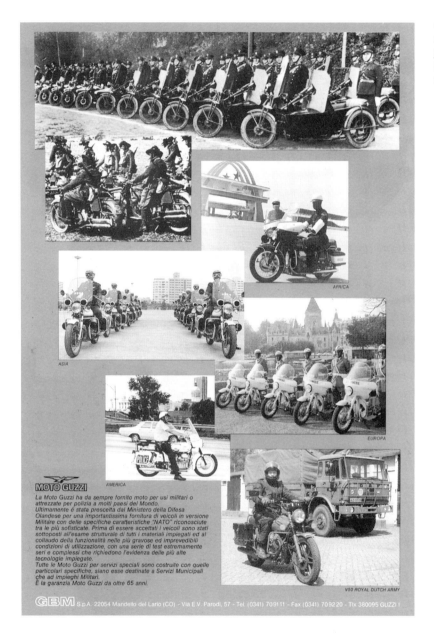

*Guzzi has been supplying motorcycles suitable for police and army forces for most of its history. Here are a few examples.*

AFRICA

ASIA

EUROPA

AMERICA

**MOTO GUZZI**

*La Moto Guzzi ha da sempre fornito moto per usi militari o attrezzate per polizia a molti paesi del Mondo.*
*Ultimamente è stata prescelta dal Ministero della Difesa Olandese per una importantissima fornitura di veicoli in versione Militare con delle specifiche caratteristiche "NATO" riconosciute tra le più sofisticate. Prima di essere accettati i veicoli sono stati sottoposti all'esame strutturale di tutti i materiali impiegati ed al collaudo della funzionalità nelle più gravose ed imprevedibili condizioni di utilizzazione, con una serie di test estremamente seri e complessi che richiedono l'evidenza delle più alte tecnologie impiegate.*
*Tutte le Moto Guzzi per servizi speciali sono costruite con quelle particolari specifiche, siano esse destinate a Servizi Municipali che ad impieghi Militari.*
*È la garanzia Moto Guzzi da oltre 65 anni.*

V50 ROYAL DUTCH ARMY

GBM S.p.A. 22054 Mandello del Lario (CO) - Via E.V. Parodi, 57 - Tel. (0341) 709111 - Fax (0341) 709220 - Tlx 380095 GUZZI I

fited from continued development over many years, but also been subjected to the strictest structural tests and most demanding inspections. It was particularly suitable for VIP escort (government leaders for example). Moto Guzzi's main challenger for police (and military) contracts has in fact in recent times been BMW, and to a lesser extent Italian rivals, Cagiva. So it would appear that as the twenty-first century dawns the sight of a police Guzzi on the motorway, or the Guzzi mounted soldier escorting a convoy, will remain a regular sight around the world.

# 6  Le Mans

For over one and a half decades, one Moto Guzzi model stood head and shoulders above its brothers; this bike was the Le Mans. Named after the legendary French racing circuit the Guzzi Le Mans, in its various forms, proved to be one of the true classics of the postwar Italian motorcycle industry, and except for the on-going California, built in larger numbers and over a longer period, than any other large capacity Mandello del Lario V-twin. Originally conceived in the mid-1970s to take on rivals such as the Ducati 900SS (bevel), Laverda 3C and MV Agusta America, it outlived them all, before finally being phased out of production during the early 1990s. A prototype was track tested in the 1973 Barcelona 24 Hours

endurance race. Ridden by Raimondo Riva and Giuseppe Gazzola it came home an excellent fifth, in an event won by Ducati riders Benjamin Grau and Salvador Canellas.

## MARK I

The production model, the Le Mans I, was officially announced, and exhibited, at the biannual Milan Show in November 1975. But whereas its Italian competitors Ducati, Laverda and MV had largely created uncompromising sports machines, the Guzzi offering was equally at home in both sporting and touring roles. In fact, when asked by a

The original 1976 Le Mans Mark I, to many the finest Italian sporting motorcycle of the mid-1970s.

potential customer which machine he should buy – the choice was between a 900SS or Le Mans I – I replied, 'Well, if you want to ride the bike every day, pick the Guzzi.' When placed alongside its predecessors, the 750S3, 750S and V7 Sport, the Le Mans displayed a clean pair of heels in terms of marketing appeal, although many traditional Moto Guzzi enthusiasts still argue that the original V7 Sport (see Chapter 3) was the model which most had the heart of an out-and-out sportster, a theme which had become somewhat blurred by the time the Le Mans appeared on the scene. Nonetheless, Moto Guzzi was a commercial operation and it was the Le Mans, not the V7 Sport which generated by far the most revenue. So it has

to be said in this instance the marketing man scored a significant victory over the engineers. None of this is to imply that the Le Mans was not a grade one Sportster in its own right, just that whereas the 900SS, 3C and V7 Sport offered a more single approach, the 'Lemon' as it was commonly called, offered a wider appeal, possessing as it did an infinitely more subtle charm. Technically, the Le Mans I leaned heavily on existing Guzzi's, notably the 750S3 and 850T3. In truth, the power-unit and drive assembly was essentially an upgraded version of the T3 – with identical cylinder dimensions, gearbox and final drive. To gain extra 'umph' in its new role, the Le Mans was given higher compression pistons

*Technically, the Le Mans I leaned heavily on existing Guzzi's, notably the 750S3 and 850T3. Its styling though was pure genius.*

*Multi World Champion Phil Read with a brand new Le Mans Mark I at importers Coburn & Hughes, Luton premises in 1976.*

(10.2:1), larger valves (37mm exhaust, 44mm inlet), a more, lumpier cam profile with accelerator pumps and massive plastic bellmouths. At the machine's Milan launch, Guzzi sources claimed an optimistic 81bhp at 7600rpm and 134mph (215.6kph). The truth was somewhat different – 71bhp at 7300rpm and 124mph (199.5kph). But there was to be a production racing kit (including a pair of very noisy Lafranconi mufflers) which did provide Guzzi's figures, just that they did not mention the existence of a kit at the time! Even so, the combination of a torquey motor, surefooted handling, excellent brakes and an aggressive style finally gave Guzzi and its fans a motorcycle with of to be truly proud.

Production did not get underway until Spring 1976 and when the bikes began to appear in dealers' showrooms buyers were soon getting out their wallets. The styling of the Mark I is, even today, regarded as being the best of all the Le Mans series. With clip-ons, rearsets, a race-style bum-stop saddle, bikini fairing, drilled brake discs, matt black frame and exhaust system, silver-finished cast alloy wheels and a choice of colour scheme (bright red, ice blue metallic or

*The Le Mans replaced the 750S3. The pair are shown together at a European Show in the summer of 1976.*

white) this machine was in the very best Italian sporting tradition. Red was by far the most popular choice, being applied to tank, mudguards, side panels and fairing, it really suited the machine's character. Even though the fairing had a central section finished in a distinctive day-glo orange (surrounding the 170mm headlamp), it only served to heighten the overall appeal. The machine's more civilized aspects were subtly subdued. Although direction indicators were fitted as standard, they and their support arms were cleverly finished in matt black, thus blending more easily into the contours of the remainder of the bike than would normally have been expected. Pillion footrests were also provided, but a passenger found things difficult, given that they were expected to sit on the top of the padded bum-stop! The seat was altogether a distinctive feature of the Le Mans I, and should have been both a stylistic and ergonomic coup – for solo use! Instead, the seat was to prove one of the few really poorly finished items on the whole machine. The interesting thing about this seat was the way in which it was moulded so that the nose extended over the rear of the tank, a curiously effective feature which should have also enhanced rider comfort. The problem was that the whole contraption was moulded in one piece from dense foam rubber; this was simply not strong enough for the task in hand, the result being that whole chunks could break away, particularly from the poorly-supported front section. A favourite and practical remedy was to fit a seat from the earlier 750S/S3 models. Another component which was a source of nuisance to owners of the original Le Mans models, certainly in northerly climes, was the battery – a puny 12-volt 20-amp hour device compared with the 32-amp hour variety specified for the other models. Following extended use with lights on, such as might well be encountered in a typical cold, wet British winter's night, this frequently failed completely in its attempts to get the bike going the following morning. Without a back-up kick-starter, and a bike which was anything but easy to bump start, quite often the irate Le Mans I owner was simply stranded. Such annoyances apart, the Le Mans soon gained a loyal and enthusiastic following, for here at last was a practical Italian sportster. So maybe the Ducati 900SS did have the edge on the open road, but what of it, for the Moto Guzzi rider knew who would have the final laugh next time they hit a traffic snarl-up.

When it was launched on to the British market in June 1976, the Le Mans I cost £2,000 – some £400 more than the T3 roadster, but there was certainly no shortage of eager buyers waiting to take up ownership. Guzzi certainly had the world's motorcycle

journalists to thank for many sales, their unbridled enthusiasm often generating equal enthusiasm with the relationship. The press were virtually unanimous in dishing out rave reviews in the direction of the Le Mans. Some testers, it has to be said, were guilty of simply hype, having only ridden the bike 'round the block'. But there were also those who took things far more seriously. In this latter category came *Motor Cycle Mechanics*, whose editor Colin Mayo and features writer Bob Goddard (on a Le Mans and 850T3) took part in an extended three-day, 1,400-mile (2,250km) marathon over unknown roads through no less than six European countries.

From the outset, this expedition had looked a pretty daunting task with, as they stated, 'the cafe racer Le Mans promising to

*When it was launched on to the British market in June 1976, the Le Mans I cost £2,000 – some 20 per cent more than the T3 roadster, and to most of its owners worth every penny.*

be uncomfortable over the twelve hours we proposed to ride each day, and the T3 touring version, gasping to keep up, or so we thought!' Even the gallop back from the importers, Coburn & Hughes in Luton, to Peterborough when they collected the bikes was found to be a bit of an anti-climax. Perhaps expecting too much, Colin Mayo summed up his feelings, 'after all, the Le Mans did look as though it would crack the sound barrier and gobble up Z900s on the way. While it definitely had a bit more mid-range surge than the 750 (S3) version, the overall performance was only slightly improved and the gearchange was just as crunchy and awkward as ever.' Harsh words perhaps, but as the test wore on, the pair of riders found more and more to praise. It was soon discovered that the Le Mans could live with the T3 in the touring stakes, thanks to its 'fat spread of powerful torque' and that it could handle too, for there could be no doubt that the long, low Le Mans would go round bends quite a bit faster than many of its Oriental contemporaries, and took to sweeping roads like a duck to water! The test finished by saying, 'The Le Mans never really felt as though it were trying, despite the rapid nature of our journey, and the lop-sided rumble of the big V-twin motor had a relaxed feel to it. The luxury of not having to lubricate and adjust the chain is a strong bonus. But in many ways the Le Mans is a showpiece to be admired and envied and is not nearly so inspiring to ride as it looks.' *MCM* concluded by saying that the important thing was that the Le Mans was very different to the norm and that it thus captured the same exotic aura that Ferraris and Lamborghinis thrived on. Thoroughbred it might have been, but it was neither nervous nor highly strung. Throughout the test the Le Mans averaged 44.5mpg (6.36l/100km) despite maintaining an average speed of almost 60mph (100kph) for the whole trip. These figures were certainly at the lower end of a potential owner's expectations, even though most would use their mount as a sportster rather than as a tourer.

With its lazy, laid-back approach to power delivery, the Le Mans engine often fooled even the most expert of road testers into believing that it was somewhat lacking in performance. But as results were to prove, in production sports racing the Guzzi was often to fool the opposition too – beating the best there was out on the track.

*This frontal view of a Le Mans Mark I gives a true indication of just how sleek and aggressive it really was – later versions never quite managed to recapture this fully.*

## MARK II

Even though the factory never had any trouble selling as many Mark Is as it could produce, it still decided in early 1978 that the time had come to offer a revised 'Mark 2' version. The result was to make its debut in September that year at the German Cologne show as the Le Mans II, one of only two new Italian machines – the other being from Ducati in the shape of the pre-production Ducati five-hundred Pantah.

The Le Mans II's most obvious change was the adoption of a Spada-style three-piece full fairing, which endowed the machine with an angular stance. At the same time, the Le Mans gained most of the fairing-mounted accessories from the Spada. These were the complete instrument layout and switchgear, including the quartz clock and voltmeter. The large, moulded rubber dashboard was suitably re-labelled with the 'Le Mans' logo. While the front indicators were now integral with the fairing, the clip-on handlebars were modified to suit the fairing's upper section. The red paint finish was as before, except that there was now more of it, and the frame continued to be in matt black. However, the metallic blue/grey and white options were dropped; in their place coming a bright royal blue as an alternative to the ever-popular Italian racing red.

In their pre-launch publicity blurb Guzzi stated that the power output had been improved and the exhaust system modified. These comments were not in fact true, as the changes made were purely cosmetic, but there were a couple of significant improvements to overcome areas of discontent over the Mark I. The troublesome single saddle had already received attention and had been changed during 1977 for one which not only gave true two-up abilities but also stayed in one piece, despite being manufactured from similar material. Although the first batch of Mark IIs came with the original small capacity battery, this was replaced by a much more meaty 32-hour component from batch two onwards. There were several other more minor changes. These included the Brembo front brake calipers being relocated to the rear of the fork legs which, inci-

*Even though the original (Mark I) proved a top seller, the factory replaced it after some 2½ years with the more angular Mark II, which made its début at the Cologne Show in September 1978.*

## TECHNICAL SPECIFICATIONS
### 850 Le Mans II (1979)

| | | | |
|---|---|---|---|
| Engine | 4-stroke 90° V-twin | Wheels | rims cast in light alloy, rim size<br>front: WM 3/2.15 × 18in<br>rear: WM 3/2.15 × 18in |
| Bore | 83mm | | |
| Stroke | 78mm | | |
| Displacement | 844cc | Tyres | front:<br>Pirelli 100/90 H 18 (MT 18)<br>Michelin 3.50 H 18 (M45)<br>Metzeler 3.50 H 18 (Rille)<br>rear:<br>Pirelli 100/90 H 18 (MT 18)<br>Michelin 4.00 H 18 (M45)<br>Metzeler 4.10 V 18 (Block C7)<br>(Tyre brand fitted alternatively to comply with the different standards in each country) |
| Max torque | 7.8 kgm at 6600rpm | | |
| Compression ratio | 10.2 | | |
| Valve gear | ohv push rod operated | | |
| Carburation | two Dell'Orto carburettors PHF 36 B(D) (right) PHF 36 B(S) (left) | | |
| Lubrication | oil pressure by gear pump | | |
| Transmission | primary by gears secondary by cardan shaft and level gear sets | | |
| Clutch | dry with double plate | Frame | tubular cradle |
| Alternator | located at the front end of the crankshaft, 14V–20A | Suspension | front: Moto Guzzi telescopic front fork rear: swinging arm with externally adjustable springs |
| Starter | electric | | |
| Ignition | battery-coil with twin contact breaker | Fuel capacity | 22.5ltr (4.95lb) |
| Gearbox | 5-speed frontal engagement, constant mesh gears, cush drive incorporated | Fuel consumption | 6.5ltr × 100km (43.5mpg) |
| Brakes | front: hydraulic 300mm disc rear: hydraulic 242mm disc | Max. speed | 200km/h (124mph) |
| | | Dry weight | 196kg (431lb) |

*The dash layout of the Le Mans II followed similar lines to the SP (Spada) sports / tourer; instrumentation was mounted in a large, moulded rubber dash.*

dentally, were now finished in black rather than silver. The ignition switch and rear brake master cylinder cap were replaced for the improved type as fitted to the SP (Spada), the latter linked to a warning lamp up on the console (so the rider received a warning when the fluid started to get low) and some other detail improvements.

Out on the street, the performance figures of the fully-faired Le Mans differed little from the original. The British magazine, *Motorcycling*, recorded and electronically-timed a maximum speed of 126.89mph (204.16kph) with the rider in the prone position; at the same time averaging 48mpg (5.89l/100km) over the entire test. Editor Charles Deane faulted the switchgear, stand operation and over-firm dual seat which, in his opinion, did little to absorb road shocks and lifted only just enough to give access to the toolkit beneath; it also did not lock! But overall, Deane remained favourably impressed with the Le Mans II, in particular with its ability to match many one-litre bikes in performance and beat them in fuel economy. I, too, found the Mark II not to possess any real performance advantage over

the Mark I, but its comprehensive fairing and increased level of standard equipment offered an improvement in terms of comfort and convenience. There were many, myself included, who preferred the more rounded, more racy style of the original.

During late 1980, a series of modifications were all introduced at the same time on the Le Mans II. The chrome-plated cylinder bores were replaced by Nigusil (Guzzi's in-house coating, very similar to Nikasil) ones. The internal fork dampers (manufactured by Lispa) were improved, and the forks were converted to air-assisted operation. The rear shocks were also changed, with the substitution of Paioli-made assemblies. At the same time, British importer, Coburn & Hughes, launched a UK-market only special. This was the Le Mans II in an overall black and gold livery, gold being used for the wheels, fork bottoms and pinstriping on the black areas of the fairing, tank and side panels – altogether very much a Guzzi take-off of the black and gold colour scheme used by Ducati for their 900SS of the period. It should be remembered that Coburn & Hughes acted for both Guzzi and Ducati in the British market of that time. C&H (Moto Guzzi Con-

*A totally stock Le Mans II in the pits at Shelsley Walsh Hill Climb, Worcestershire, August 1988. Then ten years old, it had survived well.*

*During late 1980, British importers Coburn & Hughes launched a UK-market special. This was the Le Mans II in an overall black and gold livery. It was an obvious take-off from Ducati's black and gold 900SS bevel vee of the same period.*

cessionaires Ltd) marketed the machine under the Le Mans Black/Gold name, and at a price of £2,999. Of course, there was a very good reason for the introduction of this one-off model; its sole purpose being to help the importers remove excess stocks from their warehouse in readiness for a brand new version, the Le Mans III.

No Mark IIs were sold in the USA. Instead, a special model, the CX1000, was introduced in 1980 and sold through 1981. This was basically a Mark II chassis with 944cc SP engine.

## MARK III

This was no tarted-up adaptation of the previous theme, instead it was very much a major redesign in its own right. The changes were not simply skin-deep, but internal too, with the engine, in particular, receiving updates. Most noticeable of these were the new, square-finned cylinder heads and matching Nigusil cylinder barrels. Although such fundamentals as the camshaft profile

and valve sizes remained unchanged, and even though the compression ratio was actually decreased from 10.2:1 to (.8:1) in the interests of improved low-speed running and torque, the performance was still bettered by a full 3bhp, while engine torque increased to 7.6kg/m at 6200rpm. This was quite an achievement by the Guzzi design team because it came about purely by the combination of superior machining equipment improving operating tolerances, the use of aluminium rocker supports (which also help reduce tappet noise) and improved air filtration and exhaust systems. The latter was in fact the first from a European motorcycle to fully meet the stringent EEC regulation CEE 78.1015. The double-skinned exhaust pipes and mufflers were now finished in bright shiny chrome plate.

The fairing was another component to undergo radical changes, and the new design (again the product of Guzzi's own wind tunnel facilities) featured considerably smaller dimensions than the previous model. There was also a form of spoiler offering deflection of the air current past the base of the fuel tank and the top of the cylinder heads. The instrument console had been

*Working prototype for the Le Mans III. A factory hack Mark I, with revised engine, pictured in August 1979.*

*The Le Mans III was distinguished by its new, square-finned cylinder heads and matching Nigusil-coated cylinder barrels.*

*Although still angular the Le Mans III style was nonetheless attractive, and together with technical changes helped it sell in reasonable numbers.*

totally rehashed. Pride of place now went to a new 100mm white-face Veglia tachometer. This was flanked by a smaller diameter speedometer from the same manufacturer on the right, voltmeter on the left, and rows of idiot lights below. These, together with the ignition switch, were housed in a thick rubber console, as were the two green indicator warning lights. The same Italian racing red and black colour scheme as used on

*The Le Mans III fairing employed a form of spoiler offering deflection of the air current past the base of the fuel tank and the top of the cylinder heads.*

*A striking rear shot of a Mark III, taken at the town of Lecco on the southern tip of Lake Como, May 1983.*

*Making its debut at the end of 1971, the Lino Tonti-designed V-7 Sport was Guzzi's first sporting version of the V-twin line begun in the mid-1960s with the original 700 touring model.*

*The 1975 V1000 Convert automatic. Revolutionary, it failed to win many customers, but was nonetheless a landmark (with its near 1-litre engine size) in the evolution of the heavyweight V-twin series.*

The original Le Mans I was a true classic amongst Italian motorcycles of the mid-1970s. Today it is highly valued by collectors and enthusiasts alike.

In designing the 1000SP (Spada in Britain), Moto Guzzi made full use of its wind tunnel facilities, which had lain idle for almost two decades.

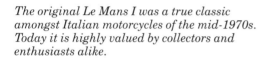

When the Le Mans III took its bow in 1981, it was no simple cosmetic makeover. The engine in particular received a considerable amount of input. This resulted in an extra 3bhp, with engine torque figures also improved.

Like the earlier V1000, SP and California II, the Le Mans was given the 948.8cc engine at the end of 1984 to create the 1000 version. A couple of factory testers are seen with the improved 'Mark 2' in 1988. The main difference over the first version was an 18in, rather than 16in, front wheel.

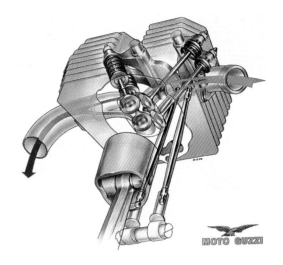

The four-valves-per-cylinder heads as used on the 1984 sporting middleweight V35 Imola II, V50 Monza II and the V65 Lario.

The California III arrived in 1988. It was available in several guises. This is the LAPD (Los Angeles Police Department) version.

*The V65 Florida was available either naked, as shown, or with screen, panniers, carrier and crashbars. It was one of Guzzi's top-selling models of the late 1980s.*

*In the late 1980s Guzzi introduced the world's first true 'retro', the 1000S. This aped the long gone, but much loved 750S3. It beat Kawasaki's Zephyr 550 by several months.*

*Arturo Magni has created several Guzzi V-twin models, including this classic-style Sfida 1000.*

(Above) 992cc (90 × 78mm) fuel injected, four-valves-per-cylinder Daytona engine; Milan Show, November 1991.

(Left) The American Dr John Wittner was largely responsible for the Daytona project.

(Below) A 1992 production Daytona out on the road.

One of the best modern Guzzi V-twins, the 1100 Sport. This is the early version with conventional front forks and Dell'Orto carbs, circa 1993.

The Nevada custom, available in either 346.2cc (66 × 50.6mm) or 743.9cc (80 × 74mm) engine sizes. These are Series I machines built from 1990 until 1994.

*A 1991 750 XPA police model, based on the NX street enduro. It, together with other specialized police models, is sold to governments around the world.*

*Love it or loath it, the V10 Centauro (introduced in 1996) is certainly a muscular-looking piece of machinery. From 1998 it was also offered in Sport and GT guises.*

*1996 California 1100 Injection; since superseded by the new EV model, but still an excellent motorcycle.*

*In 1996 Guzzi revised their popular 1100 Sport. The biggest changes were inverted front forks and fuel injection. For 1998 a limited edition 1100 Sport Corsa was offered.*

the Mark II now featured matching red fork sliders. The tanks had been enlarged to 25 litres (5.5imp gal) and were reshaped to set-off the new angular-style cylinder head and barrel finning. This in turn, provided the engine with a more muscular appearance. The Mark III was also offered in white or silver, but the latter colour was not available in the USA. The seat, too, was new but not to everyone's liking. This is what one road tester had to say, 'The seat is as long, narrow and hard as a length of railway track, and it's a long way to the controls, even for a six-footer like me!'

## MARK IV AND SPECIAL EDITION

The next move came in late 1984 with the introduction of the Le Mans 1000 (more commonly known as the Mark IV). Like the V1000 Convert automatic, California II and SP (Spada) models, the Mark IV came with the larger 948.8cc (88 × 78mm) engine, but

*The belly pan and use of a 16in wheel were both following trends set by the Japanese. The 16in wheel saga was to prove a real headache for Guzzi.*

*Late 1984 saw the introduction of the Le Mans 1000 (more commonly known as the Mark IV). Technical changes not only included the larger 948.8cc (88 × 78mm) engine, but also larger valves, higher compression pistons and bigger, 40mm Dell'Orto carbs.*

obviously in a more advanced state of tune for the Le Mans' more sporting role. The valves were both increased in diameter by 3mm over the 850 engine, to 47mm inlet and 44mm exhaust. The compression ratio was also raised, to 10:1, and the larger Le Mans came with bigger 40mm Dell'Ortos and new exhaust pipes of the same diameter. The mufflers were also different, and both they and the header and balance pipes were finished in a gloss-black chrome. The net result of these modifications gave 85bhp at the crankshaft, with maximum speed rising to 141mph (226.9kph) – a 10mph (16kph) increase over the Mark III.

As for styling, the Mark IV relied heavily on the then-current V65 Lario, itself drawing inspiration from the V35 Imola II and V50 Monza II (see Chapter 7). There was even more use of the main colour (red), including wheels and bottom detachable frame tubes. A belly pan was incorporated below the fairing, following a fashion popular in the mid-1980s. This feature was very much a case of the Italians following the Japanese, rather than the other way around. The Mark IV was also available in white. This trend of following Japanese practices was also to be seen in the fitment of a 16in front wheel – and what a disastrous move it proved, too, as I can well remember from my first ride on the new

machine in early 1985. At first I thought the tyre must be punctured but no, everything was in order, and the vague handling was due entirely to the use of that wheel without any noticeable modifications to the frame or suspension. Why change something to mimic a fashion statement without even testing to see if it *works* first? But that, unfortunately, was exactly what Guzzi did. Besides the change to a 120/80 V16 front tyre, Guzzi fitted a wider 130/80-section rear tyre, but this stayed at 18in. The brakes were still the patented linked disc system pioneered on the 850T3 series back in 1975, and used from the Le Mans I onwards, but were now a uniform 270mm all round.

Fairing and aerofoils were closely related to those of the Le Mans III, except for the front indicators, which were now sharply angular and in fact doubled in a most efficient manner as wind deflectors for the rider's hands. These streamlined front indicators were replaced by blunt, squared-off components on USA-spec Le Mans Mark IVs. The instrument console was unchanged from the Le Mans III, and also adopted from the V65 Lario. Additional items, which the Lario gave to the latest Le Mans, included switchgear, foam-rubber handlebar grips, and dog-leg control levers. Much louder dual-tone horns replaced the conventional type specified for the earlier marks.

Since it was launched, the only major set of changes to the Mark IV came in 1987. These comprised a number of modifications and the introduction of a special edition. The most significant was the replacement of the awful 16in front wheel by an 18in one, thereby restoring Guzzi's good name for sure-footed handling and cornering abilities. The 1987 Le Mans Special Edition had a black-painted engine and transmission, Bi-Turbo damper assemblies for the front forks, and a close-ratio gear cluster. Cosmetically, a one-off red and white paint job, together with a red seat covering, gave it a

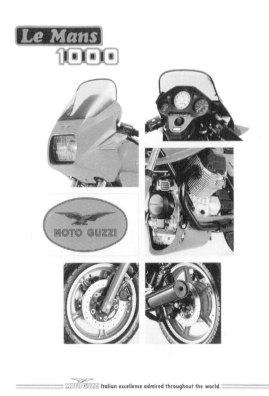

*Extracts from the 1986 Le Mans 1000 factory brochure.*

*The only major change to the Le Mans 1000 came for 1987 in the shape of an 18in front wheel. In this form the machine finally regained its handling prowess. Riders are Mike Shorten (left) and Richard Davies.*

distinctive appearance. Many of the Special Editions in the States were damaged in transit, due to salt water entering the shipping container. The bikes corroded to varying degrees and were sold at reduced prices without the normal manufacter's warranty. The revised model with 18in front wheel did not debut in America until 1989 (one year after Europe) where it was sold as the Mark V. From then until it was finally taken out of production during 1991 – to make way for the new 4-valves-per-cylinder Daytona (launched at the Milan Show in November that year) – the Le Mans remained virtually unchanged. Probably the Le Mans' long pro-

**TECHNICAL SPECIFICATIONS**
**Le Mans 1000 (1989)**

| | | | |
|---|---|---|---|
| Engine | 4-stroke 90° V-twin | Brakes | front: twin 270mm discs rear: single 270mm disc integral braking system |
| Bore | 88mm | | |
| Stroke | 78mm | | |
| Displacement | 948.8cc | Wheels | cast alloy |
| Maximum power | 78bhp | Tyres | front: 100/90 V18 rear: 120/90 V18 |
| Compression ratio | 10:1 | | |
| Timing | ohv | | |
| Lubrication | by pressure pump | Frame | duplex cradle |
| Transmission | primary by helical gear secondary by cardan shaft with cush drive rear wheel | Suspension | front: Moto Guzzi telescopic air fork with pressure equalizer rear: twin Koni shocks |
| Clutch | dry with double disc | | |
| Fuel delivery | two Dell'Orto PUBU 40 carburettors with accelerator pumps | Fuel capacity | 25ltr (5.5gal) |
| Electrical system | 12V, alternator 14V–20A, battery 24Ah | Fuel consumption | 5.4ltr × 100km (52.4mpg) |
| Starting | electric | Maximum speed | 143mph (230km/h) |
| Ignition | battery and coil | | |
| Gearbox | 5-speed | Dry weight | 215kg (475lb) |

*A 1988 Le Mans 1000. It was to remain virtually unchanged until taken out of production in 1991 to make way for the new four-valves-per-cylinder Daytona. Sixteen years for the basic Le Mans concept makes it one of the longest running Guzzi V-twins, only beaten by the California series.*

duction run was due to the fact that it could commute, tour, or sprint with the best. But as journalist Mark Revelle said during a test report of a Mark III in 1981, 'Using the Le Mans to commute is like keeping an eagle in an aviary. It is in its element beneath open skies, where the engine's torque and power can be fully exploited.' The nearest Guzzi has come to building a modern-day Le Mans is the 1100 Sport; this too has all the attributes that made the original so popular.

# 7 Middleweight Vees

During the 1970s, under the ownership of the Argentinean industrialist Alejandro de Tomaso, Moto Guzzi made significant progress. At the start of the decade, before de Tomaso purchased the marque from the government-appointed body SEIMM, the famous old company had been at rock bottom. Its original founders had effectively been bankrupt before the government moved in. Then came de Tomaso, and much as the Castiglioni brothers did for Ducati in the late 1980s and early 1990s Guzzi, was put back on its feet. One of the major building blocks in de Tomaso plans centred around the creation of a middleweight line of V-twins, in effect downsizing the long lasting and successful heavyweight into a lighter, cheaper machine and thus giving the factory a whole new range of potential customers. De Tomaso also saw this as being the key to his aim of doubling the factory's production from its 1975 figures by the end of 1978. To this end, de Tomaso again recruited the services of that talented designer Ing. Lino Tonti (the man who had earlier created the V7 Sport) to pen a suitable machine.

Before going on to describe Tonti's middleweight V-twin design in detail it is worth recalling that prior to this there had been a couple of notable failures. These were however not twins at all, but the Nuovo Falcone single (conceived back in 1969) and the Benelli-designed four cylinder models (which Guzzi marketed as the 350/400 GTSs). But with a man of Tonti's ability the situation was very different this time. As he had done with the V7 Sport a few years before, the 'new' bike was very much a com-

bination of Tonti's own thoughts and an established product. From an engineering viewpoint, the result was everything that de Tomaso could have wished for. The new design was based around the 90-degree V-twin ohv four-stroke with shaft final drive formula which had proved so successful with the larger machines.

## V35/V50

Emerging initially as the V35 and V50, Guzzi's new middleweights made their public debut at Europe's biggest motorcycle show, the biennial event in Cologne, Germany, in September 1976. Later, progressively larger engine sizes were to be added, up to a maximum of 750cc. Ing. Tonti first put pen to his drawing board in 1975 and, by the following spring, prototypes in both three-fifty and five-hundred engine sizes were up and running. These were extensively road tested following the completion of bench trials. Tonti and his team worked long and hard to ensure the middleweight series launch in Cologne. This was important, otherwise the next major show in Europe was some fifteen months later in Milan. The Guzzi publicity department also enjoyed a certain amount of luck as Cologne that year was bereft of any real launches by the major factories. In fact the only really new Japanese motorcycles to appear for the first time were the Yamaha XS 250/360 parallel twins and the Honda CB 125T (a pushrod twin of little real interest to serious motorcycle enthusiasts). This lack of competition for headlines provided Moto Guzzi

*Guzzi's first middleweight V-twins made their public bow at the 1976 Cologne Show in the shape of the V35 and V50 (shown); both entering production the following spring.*

with a unique opportunity to grab the world's biking press; the result being a number of major stories. After all, editorial is cheaper (and better!) than advertising. a typical headline concerning the launch, read 'Cologne – Guzzi's smell success'.

This, together with the factory's own efforts to publicise the middleweight range, created considerable interest, both in Italy and abroad, and in the pair of machines it potentially had a formidable duo. The smaller 346.23cc (66 × 50.6mm) V35 provided an ideal machine for the home market 350cc 'Tax Special' category; whilst the larger capacity 490.30cc (74 × 57mm) V50 offered a viable alternative to Honda's newly released CX500 V-twin. But there were problems.

In truth, de Tomaso faced two major production glitches. Both of these stemmed from the same cause – the limited manufacturing capacity at Guzzi's Mandello del Lario facilities. This had not been helped by the demand generated for the heavyweight

V-twins, led by the success of machines such as the Le Mans I and 850T3. By the end of 1976, the plant was virtually at full stretch, and was thus totally unable to cope with the considerable extra output which the V35/50 needed. This led to very few of the new machines actually being built in 1977, which was when volume production of the two middleweights should have come on stream. Also, manufacturing costs were almost the same as for the bigger models, but with far less profit per unit. As a result, the V35/50 series was not profitable to build; yet there was a massive demand for the newcomers fanned by the huge amount of publicity generated after their launch. How was this dilemma to be resolved? Although, to the outsider, the position seemed totally unacceptable, de Tomaso had already realized the situation, and furthermore was in the process of resolving it. He saw clearly that there were very good reasons why it was necessary to find alternative manufacturing space, and away from Mandello, as it could

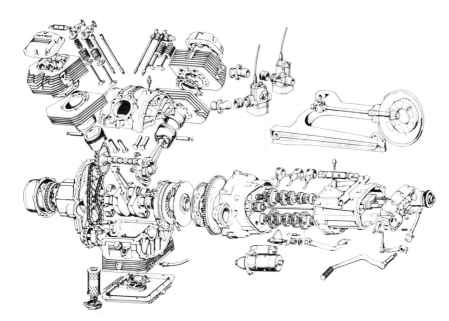

*Exploded view of the V35/50 series engine, transmission, swinging arm and final drive.*

*Outwardly, the V35 and V50 were identical, but internally there were several differences. The bore and stroke of 66 × 50.6mm for the smaller unit and 74 ×57mm for the V50 gave then capacities of 346.23cc and 490.30cc respectively. The primary drive and final drive ratios were also different for both models.*

build and sell all the 850 and 1000 class machines which it could produce at that time. Unlike rival Italian motorcycle factories, de Tomaso's empire was diverse enough so that he was able to find the answer within his own group of companies. This came in the shape of the old Innocenti plant in southern Milan. Once the home of the top selling Lambretta scooter during its boom days of the 1950s and 1960s and latterly employed in the manufacture of Innocenti's version of the British Leyland Mini and later still its own version, the de Tomaso-owned plant needed more work. The full Innocenti story is contained in a separate section within this chapter, but suffice to say de Tomaso's dilemma was solved. Using his contacts within the American automobile industry, the Guzzi boss organized a large consignment of American machine tools with which to re-equip the lines for mass production (using cost-saving robot techniques) of the middleweight V-twins. Conversion of the Innocenti factory got underway in the latter part of 1978, and by

the beginning of 1979 things were starting to buzz, with the promise both of meeting production quotas and of making a significant saving in unit cost. At last it looked as though both the Italian dealers and the various overseas distributors would be able to fulfil demand – and with the promise of a realistic retail price structure.

The world's motorcycling press had already sampled the new middleweight V-twins the previous year, even including

# Innocenti

Ferdinando Innocenti established his original workshop at the tender age of eighteen. Thirteen years later, in 1922, then aged 31, he relocated to Rome where he developed ways of improving the manufacture of steel tubing. Nine years later he moved once again, this time to the Milanese suburb of Lambrate, where he founded a steel company which was to be the basis of his future industrial might.

But none of this was to come easily, as the Lambrate plant was virtually flattened by Allied bombing during the Second World War, so Innocenti was faced with the daunting task of not only rebuilding the plant but finding a profitable niche of the metal finishing market in which to sell his wares.

The result was to be one of the true success stories of the post-war era: Lambretta. The idea of making scooters came from the realization that Italy was devastated and that a simple and cheap form of transport was a leading priority, and also that there was already a proliferation of motorcycle manufacturers.

So Innocenti and his fellow director, Giuseppe Lauro, targeted the motorized scooter as their 'baby' and in 1946 introduced the first Lambretta, the Model A. This was designed by Ing Pier-Luigi Torre. By 1950, production at the Pitteri, Milan, factory was up to 300 scooters per day and two new models, the 125C and LC, had just been introduced. At around the same time an agreement was concluded with the German company NSU for manufacture of the Lambrettta scooter in that country. This lasted until 1956, when NSU began making its own Prima scooter.

Innocenti even went record breaking with special Lambretta scooters and also built prototype racing motorcycles (including a superb 250 90-degree V-twin, which stunned everyone when it was shown for the first time in 1951). It was strongly rumoured that the racers were a warning to the likes of Moto Guzzi not to enter the scooter world. At the 1954 Milan Show Lambretta launched a 48cc moped with front and rear suspension, but it was really the millions of scooters which made the marque's reputation. Following the LC came the LD, but perhaps the most important model of all was the Li series, which came out in 1968.

After 1962 scooter sales, particularly in export markets, declined rapidly. This fall in scooter sales did not matter too much to Innocenti, as from the mid-1950s it had diversified into three divisions: one making scooters, once manufacturing steel tubing and the third specializing in machinery, including presses and machine tools. Much of the other two divisions' products went to the car industry – including not only the majority of the Italian ones, but also Ford and Volkswagen. In 1961 Innocenti moved into car production itself, initially with licence-built British cars such as the Austin A40.

At the height of its industrial success the group employed some 7,000 people, but after the death in June 1966 of its founder it lacked leadership, and by 1975 was in deep financial trouble. The result was that Innocenti passed into the hands of the Italian government, and thence to a new management team led by Alejandro De Tomaso. As related in the main text, during the late 1970s one of Innocenti's vast production facilities in Milan was being used to mass produce Guzzi V35/50 V-twin engine assemblies for another section of the De Tomaso empire.

*V35 and V50 engines in the Innocenti works in Milan; 1979*

those countries which did not actually receive any bikes. This latter section included Great Britain, where several magazines carried favourable comments. *Which Bike?*, then one of the biggest selling UK monthlies, voted the V50 top of a four-bike shoot-out between the Honda CX500, Moto Morini 500 V-twin, the Yamaha XS500 parallel twin – and of course, the V50. *Which Bike?* concluded the comparison by saying, 'So for the moment, Messrs Yamaha, Morini and, in particular Honda can rest easy, for as far as this writer is concerned, the Moto Guzzi is the best of the bunch when it comes down to enthusiast motorcycling!' This last statement was a reference to the machine not being available to buy at the time. As the *Which Bike?* test also revealed there was nothing revolutionary about the V50, simply that it was the best overall package both in terms of what it produced, and how it produced it, giving a considerable amount of rider pleasure. The design's two real strengths which made it such a viable middleweight contender was the price (after 1979), and the incredibly low dry weight (particularly for a bike having the luxury of shaft drive) of only 152kg (303lb). This was over 45kg (100lb) lighter than Honda's tubby CX500, and 36kg (80lb) off the figure for Yamaha's dohc XS500 parallel twin. Its size, too, matched its weight, with the V50 being smaller than all the Japanese companies' two-fifty four-stroke twins of the same era! Again this was a major plus in the eyes of many smaller riders. Finally fuel consumption was another strong Guzzi advantage – again its figures often beating machines half its engine size.

Ing. Tonti should also be complimented on just how clever his middleweight V-twin design really was. The machine's ultimate success (the basic design remains in production as the Nevada custom roadster today) was built on several factors:

- The use of existing technology.
- Advanced mass-production techniques.
- A resultant price saving to Guzzi and customers alike.
- An attractive, compact layout.
- Excellent power-to-weight ratio.

Moto Guzzi could well have turned the V50 (and V35) into the biggest selling motorcycle of all time. The reason this ultimately did not happen was down to three factors – marketing, quality control, and the general world recession from 1981 onwards – and only two of which were in Moto Guzzi's power to control of course. It must be said that marketing (if you discount style and race victories of course) has never been one of the Italian motorcycle industry's strong points. Generally, until very recently in the 1990s, they have either proved lazy or simply tightfisted. (I, as an Italian bike importer in the 1970s, had to pay certain marques for leaflets!) Compared with the efficiency of Japanese and German marques (the latter really meaning BMW), the Italians came a very poor third. The efficiency of the sales operation behind the V35/50 was to lend yet more evidence in support of the basic fact, that had Guzzi marketed the machines more efficiently it would probably not have been able to build enough bikes anyway. There was also a spate of early niggling component part failures which was already indicating that the middleweight V-twins were not likely to be quite so bullet-proof as their bigger brothers. The above problems were by no means insurmountable, as the factory went on to prove, but the main factor, outside of their control, the huge blip in sales during the early 1980s, was to be far less easily solved. This is an unfortunate fact of life that a manufacturer the size of Guzzi is largely unable to have any influence upon at all, since it stems from a country/continent/world recession. It would be true to say that even the mighty

Japanese bike builders suffered. As proof of this, witness Yamaha, who lost a reported £80 million in 1983 alone. National or world economic factors apart, the smaller Guzzi twins had a good deal to commend them to press and public alike. Enthusiasts familiar with the heavyweight Guzzi vees would have little difficulty recognizing these as smaller versions of the theme, starting from a very similar engine and power train.

The engines of the V50 and V35 shared identical external dimensions, but internally there were some notable differences. Besides the obvious, the already stated bore and stroke measurements, the V35 maximum crankshaft power rating was 33.6bhp at 8100rpm, while the larger engine put out 45bhp at 7500rpm. To take account of this, the primary drive ratios were different, with 1.846 on the 350 and 1.642 on the 500, and the helically-cut gears in the final drive box were also matched to the output, with 13/24 and 14/23 respectively. Like the heavyweight V-twins, their pistons (which both ran a compression ratio of 10.8:1) were offered in three sizes – Class A at 66.00 to 66.006mm (74.000 to 74.006), Class B at 66.006 to 66.012mm (74.006 to 74.012) and Class C at 66.012 to 66.018mm (74.012 to 74.018). The range of sizes enabled the pistons to be matched to the cylinder accurately, as on the bikes with chrome bores, although right from the start the bores of the middleweight vees were coated with Nigusil (Guzzi's own process similar to the more well-known Nicasil) rather than simply chromed. The pistons themselves employed three rings, and an unusual feature of their construction was the use of concave crowns. This was a result of the cylinder head layout, which did not follow traditional Guzzi procedure. Instead of the conventional hemispherical combustion chamber with angled valves, the inside of the head was flat, with both valves parallel. Space for combustion was thus provided in

the top of the piston, rather than in the head. Although new to Moto Guzzi, the system was well-tried, Heron heads, as they were termed, having been utilized on Jaguar cars and Moto Morini V-twins, amongst others. The valve sizes differed slightly between the V35 and V50. The exhaust valves were identical at 27.6mm diameter, but the inlet valves on the V35 were 30.6mm instead of 32.6mm on the V50. Twin coil springs were specified for each valve, which ran in an iron guide retained in the cylinder head by a circlip. Although the inlet valve sizes were different, both models shared identical carburettors – 24mm square slide Dell'Orto VHBZs – and the inlet ports had inward facing manifolds which were connected to the carburettor by a rubber sleeve.

A distinctive feature of the new middleweight vee series was the square finning of the cylinder heads, and this was matched by the angular rocker covers, carried by half a dozen Allen screws. The deep fins of each alloy head casting carried two anti-resonance rubber blocks, similar to those fitted to many air-cooled two-strokes to reduce fin ringing. Each cylinder head and barrel had two long and two short tie-bolts, by which they were retained to the crankcase. The crankcase itself, unlike the heavyweight V-twin series, was cast in two sections, split horizontally and held together by ten studs of varying length. The crankshaft carried a pair of bolt-up steel connecting rods with 15mm gudgeon pins running in bronze small-end bushes. Again there were Class A (blue) and B (white) con-rods which had to be matched to cranks with the same colour coding. The standard big-end diameter was between 34.987 and 34.999mm, whilst the main bearings had a diameter of 32.910 and 32.894mm for the front (timing end) bearing, and from 34.988 to 40.008mm for the rear (drive end) bearing. Engine lubrication, as on the larger V-twins, was by a lobe-type pump, circulating oil at a pressure of

**TECHNICAL SPECIFICATIONS**
**V 35 & V50 (1979)**

| | **V35** | **V50** |
|---|---|---|
| **Engine** | | |
| Cycle | 4-stroke | 4-stroke |
| Number of cylinders | 2 | 2 |
| Cylinder disposition | 90° 'V' | 90° 'V' |
| Bore | 66mm | 74mm |
| Stroke | 50.6mm | 57mm |
| Displacement | 346.26cc | 490.291cc |
| Compression ratio | 10.8 | 10.8 |
| Max. output | 33.6HP at 8100rpm | 45HP at 7500rpm |
| Nominal power | 5HP | 6HP |
| | | |
| Valve Gear | | |
| Type | OHV, push rod operated | OHV push rod operated |
| Inlet | opens 18° before TDC<br>closes 50° after BDC | opens 18° before TDC<br>closes 50° after BDC |
| Exhaust | opens 53° before BDC<br>closes 15° after TDC | opens 53° before BDC<br>closes 15° after TDC |
| Rocker clearance for<br>valve timing | 1mm (.039in) | 1mm (.039in) |
| Normal rocker clearance<br>  Inlet<br>  Exhaust | <br>0.10mm (.0039in)<br>0.15mm (.0059in) | <br>0.10mm (.0039in)<br>0.15mm (.0059in) |
| | | |
| Carburation | | |
| Type | down draught<br>Dell'Orto VHB 24 FD (right)<br>Dell'Orto VHB 24 FS (left) | down draught<br>Dell'Orto VHB 24 FD (left)<br>Dell'Orto VHB 24 FS (left) |
| Lubrication | pressure, lobe type pump,<br>oil tank in crankcase | pressure, lobe type pump,<br>oil tank in crankcase |
| Warning light | on panel board | on panel board |
| Oil filters | wire gauze and cartridge<br>type, easily replaceable | wire gauze and cartridge<br>type, easily replaceable |
| Cooling | by air | by air |

| Ignition | | |
|---|---|---|
| Type | electronic | electronic |
| Maximum advance | 34° at 5000–5500rpm | 34° at 5000–5500rpm |
| Rotor block gap | 0.15–0.20mm (0.0059–0.0078in) | 0.15–0.20mm (0.0059–0.0078in) |
| Spark plugs<br>  Marelli CW 9 LP<br>  or Bosch W 260 T 30<br>  or Lodge 2 HLN<br>  or Champion N 6 Y | long thread type dia. 14 × 1.25<br>Marelli CW 9 LP<br>or Bosch W 260 T 30<br>or Lodge 2 HLN<br>or Champion N 6 Y | long thread type dia. 14 × 1.25 |
| Ignition coils | 2 | 2 |
| Starter | electric starter,<br>pedal starter on request | electric starter,<br>pedal starter on request |
| Exhaust System | dual exhaust pipes and<br>silencers, interconnected | dual exhaust pipes and<br>silencers, interconnected |
| Alternator | fitted on front end of<br>crankshaft (14V – 20A) | fitted on front end of<br>crankshaft (14V – 20A) |

| **Transmission** | | |
|---|---|---|
| Clutch | dry type, single plate with<br>diaphragm spring.<br>controlled by lever on<br>left side of handlebar | dry type, single plate with<br>diaphragm spring.<br>controlled by lever on<br>left side of handlebar |
| Primary drive | helical gears, ratios:<br>1 to 1.846 (13–24) | helical gears, ratios:<br>1 to 1.642 (14-23) |
| Speed change | 5-speed, constant mesh gears,<br>frontal engagement, foot<br>controlled on left side<br>of machine | 5-speed, constant mesh gears,<br>frontal engagement, foot<br>controlled on left side<br>of machine |
| Internal gear ratios<br>  low gear<br>  2nd gear<br>  3rd gear<br>  4th gear<br>  high gear | <br>1 to 2.727 (11/30)<br>1 to 1.733 (15/26)<br>1 to 1.277 (18/23)<br>1 to 1.045 (22/23)<br>1 to 0.909 (22/20) | <br>1 to 2.727 (11/30)<br>1 to 1.733 (15/26)<br>1 to 1.277 (18/23)<br>1 to 1.045 (22/23)<br>1 to 0.909 (22/20) |
| Secondary drive<br>  ratio | cardan shaft with bevel gears<br>1 to 3.875 | cardan shaft with bevel gears<br>1 to 3.875 |
| overall gear ratios:<br>  low gear<br>  2nd gear<br>  3rd gear<br>  4th gear<br>  high gear | <br>1 to 19.506<br>1 to 12.396<br>1 to 9.134<br>1 to 7.475<br>1 to 6.502 | <br>1 to 17.351<br>1 to 11.026<br>1 to 8.125<br>1 to 6.649<br>1 to 5.783 |

**Cycle parts**

| | | |
|---|---|---|
| Frame | tubular structure, cradle type | tubular structure, cradle type |
| Suspension | telescopic front fork type hydraulic dampers rear swinging arm with externally adjustable springs | telescopic front fork type hydraulic dampers rear swinging arm with externally adjustable springs |

Wheels

| | | |
|---|---|---|
| Type | single piece light alloy casting | single piece light alloy casting |
| Front | WM 2/1,85 × 18" CP2 | WM 2/1,85 × 18" CP2 |
| Rear | WM 3/2,15 × 18" CP2 | WM 3/2,15 × 18" CP2 |

Tyres

| | | |
|---|---|---|
| Front | Pirelli 90/90 S18 or 3.00–18 Metzeler 3.00 – 18R (Block C5) Michelin 3.00 – 18R (M38) | Pirelli 100/90 S18 (MT15) Metzeler 3.25 – 18R (Block C5) Michelin 3.50 – 18R (M38) |
| Rear | Pirelli S18 (ribbed) Metzeler 3.00 S18 (Block C5) Michelin 3.00 S18 (M38) | Pirelli 100/90 S18 (MT15) Metzeler 3.50 S18 (Block C66) Michelin 3.50 S18 (M38) |

Brakes

| | | |
|---|---|---|
| Front | 260mm disc | 260mm disc |
| Rear | 235mm disc | 235mm disc |

**Overall dimensions and weights**

| | | |
|---|---|---|
| Wheel base | 1.395m (54.5in) | 1.395m (54.5in) |
| Length | 2.080m (82in) | 2.080m (82in) |
| Width | 0.750mm (29.85in) | 0.750mm (29.85in) |
| Height | 1.035 (39.4in) | 1.035 (39.4in) |
| Dry weight | 152kg (303lb) | 152kg (303lb) |

**Performance**

| | | |
|---|---|---|
| Max. speed | 150km/h (93mph) approx. | 170km/h (105mph) approx. |
| Fuel consumption | 3.7ltr × 100km (77mpg) | 4ltr × 100km (70mpg) |

**Fuel capacity**

| | | |
|---|---|---|
| fuel tank | 16.5ltr (3.6gal) | 16.5ltr (3.6gal) |

between 4.2 and 4.8kg/cm$^2$. But a new feature was a different type of disposable oil filter housed in the sump. Unlike the earlier twins, it was now possible for this to be replaced with the sump *in situ*.

Once again, the transmission was similar to the bigger brother, but with some important differences. As on the larger machines, the clutch was housed inside the large ring gear for the electric starter. But unlike them, the clutch itself was a true single-plate diaphragm type, consisting of a friction plate, pressure cap, pressure plate and diaphragm spring. The spring had a design load capacity of 160kg (350lb) when compressed to 4mm. The five-speed constant mesh gearbox featured frontal engagement, with a left-hand gear lever, and the internal ratios were identical on both the V35 and V50. But a major difference was that the gears themselves were straight-cut, rather than heli-cut as on the later vees. Final drive was by the traditional Moto Guzzi shaft arrangement but the rear universal joint carried a long extension as on the V1000, and was protected by a revised rubber boot. Mainly because of possible

*As is evident from this tank-off view, the chassis followed very similar lines to the bigger twins. A major difference was the cast alloy (instead of tubular steel) swinging arm.*

police/military sales, the gearbox had a provision for installation of an optional kick-starter (operated on the offside of the machine), but the normal method of starting was electric, via a Bosch DG 12-volt starter motor rated at 0.70hp.

The battery was not an especially massive affair, with Guzzi providing a 12-volt 20-amp hour as standard, and an optional 32-amp hour available if starting became a bind. But why, I ask, didn't the powers that be plump for the heavy duty component in the first place? OK, that would have meant carrying around more weight, but at least you would not have risked being stranded one dark, cold, wet night out in the wilds, would you! Luckily, Guzzi did at least provide a decent alternator to keep the battery up to scratch in the shape of a German-made Bosch GI(R) 14V 20 A21 assembly. Bosch also provided the regulator and rectifier, as well as the electronic ignition system, which comprised a pair of magnetic pick-up triggers and a matching pair of transducers. Completing the electrical equipment package was a 170mm CEV headlight with its 12-volt 40/45 watt bulb, a twin-bulb rear light, black indicators, a single Belli horn, and a wodge of four idiot lights on the instrument console. The garish 'Monopoly' handlebar switchgear was from the 1000SP and Le Mans models of the same era.

Following traditional Guzzi fashion, the new middleweight V-twins came with a double-cradle frame which followed the normal Guzzi practice of having detachable bottom rails that allowed the engine to be dropped out from below with ease. In fact, the whole drive train – engine, gearbox, drive shaft (including the swinging arm) and rear wheel – together with the exhaust system, could be parted from the frame, forks and front wheel to provide truly amazing accessibility. The swinging arm itself was an aluminium casting, pivoting on the rear section of the gearbox casing, and it was suspended from the frame by three-way or five-way adjustable Sebac suspension units with exposed chrome-plated springs. It is worth noting that Sebac now give their springs a hard-wearing black plastic coating; this is a much superior solution as chrome-plating not only potentially weakens the spring, but with the constant up and down stress will literally 'crack'. The latest (1990s) Sebac shocks are fully rebuildable to boot.

The front brakes were of Moto Guzzi's own manufacture (like the heavyweight models). Those on the V35/50 had 35mm diameter hard chrome stanchions and an effective travel of 125mm. As on the other models, these forks had sealed internal dampers, and in the case of the middleweights they were manufactured by the Lispa company. The steering head bearings were of the cup and cone variety, each carrying twenty-five steel balls. The twin piston Brembo front calipers were mounted on lugs forward of the fork sliders, and the nearside (left) front brake and rear calipers were operated by a master cylinder located next to the rear brake pedal. The offside (right) front brake was operated by a master cylinder mounted at the front of the top frame tube, between the cheeks of the fuel tank. This was in turn actuated by a short cable running from the handlebar lever itself. Among the Guzzi range, this system was unique on the V35/50, but it had been used earlier by both BMW and Kawasaki, and the theoretical advantage of the added complication was supposed to be offset by removing the otherwise vulnerable handlebar-mounted master cylinder in the event of an accident. At the time of the new model's introduction, cast alloy wheels were just becoming the motorcycling fashion accessory, so these were adopted as standard fitment. The pattern employed by Guzzi had twelve spokes and a silver painted finish. Both wheels were 18in in diameter, and carried the patented Guzzi linked braking sys-

tem. The cast iron discs themselves were smaller than for the 850/1000 models. The V35/50 employed twin 260mm discs at the front and a single 235mm component at the rear. As with the disc diameter, the machines' Brembo calipers were also smaller and in keeping with the middleweight's lighter weight.

Both models shared the same colour schemes, the choice being between red or metallic blue/grey. These colours were used on the tank, plastic side panels, mudguards and headlamp brackets, while the frame, headlamp shell and many more minor items were finished in black. Like the wheels, the fork sliders and swinging arm were painted silver, whilst the entire exhaust system was bright chrome-plated. As well as the body colour, the tank also carried a matt black central panel (like the Le Mans II), running from front to rear virtually all the way across the flat section of the tank top.

## V50 II

When the new Innocenti factory production lines came on stream in early 1979, manufacture of both the V35 and V50 was transferred completely to their new home in the industrial heartland of urban Milan. At the same time, several design changes were introduced in both engine sizes, the larger model being rebadged 'V50II'. In the original design there has been an oil capacity of 2.25 litres. This had been upped to 2.5 litres by making the finned sump deeper – this also requiring a modified gasket. In place of the polished aluminium timing cover, both bikes now sported a black plastic moulding, but the rocker covers were now polished. All the other changes were reserved for the V50 only, and were virtually entirely cosmetic rather than mechanical. The only functional alteration was to the front brake discs which were of a revised pattern although the actual diameter remained unchanged. The headlamp received a bright chrome rim and the headlamp shell was now held by a pair of Allen bolts instead of the former hexagon bolts. The black-bodied CEV turn signals had been ditched in favour of chrome-plated Larghi-made components and all these gained matching chrome stalks; one piece at the front (fixed to the bottom yoke). The yoke itself was now polished alloy rather than black. The V50 II paintwork was brightened up by the use of thin orange and yellow striping running either side of the fuel tank and on the side panels. The logos for the latter now incorporated a 'II'.

There was also a number of changes to suit individual export markets. For example, the German V35 saw its carb size reduced to 20mm with resultant changes to the main jet and needle sizes. There were matching smaller manifolds at inlet ports, and smaller valves at 27.6mm (inlet) and 26.6mm (exhaust). The Stateside V50 saw side reflectors introduced for the turn signals, a sealed beam headlight and other minor modifications to comply with American legislation. The Dutch market V50 got modified exhaust header pipes, but quite why, no-one seems to know. The British

importers, Coburn & Hughes were able to take Italian market bikes, but with the additional mph speedometer and a headlamp which dipped on the correct side (although in typical Italian fashion some bikes were not updated before being exported). When the first imports arrived in Great Britain in April 1979, the V50 (the V35 was not brought in) cost £1,475, but with the Innocenti plant coming into the picture the price was dropped to a very competitive £1,299 by August that year. After the price reduction sales boomed, and thanks to some excellent press – typified by a *Motor Cycle News* headline, 'Best handling bike I've ever ridden', the importers went on to sell over 2,000 V50s in that year, a higher figure than that for all other Guzzi and Ducati models which Coburn & Hughes imported during the same period!

But all was not quite going to plan, because behind these record sales figures there were many dealers who were far from happy. The problem was the number of warranty claims these sales were generating. But in fairness most of these were centred on a small number of components. These included the failure of flanges and oil seals in the final drive, failure of the fork oil seals, problems with ignition switches, and perhaps most of all, poor finish of the paintwork. This could be appalling, with whole flakes of paint falling off the side panels (which had not been keyed before being painted!), and rusting of the mudguards.

## V35 II

By mid-1980, these glitches had reached a point where new sales were being affected. To counter these criticisms Guzzi brought in first the V35 II and eventually the V50 III (the latter is described later). The V35 II had first been shown on the factory's stand at the Milan Show as early as November 1979

*A V50 Series II. Built in the model years 1979 and 1980, this version sold in the largest numbers, but a number of niggling problems experienced with the V50 Series II stunted sales for later versions.*

(so obviously Guzzi knew they had a problem!). Being largely intended for the home market the V35 II was easier to police, rather than the mainly-export V50 III. The new V35 was essentially a V50 II chassis but with a slightly revised engine. The main improvements were actually those detail points which had caused the flood of warranty claims, and an improved level of finish – still not perfect, but better than on the original bikes. The front mudguard was replaced by a plastic one (some very late V50 IIs came similarly updated). A new headlamp with a halogen quartz bulb was fitted, giving much improved illumination at night. The front master cylinder was moved up from under the tank to the more normal handlebar location, whilst the front brake discs were now drilled (again some late V50 IIs had these) and the front calipers were moved behind the fork sliders. The area formerly occupied by the master cylinder reservoir was now taken up by a modified cover for the fuel filler cap. On the V50 II, this was a simple hinged plastic flap, but now the cover was metal and hid a chrome filler cap.

The saddle and silencers were also entirely new – and there was a choice of new colours of red or silver (also from the 1982 model year, metallic green). The fuel filler flap was colour coded, rather than its former separate matt black finish. Together these changes contributed to an improved, more integrated appearance. But it was not just a case of cosmetic improvements which were significant. The carb size was increased from 24 to 26mm, with main jet sizes also increasing from 102 to 108. To cure an annoying flat spot in the mid range, the Bosch electronic ignition was swapped for Dansi contact breakers and condensers. Together with other fine tuning, the power output rose from 27 to 29.07bhp, with maximum rpm staying at 7750.

When testing a V35 II in the autumn of 1984 for *Motorcycle Enthusiast*, I found it

*The V35 II. This was produced from the 1980 model year and conversely was based on the Series III, not the Series II V50. This meant points instead of the original electronic ignition to cure an annoying mid-range flat spot, and a much improved finish.*

marginally quicker than the original, with a top speed of 93mph, but considerably smoother and with none of the former hesitancy encountered with the first batches of V35 in the mid-range. I also discovered that the smallest Guzzi V-twin had a clunk-free gearchange with which first gear could be engaged noiselessly every time – even from a cold start situation. It was fully capable of holding 70mph (110kph) on the motorway for long periods, and its smoothness made up for the lack of outright performance compared with the V50 series. Obviously it suffered most in a two-up situation, but solo I was impressed – such an easy, pleasant all-purpose bike. One of a dying breed. No fancy frills, it just got on with providing fuss-free travel. I also found it remarkably economical 65–70mpg (4.35–4.04l/100km) could be achieved with careful use of the throttle.

## V50 III

Introduced a year after the V35 II, the V50 III was actually a twin of the smaller bike, with virtually the same improvements.

*The V50 Series III arrived in 1981. It put right most of the faults found on the Series II. Although a much better bike the worldwide sales recession of the early 1980s and experiences with the earlier bike kept sales below what the machine itself deserved.*

Power increased from 45 to 47bhp (crankshaft readings). This was achieved by increasing the inlet and exhaust valve diameters to 34 and 30mm respectively. The carburation was also uprated by not only increasing the choke size from 24 to 28mm, but also using round PHBH BS/BD instruments in place of the original model's square slide VHB Dell'Ortos. To take full advantage of the freer breathing, larger diameter inlet manifolds and exhaust pipes were employed. In the transmission, the gear selectors and gears themselves were modified (also found on the V35 II) and all the other improve-ments from the smaller machine – including the points ignition, new seat and silencers, were also fitted. But the two models could easily be told apart. The V50 III had oblong (black) turn signals and a new instrument dash and headlamp mounting arrangement, plus a grill-like affair under the headlamp which also supported the front turn signals. Like the V35 II, it was out on the road where the V50 III really excelled over its forerun-ners. That and a much improved finish should have made it a winner – but this was not to be – for the reasons already explained elsewhere in this chapter.

## V35 IMOLA/V50 MONZA

For those wishing for a more sporting style (if not performance!) Guzzi obliged by creat-ing first the V35 Imola (launched at the Milan Show in November 1979 – at the same time as the V35 II) and the larger V50 Monza at the Bologna Show the following year. Both machines benefited by having, right from the off, the changes introduced by their touring brothers the V35 II and V50 III. Essentially the Imola and Monza appeared much more sporting than they actually were. They even used the same compression ratio and carburettor type/size as the tourers. The factory quoted an addi-tional 1bhp for each model. This was achieved by fitting larger valves; on the V35 Imola these were increased to a 30.5mm inlet and 27.5mm exhaust. Most of the run-ning gear was shared with the standard models, but the sportsters gained a neat bikini fairing, clip-on handlebars, rearset controls, a new dual seat with a racing-style tail-section, upswept silencers and the oblong turn signals from the V50 III. Han-dling was assisted by air suspension front and rear, the latter units now being exclu-sively of Paioli manufacture. The fuel tank capacity was upped to 16 litres (3.5gal) and the finish was Italian racing red (V35 Imola); for the V50 Monza there was also a colour option of metallic grey/blue. These colours were used on the fairing, tank (with a black base and top), mudguards, side panels, fork sliders and seat tail-section. There were no badges or lining, simply a gold 'Moto Guzzi' logo on the front of the fairing and each side of the tank, and either 'V35 Imola' or 'V50 Monza' on the side panels. A word of praise should be given to the stylist who, for minimum cost, transformed a humble tourer into a sleek sportster. Just a shame that those attractive looks did not actually mean much in the way of increased performance

levels. Maximum speeds were 99mph (159kph) (Imola) and 106mph (170kph) (Monza). What increases there were coming from the more sporting riding stance, the small fairing and the better breathing of the motor thanks to the larger valves. To cope with their performance gains the primary gearing of each machine was altered to suit.

Unlike the Imola, the Monza was imported into Great Britain by Coburn & Hughes, with first deliveries arriving in February 1981 at a retail price of £1,699, some £200 more than the V50 III. Even so the Monza soon found willing buyers, although like the V50 III, it never approached the

*More sporty styling but hardly any more performance the V35 Imola (1979–1983) and shown, the V50 Monza (1980–1983).*

sales figures enjoyed by the earlier V50 II during 1979 and the first half of 1980. When *Motorcycling* tested a Monza during the summer of 1981 they recorded a top speed of 105.35mph (169.5kph) with the rider prone and a fuel consumption figure of 58mpg (4.88l/100km) – the average over the entire test.

## V35C/V50C/V65C

'C' stood for Custom, and together with the new V65 series made their bow late in 1981 at the customary Milan Show venue. There were clear commercial reasons why Moto Guzzi should go for the 'Easy Rider' laid-back biking scene. Not only had Honda already introduced a CX500 Custom, but the American Custom Cruiser concept was fast gaining ground on the Italian home market at this time, where, following hard on the heels of a boom in enduro-style machining at the end of the 1970s, Italian riders were rapidly switching to cruising the streets on bikes that were more in keeping with Los Angeles than Rome, Milan or Bologna. Guzzi's development team had obviously

*The cover of the 1984 V65C brochure, showing a number of optional extras, including screen and hard panniers.*

*Custom cruiser. Guzzi came up with the V35C (seen here), V50C and V65C. All three ran from 1982 through to 1985. Popular in the home market, very few were sold in Britain.*

closely followed Honda's thoughts with a machine which was superficially very similar to the Japanese company's CX500 Custom. All three engine sizes of Guzzi's custom shared the same cycle parts. There was the customary Ape-hanger bars, 15-litre (3.3gal) peanut tank, the chrome fenders, 'King and Queen' seat, chrome grab rail, and fat 16in rear tyre. Again, like their Japanese rivals, Guzzi were building on much of the original motorcycle and using entirely standard engines. The frame and forks, linked braking system and electrics were also stock Guzzi, and even though the rear light and headlamp brackets were from the 850T3, rather than the middleweight range, the kicked-up silencers were from the Imola/Monza. Only the side panels were exclusive to the Custom range.

As for colour schemes there was at first a choice of two: Italian racing red or metallic steel blue/grey, with the former having black/gold lining, the latter blue/black. Later, other colours were made available of which white became the most popular.

## V65/V65 SP

The 1981 Milan Show not only heralded the Custom series, but also, more importantly for the long term, a move into a larger engine size. The six-fifty parallel twin had been the definitive British bike of the 1950s and 1960s with a whole range of models from AMC (AJS and Matchless) Ariel, BSA, Norton, Royal Enfield and Triumph. But the new Guzzi shared nothing in common with the Brit iron of yore except pushrod-operated valves. Instead, the new engine followed its smaller brothers in layout, even though both the bore and stroke (80 × 64mm) were different from either the V35 or V50. This gave an exact cubic capacity of 643.4cc and except for this and the adoption of the larger 30mm Dell'Orto PHBH carbs, everything else was close to V50 III specification.

Besides the Custom version, there were two other V65s at Milan – the Normale and the Speciale. The only real difference between these two was that the Speciale came with an 1000SP-type three-piece fairing. Strangely this fairing simply did not suit the middleweight model. There were two problems The bottom sections of the three-piece fairing had to be removed for use by taller riders because they were unable to tuck their knees inside the fairing, and the upper section generated unwanted wind noise (mainly because the screen was poorly designed) and buffeting of the rider's head

and shoulders at higher speeds. All this is strange because of the factory's in-house wind tunnel facilities.

In many other ways the V65SP and the unfaired brother scored over the smaller engined V35/50 models, by way of an improved power-to-weight ratio. The only disadvantage was increased engine vibration. By the time of the V65's introduction all the middleweights had benefited from a number of detailed improvements including double-skinned exhaust pipes and an improved gearbox. *Motorcycle Enthusiast* tester Rosemary Swindells commented in the August 1984 issue, 'The gearchange was surprisingly smooth, with neutral easy to find, I would have expected such a new bike (it had only done 500 miles when the test started) to have had a stiff gearbox.' However, there were aspects of the V65's gearbox the tester did not appreciate quite so much. 'First could be a little difficult to engage from standstill, feeling rather vague, and there seemed to be too great a jump in ratios between 4th and 5th. Upwards there were

*Built from 1981 until 1985, the V65SP (there was also an unfaired standard V65 roadster) proved a much sought after machine. The combination of light weight, punchy engine and comprehensive weather protection was much appreciated; at least by smaller riders.*

many times when the engine was over revving in 4th, yet labouring in top, so I found in some instances that I was constantly changing gear just to find a happy medium.' In contrast the same tester, 'was pleased by the acceleration, which had been the cause of complaint by some V50 owners, just open the throttle and the 650 would go'. For once the electrics, so derided on certain Italian motorcycles of the period came in for praise. 'On removing the petrol tank, instead of the expected heap of spaghetti type wiring I found a neat wiring harness.' The electrics were a real EEC mixture, British Lucas starter solenoid, German Bosch regulator and Spanish Motoplat coils for example. If the electrics won praise, the stands certainly did not. Again Rosemary Swindells in the 1984 *MCE* test takes up the story, 'I have come to expect little from Italian side stands, but at least they usually work for the duration of the time it takes to get off the bike and park it on its main stand. On the V65 it was impossible to put the stand down whilst on the bike, thus rendering it useless and it would be impossible to leave the V65 on its sidestand at all as it just over-balanced. The main stand was not marvellous and provided, to my mind, too narrow a base for the bike to stand on securely.' By the time of the *Motorcycle Enthusiast* test, Coburn & Hughes had been replaced as British importers by Three Cross Motorcycles of Three Legged Cross, Wimborne, Dorset. The standard V65 cost £2,299, with the SP version going for an extra £100.

During another road test, this time by *Motorcycle Mechanics*, an electronically timed 111mph (178.6kph) was obtained; this against the factory's claims of 115mph (185kph), making the V65 some 5mph (8kph) quicker than the V50. Perhaps more important was the improved mid-range torque and superior throttle response. Tester Colin Mayo called it 'the Practical Italian' and considered that the 'nicest aspect of the V65 (unfaired model tested) was its combination of excellent roadholding and chunky, mid-range torque'.

## V35 IMOLA II, V50 MONZA II AND V65 LARIO

Launched at the same Milan Show in November 1983 at the same time as the TT street enduro bikes (see Chapter 10) was a new series of middleweight sportsters. Available in 350, 500 and 650 classes, what set these models apart from the earlier Guzzi V-twins was their four-valve per-cylinder heads. Unlike their two-valve brothers of the same engine sizes, they employed angled, not parallel valve layout. The new trio was clearly aimed at the sporting rider, and shared a common styling package. This included a sculptured 18-litre (4gal) fuel tank and equally curvaceous side panels, and a matching seat tail section which blended in to provide what are best described as swoopy lines. Many of the lessons learned in the development of the 850 Le Mans III styling exercise were applied to the smaller sportsters – displayed best by the way the miniature cockpit fairing and separate air-foils were designed to deflect the air stream away from the rider, under the fuel tank and on to the cylinder heads.

The front mudguard featured a built-in fork brace, for Guzzi had by then learned from other models with plastic guards that, without bracing, fork legs were liable to flex under severe braking; thus impairing both handling and road-holding characteristics. The forks themselves were Guzzi's own well tried and tested air-assisted units, but the fork sliders were modified so the axle was now actually slightly trailing. The gas rear shocks (like those specified for the standard V65 and SP) were of Paioli manufacture. Following contemporary (Japanese inspired) fashion, both wheels were of the 16in variety. The ten-spoke (enclosed in close grouped pairs) cast alloy wheels were fitted with 100/90 H16 front and 120/90 H16 rear Pirelli tyres. The braking system employed a trio of 270mm drilled discs with twin-piston Brembo calipers. The rider's view was dominated by a thick rubber instrument console, the centre of which sported a huge white-face Veglia racing tacho, with a smaller speedo and matching voltmeter, as on the Le Mans III. All three of the four-valve models were given the same colour choice – red, silver or white. The main colour was applied to tank, fairing, seat base, fork sliders, side panels, mudguards, and belly pan (another fashion accessory 'stolen' from Japanese trends).

So how did the four-valve sports bike perform? In typical fashion, to anyone familiar with four valves in bikes or cars, they needed revving. At the lower end of the rev range there initially seemed no real improvement over the two-valve models. However, by mid-range the extra punch was beginning to make itself noticed, and by around 4500rpm it was definitely much better. This improved breathing and a higher

rpm also gave a higher maximum speed. During a 1985 *Motorcycle Enthusiast* test I recorded almost 115mph (185kph) with a V65 Lario. The two really lasting impressions I took away from that test were of a cobby, supremely compact, 'Boy Racer' riding stance, and how the machine would literally 'sit up' if the brakes were applied in a corner, the latter a trait of the 16in wheels. But even so, I was pleased with the safe handling and road-holding. These displayed none of the horrors associated with the use of 16in front wheels on the Le Mans 1000 and 1000SP II machines. In fact, generally, I was impressed enough to know that I would be quite happy to have spent my own money buying a V65 Lario – the ultimate tester's seal of approval! There was a mechanical snag, however. When the Moto Guzzi engineering team carried out the conversion to four valves, it chose to keep costs to a bare minimum. This involved retaining as many standard production components as possible, including cams, followers, and valves. The conventional camshafts were solid, and these were unable to provide adequate lubrication to the valve gear. The result was a spate of warranty claims, the like of which

*Named after its birthplace, the Lario was Guzzi's first four-valves-per-cycle production V-twin, entering the market in early 1984. There were also the identical looking V35 Imola II and V50 Monza II.*

*Four valves in its middleweight twins caused problems at first, but a retro-fit kit was soon on the scene which sorted things out.*

had been unseen since the days of the V50 II problems back in 1979 and early 1980. To the factory's credit these were effectively sorted out (under warranty) with a modification kit comprising new hollow camshaft, modified followers (these can be detected by a matt blue finish, rather than the original component's polished bright metal), and new valves. Only during the last few months of production (which eventually finished in 1987) were these uprated parts fitted as standard, so most had to be carried out by the various distributors and their respective dealer networks. By now all should have been changed, but check before buying.

## V35 III/V75

Everyone – the press, Guzzisti and most of all the factory – expected the long-awaited V75 to be a winner. Instead it turned out to be the biggest sales flop of the entire middleweight V-twin series. The formula sounded ideal – on paper. Prior to its launch, Guzzi owners and those thinking of joining the fold were eagerly awaiting its coming (which had been known for some time). The factory brochure claimed 200kph (125mph)

from the 175kg (383lb) machine – again, on paper this sounded highly promising. But what was not promising was a re-run of the four-valve head saga (but worse), the vague steering (thanks to a combination of 16in front and 18in rear tyres) and a distinctly weird styling job. There was also a new electronic ignition system with two independent circuits synchronized for each cylinder. The 743.9cc (88 × 78mm) engine again used the familiar 90-degree, pushrod operated valves (albeit four rather than two per cylinder). The same 30mm Dell'Orto PHBH round slide carbs were to be found from the V65 series; as was the use of the Guzzi Nigusil coated alloy cylinder barrels. Other notable features of the V75 specification included the patented integral braking system (using in this case twin 270mm front discs and a single 235mm disc at the rear – all with twin piston Brembo calipers), a 17 litre (3.7imp gal) fuel tank capacity and an 850T5-type cockpit fairing with speedometer, tachometer, voltmeter, fuel gauge and a series of warning lights.

The press did not help sales, typified by this cutting extract from *Motor Cycle International*: 'A potentially nice motor, with four-valve heads, ruined by restrictive carbs

*The two-valve V35 III (left) and four-valve 743.9cc (80 × 74mm) V75 shared the styling and 16in front wheel syndrome. The larger machine was particularly troublesome in this latter respect.*

## TECHNICAL SPECIFICATIONS
## V 35 III (1986)

| | | | |
|---|---|---|---|
| Engine | 4-stroke 90° V-twin | Brakes | front: twin disc, 260mm diameter, drilled, operating independently rear: single disc, 235mm diameter integral brake system |
| Bore | 66mm | | |
| Stroke | 50.6mm | | |
| Displacement | 346.2cc | | |
| Compression ratio | 10.5:1 | Wheels | light alloy casting |
| Timing | ohv | Tyres | front: 100/90 H 16 rear: 110/80 H 18 |
| Lubrication | by pressure pump | | |
| Transmission | primary by helical gears secondary by cardan shaft and gears | Frame | tubular cradle |
| | | Suspension | front: Moto Guzzi telescopic air fork with pressure-equalizer rear: swinging fork with hydraulic dampers |
| Clutch | dry with single disc | | |
| Fuel delivery | two carburettors VHBZ 26, with air filter and engine gas recycling | | |
| Electrical system | 12V, alternator 14V–20A fitted on driving shaft, battery 12V-20Ah | Instruments | speedometer, rev-counter, fuel level indicator, voltmeter and warning lights |
| Starting | electric | Fuel tank capacity | 17ltr (3.7gal) |
| Ignition | electronic, two circuits (one per cylinder) operating independently, with automatic spark advance | Fuel consumption | 4ltr × 100km (70.75mpg) |
| | | Speed | 150km/h (94mph) approx. |
| Gearbox | 5-speed | Dry weight | 160kg (350lb) approx. |

and exhaust. The seat is uncomfortable, the styling odd, and the finish shoddy'. To help poor sales the British importers, Three Cross Motors, brought out their version of the V75 in July 1986. This not only had a new seat (which the factory had introduced), but there was also a new fairing which, together with a belly pan, cost an extra £260 plus VAT. These measures did not really help sales, although the combination of a much more comprehensive fairing and a more comfortable seat made the bike better than before.

The V35 III was essentially a smaller engined V75. Differences were: VHBZ 26mm carbs; 5kg (11lb) less dry weight; narrower tyres, front 100/90 (110/90), rear 110/80 (120/80) and a revised front mudguard; and only two-valve heads. The factory claimed 150kph (93mph). If anything, the V35 III was even less successful than its bigger V75 brother, and both machines marked a low point of Guzzi V-twin sales in the middleweight sector. Both were built in the period late 1985 until early 1987.

## V35/V65 FLORIDA

If the V35 III and V75 roadsters were a failure just the reverse could be said of the V35/65 Florida Custom models. Making their debut in late 1986, they went on to become the top selling middleweight Guzzi V-twins of the late 1980s and early 1990s. Although clearly developed from the earlier 'C' models, the Florida much more closely followed its bigger brother, the best-selling California. The Florida used the same 'Cali' style, but in a lighter more agile and of course cheaper format. This light weight made it an ideal town bike, yet with the addition of panniers, windshield, crashbars and the like it provided a viable option for longer distances. The V65 Florida could be purchased with or without accessories. Naked it weighed in (dry) at 170kg (374lb) against the V35 Florida's 165kg (363lb). Soon after its launch in 1987 it was realized that Guzzi had found a winner. The bike looked the part, and by the end of 1988 over 60 per cent of custom bike sales in Italy were being claimed by the California and Florida – against several rivals including Ducati (350, 650 and 750cc Indianas) and Moto Morini (350 and 501 Excaliburs), plus of course the Japanese and Harley-Davidson. The use of epoxydic compound painting also gave a higher resistance to corrosion. Other fea-

*A fully dressed V65 Florida. It was purchased by those who wanted a custom, but were put off the California either by price or size.*

tures such as large capacity panniers with watertight sealing, the higher use of alloy and plastics and convenience features such as the 'Highway Footpegs' which allowed for a relaxing position on long distance touring all conspired to help the Florida series' success. Even the handlebar switchgear was almost on a par with Japanese levels. As for wheel size and tyre choices Guzzi came up with just the right combinations. The figures given here show the V65 Florida, with the V35 Florida in brackets. Front 100/90 18in (90/90), rear 130/90 16in (120/90). The two machines shared most details of specification including brakes (twin 260mm front discs, single 235mm rear), 17 litre (3.7gal) fuel capacity and virtually all the other cycle part components. The larger model had Dell'Orto PHBH 30mm carburettors. Colour choices included white or black.

Up to the 1990 model year there were cast alloy wheels and a right-side-mounted rear disc. From the 1991 model year, wire wheels were specified, together with a left-side-mounted rear disc. In addition, all the Florida series used two-valve cylinder heads, thus preventing the disasters that

*Although clearly developed from the earlier V35/65 C custom models, the Florida series was a much superior machine. This is the home-market three-fifty.*

## TECHNICAL SPECIFICATIONS
### 350 Falco (Prototype only) 1987

| | | | |
|---|---|---|---|
| Engine | 4-stroke 90° V-twin | Frame | square tubular steel frame |
| Bore | 66mm | Suspension | front: Moto Guzzi telescopic fork |
| Stroke | 50.6mm | | rear: light alloy swinging fork with oil/air dampers |
| Displacement | 346.22cc | | |
| Compression ratio | 10.5:1 | | |
| Timing | ohc, four valves per cylinder | Instruments | speedometer, electronic rev-counter, fuel level indicator and warning lights |
| Lubrication | forced, by pressure pump | | |
| Transmission | primary by helical gears secondary by cardan shaft and gears | Fuel tank capacity | 16ltr (3.5gal) |
| | | Fuel consumption | 4.8ltr × 100km (59mpg Imp/49mpg US) (CUNA Norms) |
| Clutch | dry with single disc | | |
| Fuel delivery | two carburettors PHBH 30 with air filtering and engine gas recycling | Speed | over 170km/h (106mph) |
| | | Dry weight | 179kg (394lb) |
| Electrical system | 12Vr, alternator 14V–20A fitted on driving shaft, rectifier and regulator | | |
| Starting | electric | | |
| Ignition | electronic | | |
| Gearbox | 5-speed | | |
| Brakes | front: two drilled discs 270mm, independently operated rear: one disc 235mm integral braking system | | |
| Wheels | light alloy casting | | |
| Tyres | front: 100/90 V 16 or H 16 rear: 120/90 V 16 or H 16 | | |

*The little-known 4-valve overhead cam 350 Falco remained a prototype only. Only appearing as a prototype at the Milan Show in November 1987, it was destined never to reach production. Its fate probably sealed by a too high unit cost*

accompanied bikes like the V65 Lario and V75. Maximum speeds (without accessories, including the windshield) were: V35 Florida 94mph (150kph) and V65 Florida 106mph (170kph). Production ceased in 1992 when it became apparent that the buying public had accepted the more radically styled Nevada range.

## 350 TRENTACINQUE GT AND 650 SESSANTACINQUE GT

Boasting probably the longest model names in history, the 350 Trentacinque GT and the 650 Sessantacinque GT were largely intended to replace the V35/50/65 roadster series. Only the largest of the two was exported in any quantity; the smaller bike was intended purely for the home market. After the V75 sales debacle, Guzzi's management obviously played safe and basically restyled the old but popular V65. The pair of newcomers' styling mirrored that of the Mille GT (see Chapter 4) from the same era, with the duo sharing several components such as handlebars, lights, instrumentation, horns, turn signals and mirrors. In a 1988 road test *Motorcycle Enthusiast* got 114mph (183.4kph) from the larger version and found the engine 'smooth and torquey'. But although tester Rick Kemp liked much about the 650 Sessantacinque GT he thought it was spoiled from being a great all-rounder by its 'lack of comfort for any trip of more than an hour and a half'. This

in Kemp's opinion was due not just to the seat but to over-hard rear shocks. Of course the latter could after all be dialled out of the equation by fitting a decent pair of after-market assemblies. Again, Guzzi played safe by opting for two- rather than four-valve cylinder heads. Also, although the larger model had 18in wheels front and rear; the smaller machine had a 16-incher. The author's own view is that Guzzi needed to shift an excess of any by now obsolete stock.

## 750SP

The 750SP was first exhibited at the Milan Show in November 1989. It was an unsuccessful attempt to offer a touring roadster in

---

**TECHNICAL SPECIFICATIONS**
**650 Sessantacinque GT (1987)**

| | | | |
|---|---|---|---|
| Engine | 4-stroke 90° V-twin | Brakes | front: twin 260mm disc |
| Bore | 80mm | | rear: single disc |
| Stroke | 64mm | Wheels | cast alloy |
| Displacement | 643.4cc, Nigusil cylinder lining | Tyres | front, 100/90 H 18 |
| | | | rear, 110/90 H 18 |
| Compression ratio | 10:1 | | |
| Timing | ohv | Suspension | front: Moto Guzzi telescopic |
| Transmission | primary by helical gears secondary by cardan shaft and gears | | rear: twin shock |
| Clutch | dry with single disc | Instruments | speedometer, rev counter and warning lights |
| Fuel delivery | two Dell'Orto PHBH 30 carburettors | | |
| | | Fuel tank capacity | 17ltr (3.74gal) |
| Electrical system | 12V, alternator 14V-20A fitted on driving shaft, rectifier and regulator, battery 20Ah | Fuel consumption | 5.5ltr × 100km (51.5mpg) |
| Starting | electric | Maximum speed | 105mph (170km/h) |
| Gearbox | 5-speed | Dry weight | 165kg (364lb) |

## TECHNICAL SPECIFICATIONS
### 750 SP (1989)

| | | | |
|---|---|---|---|
| Engine | 4-stroke 90° V-twin | Brakes | front: dual discs of 270mm diameter, drilled rear: single fixed disc of 235mm diameter, drilled integral braking system |
| Bore | 80mm | | |
| Stroke | 74mm | | |
| Displacement | 743.9cc, 'Nigusil' cylinder lining | | |
| | | Wheels | light alloy casting |
| Max. power | 34kw (46HP) at 6600rpm (IGM rules) | Tyres | front: 100/90 V18 tubeless rear: 120/80 V18 tubeless |
| Max. torque | 59.44Nm (6.06kgm) at 320rpm (IGM rules) | | |
| Compression ratio | 9.7:1 | Frame | steel tubular duplex cradle |
| Timing | ohv, two valves per cylinder | Suspension | front: Moto Guzzi hydropneumatic telescopic fork with pressure equalizer rear: swinging fork, light alloy die-casting, with Koni adjustable shock-absorbers |
| Lubrication | by pressure pump | | |
| Transmission | primary by gears secondary by cardan shaft with double universal joint and bevel gears | | |
| Clutch | single plate, dry type | Instruments | speedometer, rev-counter, quartz clock, voltmeter and warning lights |
| Fuel delivery | two Dell'Orto carburettors PHBH 30 | | |
| Electrical system | 12V, 14V-20A alternator, battery 20Ah | Fuel tank capacity | 17ltr (3.74gal) |
| Starting | electric | Fuel consumption | 5.4ltr × 100km (52.4mpg) (CUNA rules) |
| Ignition | electronic, motoplat double pick-up | Max. speed | 170km/h (106mph) approx. |
| Gearbox | 5-speed, constant mesh gears | Dry weight | 185kg (408lb) |

*The 650 Sessantacinque GT was introduced for the 1988 model year, it and the 750T (introduced in the early 1990s) were genuine attempts to provide sound, budget priced all-rounders.*

the same vein of the earlier V65SP, but using the V75 as a base and with two- instead of four-valve heads and 18in wheels front and rear. It came equipped with a useful three-quarter fairing with a tall, curved screen to provide decent rider protection – at least for the head and shoulders. There were also a large grab rail for the pillion, optional hard luggage and a choice of colours including dark turquoise or silver. Other parts of the specification included: 30mm PHBH Dell'Ortos, a compression ratio of 9.7:1, Motoplat electronic ignition, a 24-amp hour battery, and full instrumentation. It also used the improved switchgear from the

Florida series. Performance details included 106mph (170kph) and a dry weight of 185kg (407lb) without panniers but with the fairing. If this motorcycle had come in the place of the ill-fated V75 earlier in the decade who knows what it might have achieved. As it was, sales were never more than a trickle and it was only offered for sale for a few months during 1990 and the first part of 1991.

## 750 TARGA

Much more successful was the 750 Targa which debuted in 1990. With a styling akin to the Le Mans, it was a budget-priced sports model, but one which was very much a sheep in wolf's clothing. By the time it appeared it was totally outclassed by the Japanese 600s, let alone the 750s. But it did enjoy a much lower purchase price. In reality it should be compared with Japanese five-hundred twins, such as Kawasaki's GPZ500S or Suzuki's GS500, both having similar performances and price structures. Its 116mph (186.6kph) was quite respectable, also its physical size

and low weight of 180kg (396lb) made it a popular choice with smaller riders, particularly women, in much the same way as the original V50 over a decade before. The seat and tank were obviously stolen from the V65 Lario, but the 18in wheels and larger upper half-fairing were major improvements over the earlier model, as was the use of two-valve instead of four-valve cylinder heads. All Targas came in a bright Italian racing red which extended to the cast alloy wheels. Most Targas, at least in Great Britain, were sold with a belly pan as original equipment to complement the fairing. The last Targas were sold in 1993.

## 750T/750 STRADA

Launched a year after the Targa, the 750T was the closest you could get to the original V50, but with a seven-fifty motor. It really did look like a V50 II or III, except for its Targa engine, carbs, wheels and exhaust. This showed in its purchase price. When it went on sale from the British importers Three Cross Motorcycles at £3,999, it was

*Introduced in 1990, the 750 Targa was another low price effort. With a maximum speed of 116mph (185kph) it was not really a sports bike, but its small physical size and low weight 180kg (397lb) made it a popular choice with smaller riders, particularly women.*

*Developed from the 750T (1992–1993), the new 750 Strada made its début during 1994. It was then the cheapest 750-class machine on the British market.*

not only the cheapest 750 on the UK market, but also cheaper than many smaller-engined bikes, too. For 1994, the 750T (at least in Britain) was replaced by the 750 Strada (which was based on the now defunct 650 Sessantacinque GT). It was very much a rehash of old ideas and nothing really new. The Strada had in fact gone on sale two years earlier on the home market – as had its bigger brother, the 1000 Strada (see Chapter 4). Very few were sold before they were discontinued.

## 350/750 NEVADA

In many ways the Guzzi Nevada can be seen as a motorcycle in a similar catchment to the Ducati Monster. However, although they lack any real muscle both still have lots of street cred. However in terms of sales figures the Ducati has proved the clear winner. Some of this may be due to a wider capacity range (600, 750 and 900) against the Guzzi's 350 and 750cc. But also the Ducati has had much more attention from the press, and has benefited from brothers which have

*The 750 (and the 350) Nevada replaced the Florida as Guzzi's middleweight custom cruiser. This is the original version which first went on sale during 1990.*

included famous names such as 916 and 748 – even though they share no common components. The Nevada also arrived some three years before the Ducati, its public debut being at the end of 1989. In several ways the Guzzi (at least in 750cc form) is a superior option to the Ducati series. It has usually been cheaper than the 600 Monster on the British market and a full third less than the cost of a 900 Monster. It also has shaft, rather than chain drive.

Both Italian designs can trace their heritage back to the late 1970s; the Guzzi to the V50, the Monster to the Pantah. But of the two, the Guzzi is the least radical, being more of a conventional custom bike, rather than Ducati's street fighter image. And this, I am sure, is why the Guzzi has not matched the Ducati saleswise. When I first viewed the Nevada back in 1990 I thought it looked a strange, weird beast, with its garish chrome-plated steel pressing which dominated the space between the fuel tank and the two-valve cylinder heads on each side of the machine and the equally noticeable 'King and Queen' saddle and distinct rear mudguard and supporting chrome rails. There were also the wire wheels (18in at the front and 16in rear) with twin 270mm discs at the front, and a single 260mm assembly at the rear. Like its big brother the California, the Nevada was offered in both naked and dressed form (the latter comprising of the usual touring goodies such as windshield, crashbar, backrest, carrier, hard or soft saddlebags). A tote bag and a 40-litre hard top box were also available as optional extras.

## 350/750 NEVADA NT

From September 1994, (in other words the 1995 model year) the Nevada was subtly changed from the original model (officially coded at the works as the Nevada Comfort)

## TECHNICAL SPECIFICATIONS
### 750 Nevada (1990)

| | | | |
|---|---|---|---|
| Engine | 4-stroke 90° V-twin | Brakes | front: dual floating discs of 270mm diameter, drilled |
| Bore | 80mm | | |
| Stroke | 74mm | | rear: single fixed disc of 260mm diameter, drilled integral braking system |
| Displacement | 743.9cc, 'Nigusil' cylinder lining | | |
| Max. power | 34kW (46HP) at 6600 rpm (IGM rules) | Wheels | wire with light alloy rim |
| | | Tyres | front: 100/90 V28 Tube type |
| Max. torque | 59.44Nm (6.06kgm) at 3200 rpm (IGM rules) | | rear: 130/90 V16 Tube type |
| Compression Ratio | 9.7:1 | | |
| Timing | ohv, two valves per cylinder | Frame | steel tubular duplex cradle |
| Lubrication | by pressure pump | Suspension | front: Moto Guzzi hydropneumatic telescopic fork with pressure equalizer |
| Transmission | primary by gears secondary by cardan shaft with double universal joint and bevel gears | | rear: swinging fork, light alloy die-casting, with Ohlins adjustable shock-absorbers |
| Clutch | single plate, dry type | | |
| Fuel delivery | two Dell'Orto carburettors PHBH 30 | Instruments | speedometer, rev-counter and warning lights |
| Electrical System | 12Vr, 14V-20A alternator, battery 20Ah | Fuel Tank Capacity | 17ltr (3.74gal) |
| | | Fuel consumption | 5.4ltr × 100km (52.4mpg) (CUNA rules) |
| Starting | electric | | |
| Ignition | electronic, Motoplat double pick-up | Max. Speed | 170km/h approx (106mph) |
| Gearbox | 5-speed | Dry Weight | 177kg (390lb) |

to the Nevada NT (New Type). As with the 1000SP, the NT variant really is a considerable improvement. Besides the aforementioned chrome-steel pressing at the base of the tank and new rear carrier/backrest assembly, there were numerous other less obvious changes/improvements. A larger headlight, new horns, repositioned front twin signals, round (instead of oblong) chrome mirrors, redesigned brake discs, new mudguards, deletion of the early-model guards which had covered joining areas of the centre exhaust area and new colour schemes including yellow/black and blue/gold. Perhaps most significant of all was the new Marelli Digiplex ignition system which cured at a stroke the previous poor low rpm running and much of the unwelcome vibes encountered on the original Nevada series. Another area of improvement, albeit less obvious, has been to the overall finish. The Nevada NT, together with other current Guzzis, benefits from stricter quality targets (and now underwritten by a

*The Mark II Nevada (NT) arrived in September 1994. This was subtly changed from the original (known as the Comfort) to the NT (New Type). There was a host of small improvements which, added together, produced a much better motorcycle.*

*Latest, 1998, incarnation of the middleweight Guzzi V-twin, the Nevada 750 Club. Intended as a budget custom competitor to Ducati's newly released 600 Monster Dark.*

*New for 1998, the budget priced 750 Nevada Club. New features include individual seats and two-tone paint finish*

comprehensive three-year manufacturer's warranty from 1998), thicker paint, deeper chrome and improvements to components such as the suspension and gearbox. All-in-all the Nevada has come a long way during its production life. Price is still a vital factor with this model and with Ducati launching its new budget Monster Dark 600 for 1998, Guzzi have responded with the Nevada Club. For the British market this, like the Monster Dark, has a sub-£5,000 price tag (£4,999). And this is an on-the-road figure

fully inclusive of manufacturer's delivery, pre-delivery inspection, twelve months' vehicle excise duty, petrol, numberplate, first service labour content and VAT.

So today the Nevada is the sole surviving middleweight Moto Guzzi V-twin series – the entry level range in fact. As before, it is an ideal stepping stone, and without it there would only be models at the top end of the cubic capacity and price league tables. It is a vital brick in the company's foundation as it approaches the twenty-first century.

# 8  California

Without dispute the California is Moto Guzzi's longest running model series – even though today's Evolution is far removed from the original V7-based model which debuted in the spring of 1971.

## V7 CALIFORNIA

That first machine was basically a dressed 757cc (83 × 70mm) V7 Special (Ambassador in the USA) with laid-back hi-and-wide western bars, a black and white buddy saddle with a chrome wrap-around tail and footboards, a massive, four-point toughened Perspex screen, and chrome-plated crashbars front and rear. It was in fact the nearest an Italian-made bike got to playing the role of a custom cruiser – and in many ways

still does. Except for the fact that the cylinders were pointing in the wrong direction it was clearly aimed at the same market as that 'American Dream Machine', the Harley-Davidson. However, right from the start the California won a whole new crop of owners. These people wanted a lighter, better handling machine than the Harley, and the new Guzzi filled this role admirably.

## 850GT CALIFORNIA

The original 'Cali' as it was soon christened, ran for only a few months before being replaced by, the larger-engined 844.06cc (83 × 78mm) – achieved by increasing the stroke rather than the bore. The new, larger displacement Guzzi vee was first shown to

*The 850GT California made its début at the Milan Show in November 1971. Its last year of production was 1974. For this year only, a single 300mm cast iron Brembo disc replaced the original 200mm twin leading shoe, single-sided drum front brake.*

the public in the Italian industry's traditional manner, the biennial Milan Show, in November 1971. Beside the 850GT California, the factory also introduced the V850 GT tourer. Throughout 1972 and 1973 the California (and its GT brother) continued unchanged, but in 1974 they were given something of a facelift, swapping the massive drum front brake for a single 300mm cast-iron disc operated by a Brembo caliper mounted at the front of the right-hand fork leg.

## 850T3 CALIFORNIA

That year, 1974, also saw the debut of the 850T (see Chapter 4), a motorcycle which was not only to reshape the California series, but also the company's entire V-twin range. The 850T owed its origins to the V7 Sport, using as it did Ing. Tonti's more sporting frame and suspension changes. Although only produced for some twelve months, and never in California guise, the 850T led directly to the highly successful and popular 850T3. The T had introduced not only the improved, lighter cycle parts, but also the replacement of the belt-driven Marelli generator. Previously, except on the sport model, the position of this above the crankcase between the cylinder barrels had meant that the front of the engine was dominated by a massive aluminium outer casing. Now, like the V7 Sport and 750S, the 850T/T3 series employed a much neater (and vastly more effective) 180-watt Bosch-made alternator mounted at the front of the crankcase assembly and encased in a circular, highly polished alloy cover. Although no 'Cali' had been offered in 850T form, when the 850T3 made its bow in the spring of 1975, it certainly was then. Known simply as the 850T3 California the additional package over the standard T3 included a toughened, tinted Perspex screen, a pair of braced,

laid-back western handlebars, a hydraulic steering damper, knee protectors on the cylinder heads, a black and white 'buddy' seat with chrome grab rail, lockable fibreglass panniers on substantial frames and a chrome-plated carrier, and front and rear crashbars. The 'Cali' specification was topped up with a pair of rider's footboards, a set of revised foot controls which included a heel-and-toe gear lever and an effective prop stand which could be operated by the rider from the saddle. This final item was in stark contrast to the awful mousetrap device which Guzzi insisted on putting on its other

*Mick Walker (right) with British road race Champion Dave Croxford trying a T3 California for size, February 1976.*

V-twin model. Both the standard T3 and its California variant's biggest innovation was in the braking system. For the first time the new models carried the factory's exclusive, patented integral triple disc layout. Guzzi sources claimed it provided more stopping power and braking security than any conventional system on a series production motorcycle at the time. Applying the footbrake pedal did not only operate the rear brake in the normal fashion, but instead it applied both the 242mm rear disc brake and the 300mm nearside front disc. The braking pressure was automatically balanced to produce the correct bias needed to bring the rider to a steady, even stop. For emergencies, or simply to hold the bike stationary, the front brake lever could also be used to apply the offside disc only. The front master cylinder had been changed for one of smaller capacity. More information, together with detailed illustrations, are to be found in Chapter 4.

There was a host of other, but less significant changes, which, allied to those introduced by the 850T, made the T3 California a very different machine to the V7-based models. Rather than risk repeating masses of technical information the reader is advised to refer to the chapter dealing with the T/T3 models. Like the original, the T3 California was only produced in black with contrasting white stripes. Coburn & Hughes had become the British importers, and the T3 California was one of the principal five models imported by the Luton-based organization. Priced at £1,699, it was £100 more than the 850T3 – well worth the premium when one considers the level of 'extras'. Besides its undoubted style this list of equipment no doubt influenced many to pay the extra for the 'Cali' option. In Britain as elsewhere it soon built up an enthusiastic and loyal following.

Besides its style and value-for-money, many also chose the California for its laid-

*The T3 California proved a popular choice with touring riders, and for a £100 premium on the standard 850T3 model came fully kitted out with western bars, buddy seat, crashbars front and rear, footboards, hard panniers and screen.*

back, 'Easy Rider' approach. In truth, anything over 70mph (110kph) produced unwanted wind buffeting from the barn door-like screen but with such a machine the enjoyment was in the cruising rather than speeding. The fitment of panniers also increased its convenience and suitability for a serious touring role. Some owners also exchanged the screen for a more serious fairing to provide additional protection on long journeys. The model ran unchanged until late 1976, when an economy version was offered. This budget-buy, known in Britain as the California Rally, sold at the old price of £1,699, even though the conventional 'Cali' had now gone up to £1,799. The differences included painted (white) steel mudguards, in place of polished stainless steel components and a large speedometer (as on the V1000 Convert automatic) with no tachometer. In 1979 came the first real update. On the California this amounted to a locking petrol filler cap, black plastic alternator cover, CEV headlamp, and SP (Spada) switchgear.

# CALIFORNIA II

Although the T3 became the T4 the following year, the California remained unchanged, until a brand new version made its bow at the Milan Show in November 1981. This newcomer was very much a mixture of old and new features. Its general styling hinting strongly at the original V7-based model of the early 1970s, while its motive power was entirely up-to-date, employing as it did the latest square 'slab' style cylinder heads and barrels introduced on the Le Mans III (see Chapter 6). Like the Le Mans III, the new model, called the California III, was substantially different from the motorcycle it superseded. Not only was its detail specification and appearance altered, but its engine displacement rose to 948.81cc. This was achieved in precisely the same way it had been earlier with the V1000/G5 series, by upping the bore size to 88mm. This was not simply a matter of fashion, but it also had the useful advantage of improving the torque figure, now 7.7kg/m at 5200rpm. Guzzi's publicity claimed an optimistic 118mph (189.9kph) for the 'Cali II', but the truth was

*Like the Le Mans III, the California II was a substantially different motorcycle from the one it replaced. Making its public début in November 1971, it had the V1000-derived 948.81cc (88 × 78mm) engine size.*

somewhat different. With all the standard equipment in place, the very most it could achieve was 105mph (168.9kph). Not only this, but at around 90mph (145kph), or sometimes a shade less, depending on precise road or wind conditions, an unnerving weave could set in. This was also a problem experienced on other large capacity Guzzi V-twins using the large windshield. In my experience this is caused entirely by that slab of toughened Perspex, although the combination of the windshield and panniers simply aggravates the experience. However, this is largely academic as wind resistance above 80mph (125kph) makes the whole thing impractical anyway. Put simply, ride the California as it was designed to be ridden and you won't have any problems. It is the machine's ability to combine, at low and medium speeds, a sweetness of handling and roadholding with a laid-back style which has ensured its popularity over the years; and one that survives today. The California II was launched on to the British market in March 1982. The price was £2,899, but two years later this had risen to £3,599. Unlike the T3 California, buyers could opt for two colour choices: either dark chocolate or white, with red and yellow stripes for the fuel tank, central sections of both mudguards, and the side panels. The latter were emblazoned with a 'California' sticker in place of the metal badge of the previous model. One notable change to the technical specification concerning the frame assembly was the swinging arm which had been lengthened to 470mm (18.504in) between centres and given additional bracing.

In engineering terms the California II benefited from Moto Guzzi's improved machining equipment, which enabled tighter tolerances to be used. Along with the use of aluminium rocker supports, this gave a much quieter engine and the addition of the improved air filtration system pioneered on the Le Mans III, plus the fitment of an

improved exhaust system, made the larger California considerably more civilized than before. Like the earlier California, the II proved an excellent seller, and factory records demonstrate that style has consistently triumphed over function with both this machine and the Le Mans outselling the standard versions, the T, T3, T4 and T5. In fact, as proof that Guzzi had hit the right formula, the California II proved the factory's top selling model during the early 1980s, creating as it did a niche market position all for itself between the ultra expensive and heavyweight Harley-Davidson Electra Glide and the cheaper but generally unloved Japanese custom bikes.

## CALIFORNIA III

The next variant, the III, arrived in time to be displayed on the company's stand at the Milan Show at the tail end of 1987, going on sale early in 1988. Basic versions were made

*The California II continued the tradition of providing customers with a comprehensively kitted out touring motorcycle, with a cruiser image; a combination which was to prove eminently successful.*

*The next variant, the III, arrived in time to be displayed on the company's Milan show at the end of 1987; going on sale early the following year.*

## TECHNICAL SPECIFICATIONS
### 1000 California III (Carburettors) (1988)

| | | | |
|---|---|---|---|
| Engine | 4-stroke 90° V-twin | Brakes | front: twin disc 300mm rear: single disc 270mm integral braking system |
| Bore | 88mm | | |
| Stroke | 78mm | Wheels | light alloy casting (spoke wheels as option) |
| Displacement | 948.8cc, 'Nigusil' cylinder lining | | |
| | | Tyres | front: 110/90 18in rear: 120/90 18in |
| Max. power | 65HP (DIN) at 6700rpm | | |
| Max. torque | 7.7kgm at 5200rpm | Frame | tubular duplex cradle |
| Compression ratio | 9.2:1 | Suspension | front: Moto Guzzi telescopic fork with adjustable operation rear: swinging fork with hydraulic Koni shock-absorbers |
| Timing | ohv | | |
| Lubrication | by pressure pump | | |
| Transmission | primary by helical gears secondary by cardan shaft and bevel gears | | |
| | | Instruments | fully integrated panel including speedometer, electronic rev-counter, voltmeter, quartz clock and warning lights |
| Clutch | double plate, dry type | | |
| Fuel delivery | gravity system by two Dell'Orto carburettors PHF 30mm; main jet 125/100 | | |
| | | Optionals | pannier set consisting of two side bags and one rear top-case |
| Electrical system | 12V, alternator 14V-20A, battery 24Ah | | |
| | | Fairing | integral type |
| Starting | electric | Fuel tank capacity | 25ltr (5.5gal) |
| Ignition | current distributor | Fuel consumption | 5.8ltr × 100km (49mpg) (CUNA Norms) |
| Gearbox | 5-speed | Dry weight | 270kg (595lb) |

available. There were several choices, not just of model specification, but also, wheel type, and most notably the extra cost option (for the first time on a Moto Guzzi) of electronic fuel injection. Three basic variants were offered: the LAPD (Los Angeles Police Department), FF (Fully Faired) and the budget priced Classic model without accessories such as saddlebags or any form of protection from the elements by way of screen or fairing. Customers could also make the choice of cast or wire wheels. Additionally, with both the LAPD or FF models, buyers could choose either conventional 30mm Dell'Orto carbs or digital electronic ignition and fuel injection, from the Weber-Marelli IAW Alfa-N system. Although at first at a considerable cost difference, the fuel injected version provided much enhanced performance, particularly in terms of low speed and cool start running. Other benefits included improved engine smoothness, sharper throttle response and better fuel consumption. All in all, the California III did much to cement the series as Guzzi's most popular model during the late 1980s and early 1990s.

*The California III series was offered in a variety of specifications, including the choice of wire or cast alloy wheels and carbs or fuel injection. Three basic versions were offered: the LAPD (Los Angeles Police Department), the FF (fully faired) and the budget priced, naked Classic model.*

## 1100 CALIFORNIA

The year 1994 heralded an increase in engine capacity to 1064cc ($92 \times 80$mm), to create the new 1100. Besides the popular (and now much cheaper and therefore affordable) option of the Weber-Marelli fuel injection, the carburettor version now came with 36mm instead of 30mm Dell'Orto with accelerator pumps. Moto Guzzi claimed the power output for both versions to be identical at 75bhp at 6400rpm, but the truth was, out on the road, the injected 1100 California was notably superior. Sales too reflected this with a clear trend from carbs to injection,

customers by now realizing the benefits and voting with their wallets. If anyone thought that the larger model was simply a case of increasing the bore and stroke dimensions they would have been spectacularly wrong, because in all there were more than 200 changes between the 1000 and 1100 California models. This was no mere labelling exercise, but instead a genuine effort to notably improve what had become the Mandello del Lario factory's best-selling model. Engine improvements included new cylinder barrels (with an improved bore coating process), new pistons (9.5:1 ratio), and a newly designed crankshaft, with longer, stronger

## TECHNICAL SPECIFICATIONS
### California FF Injection (1990)

| | | | |
|---|---|---|---|
| Engine | 4-stroke 90° V-twin | Gearbox | 5-speed |
| Bore | 88mm | Brakes | front: dual discs 300mm |
| Stroke | 78mm | | rear: single disc 270mm |
| Displacement | 948.8cc, 'Nigusil' cylinder lining | | integral braking system |
| Max. power | 49 kW (67HP) at 6800 rpm (IGM rules) | Wheels | light alloy casting or wire with Akront rims |
| Max. torque | 75Nm (7.6kgm) at 5200 rpm (IGN rules) | Tyres | front: 110/90 V 18 tubeless or tube type for wire wheels |
| Compression ratio | 9.2:1 | | rear: 130/80 V 18 tubeless or tube type for wire wheels |
| Timing | ohv, two valves per cylinder | | |
| Lubrication | by pressure pump | Frame | steel tubular duplex cradle |
| Transmission | primary by gears secondary by cardan shaft with double universal joint and bevel gears | Suspension | front: Bitubo hydraulic telescopic fork rear: swinging fork with Köni hydraulic shock-absorbers |
| Clutch | double plate, dry type | Instruments | speedometer, electronic rev-counter, voltmeter, quartz clock, check-lamp and warning lights |
| Fuel delivery | digital electronic injection WEBER IAW ALFA-N system with electric feeding pump | | |
| | | Fuel tank capacity | 25ltr (5.5gal) |
| Electrical system | 12V, 14V-20A alternator, battery 24Ah | Fuel consumption | 5.7ltr × 100km (49.6mpg) (CUNA rules) |
| Starting | electric | Max. speed | 190 km/h (119mph) approx. |
| Ignition | digital computerized electronic WEBER IAW system, inductive spark | Dry weight | 279kg (615lb) |

connecting rods (similar to those found on the 1100 Sport). The gearing in the rear-drive bevel box had been altered (from 33.7 on the 1000 to 33.8 on the 1100). The gearbox action had been improved further by the use of Daytona-based components. A new higher-output oil pump and other improvements to the lubrication system (also found on the 1100 Sport) provided greater engine protection – and thus expected life. The exhaust system had been increased in its capacity to reduce noise (down from 84db on 1000cc models to 81db on 1100 models), but at the same time giving an increase in power output.

Several improvements had been made to the electrical system including a PO8 computer instead of a PO7, modern mini-relays instead of the traditional Bosch components, new lighting equipment, new front indicators and new horns. The braking power was improved thanks to a new front master cylinder with an 11mm piston together with higher quality, plated, fully floating discs all round. Suspension was another area on which the development team had been hard at work. The previously fitted Dutch Koni Dial-a-Ride rear shocks had been pensioned off in favour of Italian-made Bi-Turbo assemblies, while at the front there were

*For the 1994 model year the factory created the new 1100. With a larger 1064cc (92 × 80mm) engine there still came the choice of the by-now-popular Weber-Marelli fuel injection or carbs, the latter upped in size from 30 to 36mm.*

improved forks. These were not only multi-adjustable, but they also featured extended travel, and sliding friction had been reduced by the addition of anti-wear Teflon bushings. A new frame (based on the 1000 model) featured additional bracing at the top of the

gearbox and a more rigid lower section; the swinging arm was also new. Unlike earlier versions only wire wheels were offered. These came with Spanish-made Akront aluminium rims, instead of Guzzi's own type. The rear rim diameter had dropped from 18in to 17in, while the front remained at 18in. The smaller rear rim meant a decrease in seat height. German Metzelers replaced Italian Pirellis as the favoured tyre choice as original equipment. An important addition to the standard equipment list was a new purpose-built rear carrier, together with a fully integrated backrest and rear shock/pannier support assembly. There was also an entirely new rear light and twin signals exclusive to the model. More minor changes included new tachometer (still by Veglia), fuel filler cap, fuel taps of modified design, redesigned seat hinge (now cable operated), multi-use keys (instead of the handful needed on the earlier models), a revised handlebar with anti-vibrational mountings and finally a choice of no less

*By now the fuel injection was the preferred choice among California buyers. It not only offered much smoother running, but improved warm up from cold start and mid-range power.*

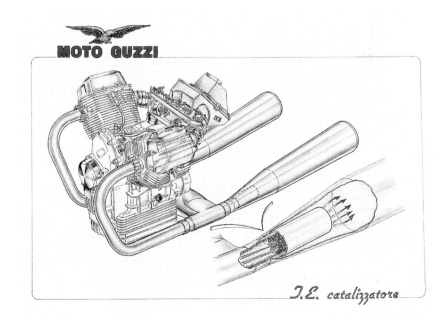

MOTO GUZZI

*I.E. catalizzatore*

than four colour schemes: anthracite/silver, black/red, black/yellow and plain black.

The factory also provided a useful number of optional extras for the new 1100: two windshield sizes (the fully faired version was not offered for the 1100); panniers and fittings in either 30 or 40 litre capacities; rear crashbars and sideplates; a 40-litre top-case (with mounting kit); leather saddlebags and fittings; and a leather tool roll. As delivered, the basic machine weighed in at: (fuel injected) 240kg (529lb); (with carbs) 245kg (540lb). Both versions could also be ordered with a catalytic converter at additional cost. By the 1996 model year the 1100 California not only benefited from a much improved paint finish, but was also available in four colour schemes: navy blue/beige; bright red/black; amaranth/cherry red and metallic green/black.

The engine type of the 1100 was referred to as the 'KD'. In the factory's in-house magazine, *Moto Guzzi Flash* the California was described thus, 'Quiet strength. Elegance, tradition, safety and style: living freely and tranquilly in a world of unending horizons. The world of the California.' Going on to say in enthusiastic PR speak, 'There she goes: the evergreen, inimitable classic California. In its twenty-year-old success story the leading players' secret is a meticulous constant development without ever betraying its unique character: a fascinating custom-built bike with the heart of the grand tourer. The California sums up a way of life: travel, freedom and the quest to explore those wide open spaces, all over the world.'

## 75TH ANNIVERSARY LIMITED EDITION

To celebrate its 75th Anniversary in 1996, Moto Guzzi selected the Cali for special model treatment. This resulted in the Limited Edition California of which only 750

*Only 750 75th Anniversary Limited Edition California models were built (during January–April 1997). Unique features included metallic silver and red finish, leather saddle, silver commemorative 75th anniversary plate on front mudguard, alloy alternator cover and chrome-plated, shrouded rear shocks.*

**TECHNICAL SPECIFICATIONS**
**California 75th anniversary**

| | | | |
|---|---|---|---|
| Engine | 4-stroke 90° V-twin | Brakes | front: twin discs 300mm |
| Bore | 92mm | | rear: disc 270mm |
| Stroke | 80mm | | integral braking system |
| Displacement | 1064cc, Nigusil cylinder | | device |
| | lining | Wheels | spokes, front rim 2.50 × |
| Max. power | 55kW (75CV) at | | 18in; rear 3.50 × 17in |
| | 6400rpm (DIN) | Tyres | front: 110/90 VB 18 |
| Max. torque | 95.1Nm (9.7kgm) at | | rear: 140/80 VB 17 |
| | 5000rpm (DIN) | Frame | detachable tubular |
| Compression ratio | 9.5:1 | | duplex cradle in special |
| Valves and operation | two valves per cylinder, | | high strength steel |
| | pushrod | Suspension | front: hydraulic |
| Lubrication | gear pump | | telescopic fork with |
| Transmission | primary by gears; | | adjustable preload |
| | secondary by cardan | | springs and antifriction |
| | shaft with double | | bearings |
| | universal joint | | rear: swinging fork with |
| Clutch | double disc, dry | | adjustable preload |
| Fuel delivery | fuel injection Weber | | springs |
| | 1AW a – n; two 40mm | | |
| | throttle bodies with | Instruments | speedometer, rev |
| | Weber 1W 031 injectors | | counter and warning |
| Electrical system | 12V, 14V-25A alternator, | | lights |
| | battery 30Ah | Fuel tank capacity | 18.5ltr (4.1gal) |
| Starting | electric | Fuel consumption | 5ltr × 100km (56.6mpg) |
| Ignition | Weber 1AW electronic | | (CUNA) |
| | digital ignition with | | |
| | inductive spark | Dry weight | 251kg (553lb) |
| Gearbox | 5-speed | Max speed | 125mph (200km/h) |

were built, each individually numbered. The first batch of twenty machines arrived in Great Britain during April 1997, costing £8,250 each.

Essentially an 1100 injection motorcycle, its unique features were: Metallic Silver/Red paint; leather saddle; silver commemorative 75th anniversary plate (on the front mudguard); an alloy alternator cover; and chrome-shrouded rear shock absorbers. Otherwise the Special Edition was unchanged from the standard model.

# CALIFORNIA EV

At the end of June 1997 the factory launched a new era, with the announcement of a much improved machine. Boasting more than 150 refinements large and small, the California EV (Evolution) blended mechanical improvement with a revised, tidier style and was hailed as being in the vanguard of a series of new machines planned by the revitalized company over the next few years.

*The new California EV brought the concept bang up to date in June 1997. Boasting over 150 individual refinements, both large and small, the EV (Evolution) ushered in a new level of quality for Guzzi buyers.*

More than 40,000 Californias had been purchased by customers worldwide in the previous twenty years. In updating the design, Guzzi's design and engineering staff had sensitively retained the unmistakable features that made the model so popular, whilst introducing improvements to ensure its progress into the 21st century.

At the heart of the EV the familiar 1064cc horizontally opposed 90-degree pushrod V-twin engine had been given lighter yet stronger con-rods, but otherwise the fuel-injected motor was largely the same as the model it replaced. The potentiometer and fuel injection bodies are brand new, the carb version having been finally pensioned off.

But if the power unit was familiar, the suspension and braking systems were markedly different. The suspension had been radically improved with brand new 45mm Marzocchi front forks (the previous forks were 40mm) and equally new Dutch White power rear dampers. Both front and rear systems were multi-adjustable for both compression and rebound damping to ensure compliance whatever the conditions.

The factory's renowned integral braking system had been given superior response and feel, thanks to sophisticated new valving that varied its response depending on the load carried, and new front 320mm-diameter stainless steel Brembo discs with four-piston Gold-Line calipers and a single 282mm disc with a smaller twin-piston caliper. New, lighter lower-profile rims have been adopted which allow tubeless tyres to be fitted.

The overall build and component quality had also been given considerable thought

*At the heart of the machine was the familiar 1064cc 90-degree pushrod V-twin engine, which except for lighter, yet stronger connecting rods, was largely as before. Fuel injection was now standardized.*

## TECHNICAL SPECIFICATIONS
### California EV

| | | | |
|---|---|---|---|
| Engine | 4-stroke 90° V-twin, KD-type, air cooled | Gearbox | 5-speed, constant mesh gears with built-in cush drive |
| Bore | 92mm | | |
| Stroke | 80mm | Brakes | front: two floating stainless steel discs diameter 320mm rear: fixed stainless steel disc diameter 282mm integral braking system |
| Displacement | 1064cc, light-alloy surface-hardened cylinders | | |
| Max. power | 54kW (73.5HP) at 6400rpm (CE standards) | Wheels | radial with patented BBS tubeless rims front: 2.50 × 18in rear: 3.50 × 17in |
| Max. torque | 94Nm (9.6kgm) at 5000rpm (CE standards) | | |
| Compression ratio | 9.5:1 | | |
| Valves and operation | light-alloy pushrod and rocker arm with two valves per cylinder | Tyres | front: 110/90 VB18 rear: 140/80 VB17 |
| Lubrication | high volume geared pressure pump, pressure regulator | Frame | detachable tubular duplex cradle in special high-strength steel |
| Transmission | primary by helical gears secondary by cardan shaft with double universal joint | Suspension | front: Marzocchi 45mm diameter hydraulic telescopic fork, separately adjustable rear: swinging fork with two WP adjustable hydraulic shock absorbers |
| Clutch | double disc, dry, mechanically operated | | |
| Fuel delivery | Magneti Marelli IAW Multipoint electronic phased sequential fuel injection; alfa-n type; two 40mm diameter throttle bodies with Weber IW 031 injectors | Instruments | speedometer with odometer and trip meter (total and partial), electronic rev counter and warning lights |
| Electrical system | 12V, 14V-25A alternator, battery 30Ah | Fuel tank capacity | 19ltr (4.18gal) |
| | | Fuel consumption | 5ltr × 100km (56.6mpg) (CUNA standard) |
| Starting | electric with starter motor | | |
| | | Max speed | 200km/h (125mph) (CE standard) without accessories |
| Ignition | Magneti Marelli IAW electronic digital ignition with inductive spark | | |
| | | Dry weight | 251kg (553lb) |

*A 1998 California EV out in the Dorset countryside whilst under test by the author.*

*EV rider's-eye view. Clear-to-read white face instruments, a flush fitting (stainless steel) fuel cap and a general air of real improvement marks Guzzi's latest incarnation of its longest running model series.*

and attention. This resulted in a number of features including a chrome-plated stainless steel double-skin exhaust system, an ele-

gant new instrument console, backrest, rear carrier and increased usage of better quality, thicker chrome-plating. There is also a new flush-fitting stainless steel fuel cap and electric fuel tap.

Going on sale in Britain during July 1997, at £8,249, it was initially available in three colour options: Red/Cream, Metallic Black/Metallic Silver and Metallic Dark Blue/Metallic Grey; these were later joined by Metallic Black/Metallic Gun Metal Grey and Yellow/Orange. Like all Moto Guzzi models, it was sold with a 24-month (from March 1998 increased to 36 month) unlimited mileage warranty and a year's RAC membership which included roadside recovery in the event of a breakdown – even including punctures (in any case, tubeless tyres make this possibility far less likely than in the days of yore).

# 9  Racing and Records

With its glorious Grand Prix history, it is hardly surprising that although the majority of Moto Guzzi V-twin production has been clearly aimed at the road rider with touring aspirations, the factory's products have still been successfully employed for both racing and record breaking. As described in Chapter 1, 1957 had marked a dramatic end to Guzzi's participation in GP racing, when along with fellow Italian companies FB Mondial and Gilera, the Mandello marque had announced their retirement on what in retrospect is seen by many as the golden age of road racing. Also, as described earlier, the simple reason was finance.

## RECORD BREAKING

When Guzzi did make a return in 1969, it was with lightly modified versions of their V7 touring machine, with the purpose of getting the company's name in the record books – nothing else. But full racing effort or not, Moto Guzzi was not a factory to do things half-heartedly, and the V-twins which were built for the record attempts were nonetheless interesting in their own right, relating directly as they did to machines that the public could buy themselves. Anyone familiar with the original V7 (see Chapter 2) would be excused for seeing any possibility of turning this into a speed machine. But this is exactly what Ing. Lino Tonti did to what after all is widely viewed as a heavyweight tourer. Tonti, then only recently appointed by Moto Guzzi as their chief designer to replace the legendary Giulio Cesare Carcano, realised the importance of

proving that the factory could still produce motorcycles which could set records – and ultimately perhaps even win races. Using a standard production model as a base, only gave more importance to achieving increased sales in the future. Before its record breaking adventures, in the years since Guzzi's much published withdrawal from Grand Prix competition, the factory had maintained its links with motorcycle sport by way of participation in the field of long distance trials; notably the famous ISDT (International Six Day Trial). The highlight of its efforts came in the 1963 event, when staged in Czechoslovakia, both the Italian national Trophy and Silver Vase teams were mounted one hundred per cent on Guzzi machines. These bikes were Stornello and Lodola singles, not twins, but just how good they were can be seen by the results: all ten starters gained gold medals (the top award), and also the Silver Vase and three manufacturers' team awards! But in truth, as Guzzi found, even world-class success on the dirt was but a side show when it came to satisfying what the press and public alike wanted and expected from such a famous name. Ing. Tonti was only too aware of expectations as he himself was very much an enthusiast for road racing – with little interest in off-road activities. With such an unlikely machine as the V7 for its base, Tonti's potential record breaking effort could quite easily have been laughed off by the opposition – had they known of course. Instead he, together with a small band of engineers at Guzzi's Mandello del Lario works went to work during the winter of 1968. Construction of a batch of suitably modified specially constructed V7s began by a weight saving exercise which saw everything dumped which was not necessary to the task in hand. The result was a machine which confounded even the most enthusiastic supporters of the project, weighing in at only 159kg (350lb). Basically the only standard components left were the basic engine and gear box assembly, frame, swinging arm, wheels and front forks. To these were added a hand beaten 29 litre (6.4imp gal) aluminium fuel tank, single racing saddle, clip-on handle bars, rearset foot controls, and a final drive box. Each of the bikes was specially built in the factory's competition department, their engines being blueprinted and the balance painstakingly assembled. Once completed each motorcycle was equipped with equally special aluminium dolphin fairings. These were constructed in three sections and, recalling the works racers of the past, finished in the same pale green paint. This was applied to the fairing, tank and rear mudguard, no front guard being fitted. The V7 record machines were built in two engine sizes. Although minimal in terms of cubic capacity, this gave the factory the chance to compete

*The year 1969 saw a return by Moto Guzzi in speed competition; albeit record attempts, rather than actual racing. One of the V7 based, dolphin faired V-twins is shown.*

in two entirely different classes. The first displacement, for the category was 739.3cc (82 × 70 mm). The other for the 1000cc class and used in the V7 special production roadster that same year (1969) was 757.486cc (83 × 70mm). The result of all the effort lavished by Tonti and his team was a dyno figure of 68bhp at 6500rpm for both versions. This was quite an exceptional figure for what, after all, was essentially a touring unit. The bikes, all equipped with a large 100mm white-face Veglia racing tach, were now ready to go and the only task left was to find no less than eight suitable riders. These needed to be proficient, reliable – and have track experience. The result was a good blend of testers and road racers, including such men as Vittorio Brambilla (younger brother of Ferrari racing driver, Ernesto), Alberto Pagani and Remo Venturi, whilst the press were represented by racing journalist Roberto Patrignani. By June 1969, the squad was ready to pay a visit to the famous Monza circuit on the outskirts of Milan. Right from the team's arrival at Monza, it was obvious that the engineering team had made an excellent job of creating potential records breakers. What had formally been very much a ponderous, gargantuan even, touring mount had miraculously been turned into a fleet, purposeful speedster. Incredible but true, and soon team members had the deep melodious V-twins thundering around the circuit with an athleticism and turn of speed which would have seemed an impossible dream, but Tonti had got it to work. Team captain, Brambilla, set new 750cc class records in the three categories: the 100 kilometre at 125.6 mph (202kph); the 100 kilometre at 131.9 mph (212.2kph); and finally the coveted hour at 132.9mph (213.8kph). For the larger 1000cc class, it was Venturi, one time second string to John Surtees at MV and later a Bianchi star, who pushed the 10 kilometre record to 129.45mph (208.28kph) before quitting as a

*One of the successful Guzzi team members rocketing around the Monza speed bowl.*

result of a rear tyre starting to break up. The bike was then taken over by Italian hill-climber champion Angelo Tenconi who set a 100 kilometre record at 129.65mph (208.6kph) and put 130.22mph (209.52kph) on the clock.

Only four months after their first record spree, Guzzi returned to the banked Monza speed saucer at the end of October 1969 and captured fifteen more records – seven solo and eight sidecar. Fastest speed was set by Alberto Pagani who took the 100 kilometre record for 1000cc machines with an average of 135.71mph (218.36kph), the record already held by the factory since late June. Like Angelo Tenconi who had set the previous record, Pagani was piloting a specially prepared 757cc V-twin. But since June the power had been increased to 70bhp, giving a maximum speed of almost 150mph (240kph). Pagani went on to break the 1000cc hour record at 134.84mph (219.96kph) (previously held by Tenconi at 130.22mph (209.52kph)). Earlier he had teamed with Silvano Bertarelli and Vittorio Brambilla and had broken the 1,000 kilometre and 6-hour times for 750cc machines. Their new speeds were 125.76mph (202.35kph) and 126.20mph

(203.05kph) respectively. During the attempt a broken rocker was replaced in seven minutes.

On the bigger-engined Guzzi, Guida Mandracci, Franco Trabalzini and Roberto Parrignani set three long-distance records for the 1000cc class – 1,000 kilometres at 127.94mph (205.85kph), 6-hours at 110.60mph (177.95kph) and 12-hours at 111.53mph (179.45kph). Soon after the bike had covered 1,000 kilometres the primary drive gear broke and forty minutes were lost changing the complete gearbox assembly. But the team pressed on to capture the 6- and 12-hours distances – despite the attempt finishing in darkness and fog. This also explains why the 12-hour time was quicker than the 6-hour one. The following day, Brambilla took the 10 kilometre, the 100 kilometre and the hour records for the 750cc sidecars with speeds of 113.90mph (183.26kph), 119.43mph (192.16kph) and 120.11mph (193.26kph). Then, teaming with Giuseppe Dal Toe and the German sidecar racer Georg Auberbacher on the 757cc machine, five more records were captured; the 10 kilometre (115.57mph/185.95kph), the 100 kilometre (117.70mph/189.38kph), the hour (115.64mph/186.06kph), the 6-hour

*Giuseppe Dal Toé with the V7 sidecar record breaker.*

146

(86.99mph/139.97kph) and the 1,000 kilometre (89.54mph/144.07kph). The 'sidecar' fitted for the records was the one built by Moto Guzzi in 1948 and used by Luigi Cavanna. The constant battering from the uneven Monza bowl caused it to break three times after the first hour. Each time it took about twenty minutes for Vittorio Brambilla and his older brother Ernesto, to carry out welding repairs. Besides the huge amount of publicity, both in Italy and abroad which the record breaking achieved, it also directly initiated not only a return to racing (albeit production based), but also a new performance model, the 748.388cc (82.5 × 70 mm) V7 Sport.

## ENDURANCE RACING

Once again Monza was to be involved, this time the 500 kilometre endurance race staged at the venue in June 1971. Headed by factory-supported rider Raimondo Riva and the Brambilla brothers, plus newcomers Carena and Gazzola, the new V-twin racked up a string of tarmac success with the machine, following its Monza debut. Like rivals Ducati and Laverda, Moto Guzzi's entry into endurance events enabled the company to develop and test ideas which would otherwise have been much more difficult. As with the V7 Sport, endurance racing was to have a definite result in ultimately producing one of Guzzi's most famous and long running models, the Le Mans. The same Barcelona 24-hour race in May 1973 in which Ducati's prototype 860 V-twin made a winning debut also saw Guzzi make an equally important entry. This was a machine based in the V7 Sport, but with its engine size enlarged to 844.057cc (83 × 78 mm), as first introduced on the GT850 the previous year. Unlike its touring brother, however, the newcomer was a pure bred sportster – and unknown to

*A very wet French Bol d'Or race was staged on 11/12 September 1971. This factory-entered V7 Sport is being ridden by Vittorio Brambilla.*

observers at the time Barcelona '73 heralded the Le Mans in embryonic form. Raimondo Riva and Luciano Gazzola put up a spirited showing on the prototype which completed the distance in an impressive fifth overall. Compared with the winning Ducati's record-setting 720 laps, the Guzzi completed a total of 683 circuits of the tortuous Moutjuich Park Course. After this successful debut the factory continued to

*Another works V7 sport endurance racer is seen here during the Dutch Zolder 24-Hours, 19/20 August 1972. Ridden by Riva and Carena it was one of the very first Guzzi V-twins to be fitted with a double disc, rather than drum front brake.*

support the endurance scene until it quit in
1975. By then the groundwork had already
been laid for the entry into production of the
Le Mans, so the need to race had gone. So
for a second time it was to be left to privateers to uphold Guzzi's honour on the race
circuits of the world. But obviously this second withdrawal did not create waves like
the 1957 GP incident!

## PRODUCTION RACING

In the 1975 Isle of Man Production TT, a
750S3 ridden by the Royal Air Force Motor
Sports Association pairing of John Goodall
and the late Dave Featherstone came home
a highly credible fifth against a large entry
including Honda, Kawasaki, Ducati,
Laverda, Benelli, BMW, Norton and Triumph machines. The Production race at
Daytona in 1976 saw more Guzzi's success,
when Mike Baldwin riding expatriate Reno
Leoni's brand new 850 Le Mans scored an
impressive fifth behind the Butler & Smith
entered factory-supported BMW R90Ss of
winner Reg Pridmore and runner up Steve
McLaughlin, Cook Neilson (Ducati 900SS)
and Wes Cooley (Kawasaki Z900). The same
year also saw the factory make a brief

*A privately entered V7 sport with non-standard
British Lockheed twin front discs; 1972
Barcelona 24-Hours endurance race. Other
alterations include non-standard seat and front
guard, exhaust pipes (chopped and rewelded to
provide increased ground clearance), and
silencers.*

return, with a semi-works Le Mans, but
with a 948.813cc (88 × 78 mm) engine, making an appearance in the Barcelona 24
hours. Ridden by Guzzi veterans Riva and
Gazzola, the machine came ninth, with 701
laps completed. This compared to the even-
tual victors, the British pairing of Stan
Woods and Charlie Williams who completed
741 laps (1,755.45 miles/2,824.52km) on
their works Honda at an average speed of
73.27mph (117.89kph). Later the same year,
during mid-September, Gazzola and a new
partner, Alberto Rusconi, finished fifteenth
in the French Bol d'Or classic, with Riva,
now partnered by Davide Levieux, coming
one place further down the field, in the most
famous of all endurance race events. As the
previous season, 1977 began with Mike
Baldwin recording another fifth on Reno
Leoni's Le Mans in the Daytona Production
race (now referred to in the programme as
Superbike Production). Although the paper
result remained unchanged from 1976,
Baldwin's performance was of a higher level,
coming through from the back of the pack to

*Alan Walsh riding a stock V7 Sport, Brands
Hatch, 6 August 1972.*

catch the previous year's race winner Reg Pridmore (980 BMW), and even though Pridmore eventually passed the Guzzi rider the verdict was by the narrowest of margins.

## COUPE D'ENDURANCE

During the 1977 FIM Coupe d'Endurance series, the highest placed Guzzi in any of the rounds were the Spanish team of A. Perez Rubio and C. Morante on a Le Mans at Barcelona. It was during the same year that British competitors at last began to take the Guzzi V-twin seriously as a suitable mount for both endurance and short circuit events. One of the first to take a real interest was Jim Wells, son of the London dealer Fred Wells, who shared with co-rider Tony Osbourne a specially-prepared home-built endurance racer using a heavily-modified 750S3 engine housed in a one-off cantilever frame. Wells had to wait for a considerable time though before actually finishing a race (at the Thruxton round of the European endurance championship in September 1977). This was the result of several gremlins which cut short their earlier Coupe d'Endurance efforts, including punctures, a snapped crankshaft and oil breather difficulties. Other Brits who campaigned Guzzi's successfully during the same season included the Oxford Fairings team of John Goodall and Doug Lunn. The latter rider (who was employed by Guzzi importers Coburn & Hughes at their retail showroom in Luton) used the Oxford-sponsored bike – a race-kitted Le Mans I – in the four-lap 151-mile (243km) Isle of Man TT Formula 1 race, in which he came home in fourteenth position, averaging 86.99mph (139.97kph). The Le Mans was totally stock, with the exception of the factory race kit (comprising an open Lafranconi exhaust, 40mm Dell'Orto carbs, racing cam and a close ratio, straight-cut gear cluster), different fairing and modified brake system. The latter saw the linked braking set-up ditched in favour of conventional hydraulics with a separate master cylinder. The bike was electronically timed at a shade over 138mph(222kph).

## AVON SERIES

But without a shadow of a doubt the really big news regarding British racing involvement with the Guzzi V-twin during 1977 was the success achieved by Manchester rider Roy Armstrong. Riding a 1976 Le Mans I in the prestigious Avon Roadrunner Production series (effectively the British championships), Armstrong not only won the first round, but also the championship. As a matter of interest, both Roy and his younger brother Ian, rode a pair of virtually stock Le Mans models throughout the series. Only towards the end of the year were special high compression pistons, a B10 cam, race valve springs, lightened and polished valve gear and modified exhaust fitted. But Roy Armstrong's 1977 Avon series winning bike retained the original 36mm Le Mans I Dell'Orto carbs. As on Lunn's machine, the

*Roy Armstrong at Snetterton winning the final round (and the championship) of the 1977 Avon Roadrunner Production series (essentially the British national title).*

linked braking system had been shelved in favour of conventional hydraulics. Contrary to reports at the time, both Armstrong bikes had been bought and paid for by the brothers, even though Roy worked as a mechanic for the Manchester-based Sports Motorcycle concern headed by Steve Wynne (of Ducati fame). However Sports Motorcycles did have a direct connection with racing a Le Mans model, as their director John Sear also took part in the same series. This machine, however, was very much more highly tuned; featuring as it did a '950' conversion from the V1000, with high compression forged three-ring pistons, factory race kit camshaft, close ratio gears, and 40mm Dell'Ortos. With the race kit exhaust, this machine was tested by *Motor Cycle* at 132.01mph (212.4kph), but the tester, John Nutting, had to sit up half the length of the test strip to keep the engine from overrevving in top. The standing quarter mile was dispatched in 11.8 seconds with a terminal velocity of 112.24mph (180.59kph). An interesting aside was that Sports Motorcycles claimed to have ordered a factory-prepared engine together with a consignment of racing parts, but so the story goes, importers Coburn & Hughes held this back for most of the season.

## ISLE OF MAN TT

It is also a little known fact that the factory officially entered the 1977 Isle of Man TT. This came about when a couple of works engines were shipped over with factory mechanic Bruno Scola. These engines were then fitted into the frames of Roy Armstrong and John Sears' Le Mans Is. These two bikes were raced in the Formula 1 TT by George Fogarty (father of Carl) and Steve Tonkin, but although they proved to possess enough speed during qualifying, unfortunately they were both destined to retire in terrible weather conditions, due to sticking carbu-

*The Sports Motorcycles-entered Le Mans I ridden during 1976/7 by director John Sear. It was timed at 132.01mph (212.4kph).*

rettor slides on the 40mm Dell'Ortos. Both engines sported all the factory race kit options, plus a '950' conversion, 47.5mm inlet and 39mm exhaust valves, and sintered metal clutch plates. Additionally, the bikes were equipped with higher-ratio V1000 rear drive bevel gear sets (9/34 teeth) giving a ratio of 1:3.788, and because of this, it was also necessary to fit the V1000 universal joint with its long rear extension, and therefore the matching V1000 connecting tube to join up with the rear bevel box assembly. But if the Isle of Man had not been the success the factory had hoped for, they were secretly pleased with the result garnered at the Avon series. Not only had Roy Armstrong's Le Mans series won, but in addition, John Sears was third and Richard Gamble fourth on yet another – again with a 950 big-bore conversion. The following year, 1978, saw rules for the Avon championship revised. One of the main features was to restrict competition in having to retain the original cubic capacity as sold to customers. Compared with machines such as the Laverda Jota 981cc and the increasingly numerous 1-litre Japanese fours the Italian V-twins in the shape of the Le Mans (and

Ducati 900SS) were at an obvious disadvantage. Effectively this rule change sidelined the Guzzi challenge. And it was not just in Britain where things were getting tougher. In the FIM European Endurance Championship, it was again the Japanese who held all the aces. Honda in particular, with full factory support, were simply too good. The real home of endurance racing is France where hundreds of thousands turn out to attend the two annual 24-hour races (Le Mans in spring and the Bol d'Or in autumn). During the 1980s the endurance championship switched from European to World status. Although the Guzzi factory has never returned to long distance racing, one can still see a machine taking part in this branch of the sport on ocasions.

## BATTLE OF THE TWINS

Twins racing began in the USA as the 1980s began. One of the most popular events at the annual Daytona Bike Week, BOTT (Battle of the Twins) was fiercely contested with the home-grown Harley-Davidsons taking on Triumph, Ducati, BMW and the occasional Guzzi. The first two competitors to enter

Guzzis in BOTT racing were John Treasauro (Le Mans), and the Californian Frank Mazur on the ex-Reno Leoni/Mike Baldwin 1970s Superbike production class Le Mans-based machine. The Battle of the Twins race at Daytona on 9 March 1984 – in the heavyweight Modified section – saw race history made when a woman, Sherry Frindus from Gainesville, Florida, scored a surprise victory. This was the first ever in an AMA (American Motorcycle Association) road race and on a Guzzi V-twin at that. The Battle of the Twins was introduced to British race enthusiasts in 1983, with the *Motorcycle Enthusiast* national series. The first Guzzi to make an appearance in the BOTT series was a superbly engineered Le Mans ridden by its owner/builder, Richard Gamble, the very same who had finished fourth in the 1977 Avon Production series. Richard revealed that he had been drawn back to racing, simply by the new twins series, and his distinctive red and white showpiece featured in many of the 1977 Avon Production series. Also during 1984, the first Guzzi 90-degree V-twin appeared on the classic racing scene. Classic racing had by now become extremely popular. Ridden by Mark Wellings, the machine clearly resembled a

*Richard Gamble was the rider / builder of this immaculately prepared Le Mans-based racer, circa 1983.*

*John Armstrong returned to the fray with the BOTT racer during the mid-1980s. He is seen here with a Le Mans 1000, Oliver's Mount, Scarborough, July 1987.*

*Some of the Dr John racing components provided by Amedeo Castellani of Raceco, for the Clarke Guzzi Battle of the Twins racer.*

*The Clarke Brothers (Bob and Chris) provided this special Guzzi V-twin for Peter Warden (seen here with the bike at Donington Park in April 1988).*

750S3 and he went on to many excellent results during the mid/late 1980s at CRMC (Classic Racing Motorcycle Club) events.

Another rider who made something of a return to racing was John Armstrong who, now a Guzzi dealer himself (Italsport), was back in action with a virtually stock Le Mans 1000; notably at the Battle of the Twins events during 1986 and 1987. British Twins racing received a big lift for 1988, with the

introduction of a national series backed by Dunlop Tyres and *Motorcycle Enthusiast* magazine. After three rounds (held at Cadwell Park, Thruxton and Donington Park) the 1-litre chase was led by Peter Warden riding the Clarke Brothers 920cc Guzzi – a pretty special bike which had many tuning parts, including some from Dr John Wittner, the American tuning wizard who was subsequently to play a major role in the birth of the Daytona (see Chapter 11). Bob and Chris Clarke (the latter the owner of a dealership in Wymondham, Norfolk) were the men behind Peter Warden's machine. The first outing was at the local Snetterton circuit in September 1987. From the start it was not to be simply a standard Guzzi. Amadeo Castellani of London (now residing in Sudbury, Suf-

*Peter Warden taking third place on the Clarke/Raceco Guzzi at Thruxton in March 1988.*

folk), a Guzzi specialist, was enlisted to supply Dr John's goodies including cams, rods,
valve springs and pistons. That first Snetterton meeting was held over two days and as
each race progressed so Peter Warden
became more acquainted with the Guzzi's
handling and went on to score a fifth, two
thirds and a second from four starts. This
was against top class opposition including
four-times Formula 2 world champion Tony
Rutter and Tony Moran on Sports Motorcycles-entered Ducati V-twins. After more tuning over the winter months the Clarke Guzzi
was put on the dyno by Amadeo Castellani
and put out 85bhp (at the rear wheel). The
fourth round of the 1988 British Battle of the
Twins was scheduled for June. After the
third round, (which Peter Warden won) the

*Peter Warden after winning the third round of
the British Battle of the Twins series at
Donington Park in April 1988. A few weeks later
he died after crashing a Suzuki GSXR750 at
Cadwell Park.*

# Raceco

Amedeo Castellini was born in the London borough of Lambeth on 16 January 1956, of Italian parents. The family moved back to Italy in 1968, where one year later, the 13-year-old Amedeo rode his first motorcycle, a 50cc Moto Guzzi Dingo.

Although his parents were to stay in Rome, Amedeo moved back to the UK in 1974 (after attending art school in Italy), his first career move coming in photography. In 1981 he made the move which was to change his life, buying a brand new V50 Guzzi from the Caterham dealers, Pineways. A few months later the V50 was replaced by an SP1000.

Subsequently he quit his job as a photographer, setting up instead as a self-employed motorcycle mechanic specializing in Guzzis. He became the workshop manager at Moto Mecca, the Guzzi spares specialist, while they were still based in London. This lasted until Christmas 1985, when he became involved in Team MCN with Howard Lees and Anthony Ainslie, travelling around Europe to the various 24-hour endurance events as one of the team's engineers.

Next came a return to specializing in Guzzis, setting up the Raceco business in Isleworth. At Christmas 1989, Amedeo went to Australia to work for Ted Stolarski and, with a Daytona prototype with carbs, competed successfully at Daytona USA. Later in 1990 Amedeo returned to Britain and his Guzzi business, which relocated to Hounslow before moving to Surbiton in

*Amedeo Castellani's company, Raceco, are probably Great Britain's leading specialists for Guzzi V-twin tuning and performance parts.*

1992 where it was to remain until Christmas 1996, when Raceco moved out of the London area to rural Suffolk.

From 1987 until 1992 Raceco provided tuning expertise to Team Clarke Racing and their riders Peter Warden and later Ian Cobbing. Then from the 1993 season came a highly successful joint venture with importers Three Cross.

The Three Cross/Raceco Daytona-based twins racer began life as an ex-demonstrator with 8,500 miles on the clock. In its first year with Torquil Ross-Martin as rider it weighed 225kg (496lb) and produced 90bhp. By the time it was last raced in 1997 (by Ian Cobby) it weighed 175kg (385lb) and produced a staggering 140bhp! Besides Ross-Martin and Cobby, other riders to straddle the Three Cross/Raceco machine were Richard Defago (early 1994), Rick Lewenden (late 1994) and Aussie ex-GP star Paul Lewis in 1995.

The machine bowed out in 1997, winning every race it competed in and more than often setting pole in qualifying to boot.

*Rick Lewendon (66) leading on the Three Cross / Raceco Guzzi at Thruxton in 1994.*

*Raceco boss Amedeo Castellani (right) and rider Paul Lewis, 1995.*

*Former 500GP racer Paul Lewis with the Three Cross / Raceco Guzzi, Brands Hatch, 1995.*

*Greg Birkett with the Jim Blomley's 1000cc BOTT racer at Cadwell Park, April 1991. Specification included Astrolite wheels, race tuned engine with Carrillo con rods and Omega pistons. Cycle parts included Ohlins rear shocks and braced front forks.*

Clarke Guzzi rider held a thirteen-point lead. Peter was also leading the Norman Hyde and ACU star 750 Production series (the latter on a Suzuki GSXR750). Then came disaster, whilst racing the Japanese machine at Cadwell Park, Peter Warden suffered an accident, sadly dying two days later from the injuries he received. As the Battle of the Twins organizer Gordon Anderson was later to recall, Peter Warden was a very special person. 'He was one of the most likeable racers I ever met and who showed a remarkable talent and smooth technique belying his three years racing experience.' A decade on, as author of this book, I feel privileged to be able to give someone who provided Guzzi fans with something about which they could cheer, true credit for his achievements.

*Racing prototype commissioned by Chris Clarke Motorcycles in 1992. It was originally intended to replace the highly successful machine used first by Peter Warden and later Ian Cobby. The frame was by Spondon Engineering of Derby. Instead, Cobby rode a Ducati 900SS (belt) racer in twins events.*

# 10   Off-Road

One of Moto Guzzi's most interesting markets for its long-running V-twin series has been the off-road styled models, perhaps best described as the large capacity enduro class. This category was largely created by the German marque BMW, when they launched their famous R80 G/S in 1980. Previous to this the street enduro market had been the preserve of single-cylinder machines; at first largely two-strokes such as the Suzuki TS and Yamaha DT, but then four-strokes such as Yamaha's XT500 and Suzuki's SP370. Although Guzzi built a prototype machine which was displayed at the Milan Show in November 1981 using the 490.30cc (74 × 75mm) V50 engine the TS, as it was coded, never reached production. Instead, the first production models were the V35/65TTs. The TT designation had

nothing to do with the Isle of Man Tourist Trophy, but instead the initials stood for Tutto Terreno (all-terrain). Although it built a small series of pre-production V65TT Competition Client models – a hand-built competition-only enduro to special order for events such as the Paris–Dakar and Pharaoh rallies, the series production TTs were really more at home on the street than the rough.

## V35TT & V65TT

Like the Custom models offered during the same period during the mid-1980s, there was no change in engine specification from the standard 436.23cc (66 × 50.6mm) V35 and 643.4cc (80 × 64mm) V65 models. However, cosmetically the pair of TTs were strikingly different from the usual crop of small capacity Japanese enduro-styled machines of the era. Topped by a motocross-inspired 14-litre (3gal) fuel tank, the styling was extremely effective with smooth flowing lines which continued through the side panels, and rear seat/mudguard section. The seat covering material was a trendy bright red with the 'TT' logo emblazoned in blue and a nose at the front which extended up and out the rear of the tank. The switchgear was taken straight off the standard V35/65 range as was the matching speedometer and tachometer. There was no centre stand, only a flip-up side affair, but a couple of worthwhile additions were rubber gaiters for the special competition-based leading-axle 35mm Marzocchi front forks and a large rubber mud flap, which extended down to protect the timing cover at the base of the

*Although Guzzi had enjoyed considerable success during the early 1960s with its Lodola and Stornello singles in the ISDT (International Six Days Trial); this 1981 V50TS prototype was the factory's first attempt at making an off-road bike from their V-twin range.*

*The hand-built V65TT CC (Competition Client) model was built expressly for events such as the Paris–Dakar and Pharaoh Rallies.*

front mudguard. Another plus over the usual run-of-the-mill enduro irons was a decent set of 12-volt electrics, meaning not only the luxury of electric start, but effective lights. At the front, the square CEV headlamp came with a plastic cowling with a red numberplate at the top and a series of air grills below. This assembly supported the black plastic front turn signals, which were flexibly mounted on rubber stalks. The tail section, which doubled as part of the rear mudguard, helped support the rear light, turn signals, and rear carrier. An unbreakable, nylon motocross front mudguard was colour coded to the tank, side panels, tail section, and front cowl in either white or

---

### TECHNICAL SPECIFICATIONS
### V65TT Competition Client (1985)

| | | | |
|---|---|---|---|
| Engine | 4-stroke 90° V-twin | | 260mm, one rear drilled disc 240mm. |
| Bore | 80mm | | |
| Stroke | 64mm | Wheels | spoked wheels with light alloy rims. |
| Displacement | 643.4cc | | |
| Compression ratio | 9:1 | Tyres | Front, Desert 90/90 – 21in |
| Timing | ohv | | Rear, Desert 140/90 – 17in |
| Lubrication | by pressure pump, cooling by separate circuit. | | |
| | | Frame | tubular cradle, disassemblable. |
| Transmission | primary by helical gears, secondary by cardan shaft and gears. | Suspension | Front, Marzocchi telescopic fork MIR 42. 280mm travel. Rear, swinging fork with Marzocchi MX hydraulic dampers and external reservoir. |
| Clutch | dry with single disc. | | |
| Fuel delivery | two carburettors PHBH 30, with air filter and engine gas recycling. | | |
| Electrical system | 12 volt alternator 14V-20A fitted on driving shaft, rectifier and regulator. | Instrument panel | speedometer, oil thermometer on panel complete with warning lights. |
| Battery | 12V-9 Ah | | |
| Starting | kick-starter | Fuel tank capacity | 38ltr (8.4gal) |
| Gearbox | 5-speed, foot operated. | Speed | over 160kph (100mph) |
| Brakes | one front floating disc | Dry weight | 165kg (363lb) |

*Built in both 346.23cc (66 × 50.6mm) and 643.4cc (80 × 64mm) engine sizes, the TT (Tutto Terreno – all terrain) models were excellent all-rounders.*

steel grey, the balance of the machine being in bright red. Although effective in reducing noise levels, the black finished exhaust system was both overly complex and rust prone. It comprised a pair of exhaust header pipes, a massive collector box, and a single pipe, which joined up with the tail-piece silencer mounted high on the offside of the machine. There was also a sump 'bash-plate' to provide vital protection. Other parts of the

*During late 1985, both TTs were given a mini update. Although largely cosmetic, they also received a new exhaust system, revised sump guard and all-black engine finish.*

V35/65TT's specification included Akront alloy wheel rims, 3.00 × 21in front and 4.00 × 18in rear knobbly tyres, front and rear brakes relying on single Brembo twin-piston calipers, and 260mm discs, which, unlike the larger V-twins, were unlinked. Although the TTs were a shade too heavy for serious off-road use, they nonetheless made excellent dual-purpose models, to a degree unmatched by virtually anything else except BMW's R80 G/S. A word of warning, however. Be aware that because of the increased angle of the rear drive housing caused by the taller suspension, the bearing at the front of the bevel drive housing will starve of lubricant unless the oil level is topped up with the rear end raised to compensate.

During late 1985, the TTs were given a mini-update. This was mainly cosmetic, but there was also a new exhaust system, sump guard and all-black engine. By the end of 1986 the TT duo were coming to the end of their production life, with a new series of off-road style Guzzis waiting to make their entrance.

## 350/650 NTX

By the middle of 1987, the TT models had been phased out in favour of their replacement, the new NTX series, which had made their debut at the Cologne Show in September 1986. At first these were offered with the two engine sizes of the predecessors. Mechanically they were largely unchanged. Besides an entirely new (but still black) exhaust system, there was also a much more frequent use of black, rather than natural aluminium finish, including the entire engine, transmission and final-drive assemblies. Wheel rims were finished in gold (left in polished alloy on TTs), whilst mirrors were now standard equipment. The smaller-engined machine came with a striking yellow/white/black paint job, while the 650

*The TTs replacement, the 350 and 650 NTX models, made their bow at the Cologne Show in September 1986.*

NTX was given a far more conservative livery of red/white/black. As with early models the three-fifty was aimed largely at the domestic market, whilst the larger NTX was exported in considerable numbers, but not to Britain, which at that time had a ban on plastic fuel tanks – a notable feature of the NTX range. Besides the new colour schemes, there was also brand new bodywork, including a much taller tank and a tinted screen atop the brand new fairing (which formed an integral section of the total styling package which included the tank, panels and the fairing itself). The result was what appeared to be completely new motorcycles, but of course, underneath, were anything but.

## 750 NTX

But the real jewel-in-the-crown of the NTX family came at the end of 1989, just in time for a Milan Show launch, in the shape of a 750 version. A 'Paris Dakar' styling job transformed its appearance and image, but this time it was simply cosmetic, as the newcomer used the 743.9cc ($80 \times 74$mm) engine from the Targa sports roadster. All the basics

*As with previous models, the three-fifty was largely aimed at the domestic market, due to Italian tax laws.*

*Arriving at the end of 1989, the 750 NTX used the 743.9cc ($80 \times 74$mm) engine from the Targa sports roadster.*

**TECHNICAL SPECIFICATIONS**
**750 NTX (1989)**

| | | | |
|---|---|---|---|
| Engine | 4-stroke, 90° V-twin | Brakes | Front, 260mm disc with four little brake pistons, caliper.Rear, 235mm disc. |
| Bore | 80mm | | |
| Stroke | 74mm | | |
| Displacement | 743.9cc | Wheels | spoke wheels with alloy rims.Front, 1.6 × 21in Rear, 2.15 × 18in |
| Compression ratio | 10.3:1 | | |
| Timing | ohv, 2 valves per cylinder. | Tyres | Front, 3.00 × 21in Rear, 4.00 × 18in |
| Lubrication | forced, by pressure pump. | Suspension | Front, Marzocchi telescopic fork.Rear, light alloy swinging fork with oil/air dampers. |
| Transmision | primary by helical gears,secondary by Cardan shaft and gears. | | |
| Clutch | dry with single disc. | Instrument panel | speedometer, rev-counter on panel complete with warning lights. |
| Fuel delivery | two carburettors PHBH 30 with air filtering and engine gas recycling. | | |
| | | Fuel tank capacity | 30l (6.6gal) |
| Electrical system | 12 volt alternator 14V-20A fitted on driving shaft, rectifier and regulator. | Frame | tubular cradle, disassemblable. |
| | | Fuel consumption | 5.8ltr × 100km (49mpg Imp) (CUNA Norms) |
| Battery | 12V 24Ah | | |
| Starting | electric | Speed | 170kph (106mph) approx. |
| Ignition | electronic | | |
| Gearbox | 5-speed | Dry weight | 185kg (407lb) |

from the original NTX models were retained including the black-finished mechanics, the gold wheel rims, and the same single exhaust. Distinguishing features for the top-of-the-range 750 included a low close-fitting front mudguard and a much more comprehensive fairing which extended under the engine. A pair of plastic enduro-type, colour-coded hand protectors completed the styling exercise. At 106mph (170.5kph) the maximum speed was little changed from the 650, but there was a useful improvement in engine torque. The 750 NTX weighed in (dry) at 180kg (396lb). From 1988 (which meant

all the seven-fifty models), the NTX series benefited like other Guzzi V-twins from the fitting of the new French Valeo starter motor. This was smaller than both the previous Bosch and Spanish Lucas types. A 'planet-wheel' type with indirect drive, it provided improved starting.

## 1000 QUOTA

The same Milan Show in November 1991 which saw the arrival of the definitive production Daytona sports bike, also witnessed the launch of a very different animal, a new monster street enduro mount, the 1000 Quota. An original prototype-only had appeared at the Milan Show two years earlier in 1989. Instead of attempting to extract yet more cubes from the existing 750 NTX, Guzzi's engineering and design teams opted instead to build an entirely new machine, using an engine from the heavyweight series of V-twins.

This also placed Guzzi in direct competition with several other manufacturers, notably Cagiva (Elefant), BMW (R100GS), Honda (Africa Twin) and Yamaha (Super Teneré), in the big cubes big money on-off roadster market. Although the Quota's power source was the tried and trusted 948.813cc (88 × 78mm) two-valves per cylinder lump as found in several other big-bore Guzzi vees at the time, the balance of the machine was radically different. The Quota was also the first Moto Guzzi production bike to feature the excellent Weber-Marelli electronic fuel injection system as standard

---

**TECHNICAL SPECIFICATIONS**
**Quota 1000 (Prototype) 1989**

| | | | |
|---|---|---|---|
| Engine | 4-stroke 90° V-twin, 'Nigusil' cylinder lining. | Brakes | Front, single floating disc 300mm drilled. Rear, single fixed disc 260mm, drilled. |
| Bore | 88mm | | |
| Stroke | 78mm | Wheels | wire with aluminium rims. |
| Displacement | 948.8cc | | |
| Output | 72hp at 6800rpm (IGM rules) | Tyres | Front, 90.90 21 Tube type. Rear 130/80 17 Tube type. |
| Max torque | 75Nm (7.9kg) at 5200rpm (IGM rules) | | |
| Compression ratio | 9.5:1 | Frame | steel double beam, rectangular section, duplex cradle, disassemblable. |
| Timing | ohv, 2 valves per cylinder. | | |
| Lubrication | by pressure pump. | Suspension | Front, Marzocchi hydraulic telescopic fork.Rear swinging fork, rectangular section, with Marzocchi adjustable monoshock. |
| Transmission | primary gears; secondary by Cardan shaft with double universal joint and bevel gears. | | |
| Clutch | double plate, dry type. | | |
| Fuel delivery | Weber double body carburettor 36. | Intrument panel | speedometer, rev-counter and warning lights. |
| Electrical system | 14V 20A alternator; 12V 20Ah battery. | Fuel tank capacity | 22ltr (4.8gal) |
| Starting | electric | Fuel consumption | 5.7ltr × 100km (49.6mpg) (CUNA rules) |
| Ignition | electronic, Motoplat double pick-up. | Dry weight | 210kg (463lb) |
| Gearbox | 5-speed | Max speed | 200kph (125mph) |

*Original prototype Quota 1000 as displayed on the company's stand at the 1989 Milan Show extravaganza. A major difference to the production version which followed two years later was single instead of twin front brake discs.*

equipment. The type chosen by Guzzi was two injectors (one per cylinder) with an electric fuel pump incorporating a pressure regulator, single throttle unit, and optimised digital injection control. This digital control allowed the engine not only to produce its peak power output of 70bhp at a low 6600rpm, but also provided an abundance of torque 79nm (58.5lb/ft) at 6000rpm. The sys-

*Definitive Quota 1000 as shown at Milan in November 1991; several changes from original prototype. Fuel injection was a bonus, the massive seat height wasn't.*

tem's biggest advantage over the conventional twin Dell'Orto carburettors was a much improved spread of power throughout the entire range, notably during the warm-up stage. This is because the injection system is able to constantly monitor engine temperature, ambient air temperature, and air velocity to ensure perfect carburation. However not everything was perfect, the Quota using a P7 computer, rather than P8 as on the 1100 California. The P7 computer worked at a slower rate, thus response was less than it might otherwise have been.

At the time the factory also claimed that the Quota was the first motorcycle where the fluid-dynamic study of a long intake manifold system had allowed the bike to conform to the very strictest anti-pollution regulations without the use of a catalytic converter. As a result, the engine was unique in the two-wheel world in being able to run with an air/fuel ratio as high as 18:1, greater than stoichiometic. The frame was also a radical departure. It was a twin-beam device formed in rectangular sections of high-resistance steel. It incorporated a removable, lower duplex cradle. Guzzi's engineering team claimed this structure provided exceptional torsional rigidity, allowing both ease of control at relatively low speeds off-road, combined with excellent road handling at higher velocities. The swinging arm was manufactured from rectangular steel tubing with an adjustable single Marzocchi shock featuring rising-rate linkage. At the front of the machine a pair of air-adjustable, leading-axle Marzocchi long-travel telescopic forks, featuring a pair of useful rubber gaiters to protect the hard-chrome stanchions, ensured the big Guzzi could compete with its rivals in the suspension department.

The balance of the Quota was just as interesting. For starters, the entire exhaust system was manufactured from high-grade stainless-steel; the brake lines were of braided stainless-steel and the wheel rims of

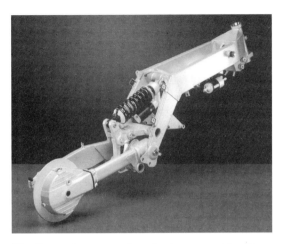

*The Quota frame was hugely strong, making it a popular sidecar machine. The swinging arm was manufactured from rectangular steel tubing with an adjustable single Marzocchi shock featuring rising-rate linkage.*

polished aluminium. Mounted on the rims were 90/90 × 21 front and 130/80 × 17 rear tyres. In keeping with its aggressive off-road looks, there was a large 21 litre (4.6gal) fuel tank with an aircraft-type filler. Only a centre stand was fitted, albeit of an extremely sturdy design. The wide, braced handlebars carried a single-pull quick-action throttle, there were twin mirrors, the latest (and much superior) switchgear, and a pair of plastic enduro-style hand protectors. A single 280mm drilled disc with a four-pot caliper at the front and a single 260mm undrilled disc at the rear had appeared on the 1989 show prototype. However, the production examples which began to leave the works in early 1992 sported twin front discs. Like the show bikes, the front braking components (except for the discs themselves which were made by Guzzi) were manufactured by Grimeca. The rear components were Brembo sourced items. The Guzzi-made front discs were to prove a constant source of problems. This was eventually found to be because of too sharp an edge on the integral disc carrier section of the disc,

causing the disc surface to warp. Eight months or so into the production cycle the disc carrier was redesigned with a smoother rounder edge, thus eradicating the difficulty. Another modification found necessary was to the rear suspension, stabilizing bars being added from the frame to the rear suspension bottom linkage.

The frame of the Quota proved to be outstandingly strong and was soon found to make it ideal for sidecar work. The Quota's bodywork was well-styled, making it an attractive overall package on the eye. There was a twin headlamp fairing, with a small smoked screen. Like the NTX 750 it was styled to join with the fuel tank, which in

*1000 Quota factory brochure cover showing the twin headlamp fairing, with a small smoked screen.*

turn flowed into the side panels and tail section. A small carrier came as standard equipment. With a dry weight of 210kg (464lb) and a maximum speed of 125mph (200kph), the Quota appeared an impressive piece of kit; at least on paper. Unfortunately, what should have been one of the very best Guzzi twins ever, ended in being just the reverse. Sales never matched expectations. A major reason for this was the seat height, which at 855mm (over 34 inches!) effectively limited ownership to those individuals over 6ft 2in (1.88m) – or sidecar enthusiasts. In fact, the British importers eventually refused to take any more until something was done to rectify the situation.

## 1100 QUOTA

As early as the beginning of 1995 Guzzi planned to bring out a modified version of the Quota, with particular attention to the seat height difficulties. This finally appeared at the beginning of 1998. But far from being simply a modified version of the original, it is in fact a comprehensive redesign, which also benefited from the larger 1064cc (92 × 80mm) engine from the new California EV. Using the later Weber/Marelli MI5 fuel injection set-up engine response is much improved which, together with the increase in cubic capacity makes for a dynamic machine. If proof is needed compare the new 1100 (factory code ES) Quota output figures of 87bhp at 6200rpm against the machine it replaced (70bhp at 6600rpm). Torque figures are equally impressive: 1100, 92nm at 3800rpm; against 1000, 79nm at 6000rpm. The seat height is now down by no less than 105mm (4.1in), so instantly making the new Quota attractive to all but the very shortest of leg. Rather than having a combination of Grimeca and Brembo braking components the new 1100 has only the latter; again in the writer's view a much more practical arrange-

*New for 1998, the 1100 Quota, with many improvements, but the really big news was the 105mm (4.1in) lower seat height so the bike could now be ridden by mere mortals.*

ment. Also the front discs (now in stainless steel rather than cast iron) are fully floating and of a larger (296mm) diameter. The rear disc size remains unchanged at 260mm. Like all the latest Guzzis the attention to detail, quality control and finish are all significantly improved; witnessed by the new management's confidence in being able to give a full three-year, unlimited mileage guarantee (from January 1998). The only downside to the 1100 Quota ES is an increase in dry weight to a beefy 245kg (540lb).

*Besides the lower seat height, another major advantage of the 1100 Quota is its much improved engine torque figures.*

# 11  Daytona

Throughout the majority of the 1980s, Moto Guzzi stagnated. It was very much a time when enthusiasts for the marque began to even wonder if it would survive into the following decade. But survive it did, and all the many prayers which had been made about something truly new were answered one overcast November day in Milan during 1991. The special occasion was the public launch of the production Daytona. Long promised, it was perhaps ironic that a former dentist, John Wittner (more commonly known simply as 'Dr John'), from Philadelphia, USA, should be the man to revitalize interest in the famous old Guzzi name. But that is exactly what transpired.

The Daytona was to be the first in a series of exciting new models to be launched throughout the 1990s, a process still going on today. Wittner had been a life-long motorcyclist, who took up dentistry after training in engineering, only to give up his new career to go endurance racing with a group of like-minded enthusiasts, and finally made contact with Guzzi owner (at the time) Alejandro de Tomaso – originally concerning funding for an all-new racing chassis.

The Doctor John race team had achieved its first major success by winning the AMA/CCS American Endurance Championship in successive years during 1984 and 1985 with the first 1000 Le Mans to arrive in the States. Then, ridden by Doug Brauneck, a Dr John Guzzi V-twin claimed the USA Pro-Twins title in 1987. De Tomaso was impressed enough by these results that he gave Wittner one of two prototype eight-valve engines (originally constructed with street use in mind) which had been designed

in the mid-1980s by veteran engineer Umberto Todero, a long serving employee who had been with the factory since the glory days of the 1950s. Armed with a specially constructed machine using Todero's engine with further development from Wittner and his team (included an American Crane camshaft), an excellent third place was secured in the bike's debut during the annual Daytona Twins race in March 1988. Further leader-board placings throughout the remainder of that year saw Wittner

*Original 1000 Daytona prototype as displayed on the factory's stand at the 1989 Milan Show with Richard Davies, son of the British importer Keith (Three Cross Motorcycles).*

*Engine of the revised Daytona at Milan two years later in November 1991.*

Using a half instead of the original's full fairing, the 992cc (90 × 78mm) 90-degree V-twin engine featured belt drive to activate each cylinder's single overhead camshaft with 95bhp at 8000rpm (maximum torque 98nm at 6000rpm) and the original production model was reasonably powerful; fitting a factory Stage 1 or Stage 2 kit (basically the former for fast road work, the latter for track use) made things even more interesting.

At the time of its launch, the Daytona was heralded as a considerable advance. Not just the four-valves-per-cylinder sohc with toothed-belt drive, but the much more modern feel to the engine and chassis once under way. From the moment you leaned forward to take a grip of the machine with the low-mounted clip-ons, and fired up the big twin, right through to the light throttle and light clutch actions, the differences between the old and the new were instantly recognizable. The throttle response was entirely due to the Weber-Marelli electronic fuel injection, with dual injectors, Alfa-N system, electric fuel pump with pressure regulator, optimized digital control of the injection times and high efficiency air filter. Not only this,

invited to Italy the next year with the exciting task of beginning work on a road-going version. The prototype street bike appeared in November 1989 at the Milan show, but it was to be a full two years longer before the production version was ready.

The 1991 machine utilized a rectangular steel space frame and cantilever swinging arm similar to that of the Dr John racer. Styling however was entirely new, and completely different to the 1989 show prototype.

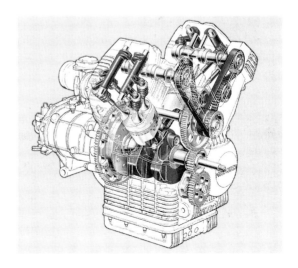

*The Daytona's four-valves-per-cylinder, belt driven ohc engine.*

*Valve cover removed to show four-valve layout.*

*An early production Daytona; circa 1992.*

but the Daytona was also unexpectedly quiet, both mechanically and through its twin exhausts. It was in this area that Wittner and his team at the Guzzi factory spent much of the time-consuming development work – and the reason why the period was greater than many considered it should have been. Another problem, certainly for a relatively small factory such as Moto Guzzi, was the amount of effort required to gain worldwide homologation.

With a high peak rpm, at least compared to previous Guzzi vees, it was good that maximum torque was produced further down the scale at 6000rpm. The abundance of low-rev and mid-range 'umph' made the standard Daytona a joy to ride. It also meant

that there was a little more need to use the five-speed gearbox which, although it contained straight-cut instead of helical-cut cogs, was still a close relation of the assembly found in the earlier Guzzi vees. If the engine generally felt like a tuned version of previous Guzzis, the chassis most certainly did not. At 205kg (420lb) dry, the Daytona was reasonably light, and with the combination of a 17in front and an 18in rear wheel, combined with modern geometry, provided a much sportier, more 'flickable' feel than the slow-steering Guzzis of yesteryear. This improved response was the more impressive because it had not taken place at the expense of straight-line stability which was as good as ever. Much of this must have been thanks to Wittner's parallelogram swinging arm linkage, which all but cured the traditional shaft-drive torque reaction found on earlier models of the V-twin line.

Another departure from conventional Guzzi big twin practice was in the braking department. Brembo brakes yes, but independent, with the usual linked system. Suspension was taken care of by a pair of flex-free 41mm Marzocchi front forks and a multi-adjustable Dutch Koni rear shock. On this latter component, a key role was played by the strut's spring rate. This was critical

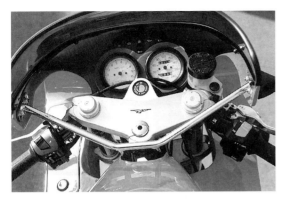

*1992 Daytona*

*(Top left)*
*Rider's eye view*

*(Middle left)*
*Fuel injection and gearbox.*

*(Bottom left)*
*Front engine.*

*(Top right)*
*Rear brake and muffler.*

*(Bottom right)*
*Front disc, caliper and fork slider.*

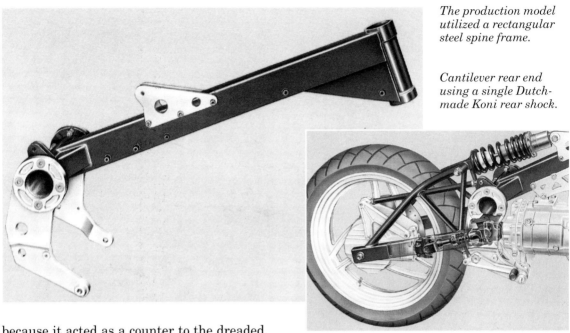

*The production model utilized a rectangular steel spine frame.*

*Cantilever rear end using a single Dutch-made Koni rear shock.*

because it acted as a counter to the dreaded shaft drive 'screwing' effect. Two springs were provided so that customers had a choice when tuning their suspension for the particular needs of rider weight and road surfaces.

The Daytona Series also played an important role in the birth of the 1100 Sport (see Chapter 12); this machine used a two-valve-per-cylinder engine based on the earlier models, but utilising much of the Daytona's running gear.

## DR JOHN REPLICA

In 1994 the limited edition Daytona 1000 Dr John made its bow. Finished in a distinctive black (including the wheels) and gold, it came with the factory B race kit as standard, complete with carbon fibre Termignoni silencers, although 'silencers' is not really an apt term for the noise these generated! The success of this machine (around 100 only were built) prompted Guzzi to build a more accessible high performance version.

## DAYTONA RS

This duly made its entrance in June 1996 as the Daytona RS. Compared with the standard Daytona, the RS engine was uprated to produce 102bhp (at 8400rpm) and featured Carrillo connecting rods, forged 10.5:1 (previously 10:1) full race camshaft, ram air intake and a larger airbox, whilst the M16

*The limited edition Daytona 1000 Dr John, with factory 'B' race kit as standard, 1994.*

# TECHNICAL SPECIFICATIONS
## Daytona 1000 (1992)

| | | | |
|---|---|---|---|
| Engine | 4-stroke 90° V-twin | Gearbox | 5-speed, straight tooth gears. |
| Bore | 90mm | | |
| Stroke | 78mm | Brakes | Front, hydraulic with adjustable lever position. Dual 300mm, drilled, floating Brembo discs and four-piston calipers of differential diameters; Rear, hydraulic with single 260mm drilled disc and floating two-piston caliper. |
| Displacement | 992cc, 'Nigusil' cylinder lining | | |
| Max power | 68kW (95bhp) at 8000rpm (DIN) | | |
| Max torque | 98nm (10kg) at 6000rpm (DIN) | | |
| Compression ratio | 10:1 | | |
| Exhaust system | in stainless steel, two separate tubes and silencers connected by a central collector. | | |
| | | Wheels | light alloy cast. |
| Valves and operation | four valves per cylinder with single overhead camshaft driven by aluminium gears and toothed belts. | Tyres | Front, 120/70 ZR 17 tubeless radial. Rear 160/60 ZR 18 tubeless radial. |
| Lubrication | high volume pressure pump. | Frame | chrome-molybdenum steel swinging fork of rectangular section with engine as a stressed member. |
| Primary transmission | straight tooth gears. | | |
| Final drive | by shaft, with two separate cardan joints and system of floating ring and pinion housing with parallel torque arm to counter torque reaction at the wheel. | Suspension | Front, Marzocchi hydraulic telescopic fork, adjustable for compression and rebound. Rear, chrome-molybdenum steel swinging fork with Koni hydraulic monoshock adjustable for pre-load, compression and rebound. |
| Clutch | double disc, dry type in extra light flywheel. | | |
| Fuel system | Weber-Marelli electronic injection with dual injector, 'Alfa-N' system, electric fuel pump with pressure regulator, optimized digital control of the injection times and high efficiency air filter. | | |
| | | Instrument panel | speedometer, electronic rev-counter and warning lights. |
| Electrical system | 12V, 14V 25A alternator, 16Ah battery. | Fuel tank capacity | 23ltr (5gal) |
| Starting system | electric | Fuel consumption | 5ltr × 100km (56.6mpg) (CUNA Standard) |
| Ignition | Weber-Marelli digital electronic ignition, inductive system with high efficiency power modules and coils. | Dry weight | 205kg (452lb) (with battery) |

Weber-Marelli fuel injection system sported a 54mm injector body with higher pressure 4-bar fuel regulator. Other details of the RS specification included fully floating 320mm Brembo racing front brake discs (the fixed rear 282mm stainless steel rear disc was also new); upside-down 40mm (stanchion) Dutch WP (White Power) front forks, with at the rear a new swinging arm with elliptical-section tubes and a WP shock adjustable in compression, rebound and preload (shorter in length compared to those of the standard model), Michelin Hi-Sport tyres (now both 17in), a TX15 120/70 at the front and a TX25 160/60 at the rear, both rated at ZR. The tyres were mounted on new lightweight three-spoke hollow wheels. There were also aluminium timing gears and toothed belts, rather than chain and toothed belts on

lesser models. In fact the RS is really best described as a race bike, but with dual seat, and homologated exhaust and airbox for the street.

## DAYTONA RACING 1000

Rather confusingly the factory also constructed a batch of 100 Daytona Racing 1000 models. Built in early 1996, twenty-one of these came to the UK and the bike was very much a mixture of the RS and original Daytona. There were the old Guzzi-made cast alloy wheels, conventional Marzocchi 40mm forks, Ysasa battery (the new RS and other 1996 bikes featured a gel-filled no-maintenance battery). There were full 'C' kit performance engine parts, a P8 computer and the

*1997 Daytona RS. Visually like the 1100 Sport, with its inverted front forks and swoopy lines.*

# TECHNICAL SPECIFICATIONS
## Daytona RS

| | | | |
|---|---|---|---|
| Engine | 4-stroke 90° V-twin air-cooled. | Starting system | electric |
| Bore | 90mm | Ignition | Weber-Marelli digital electronic ignition, with inductive spark and high efficiency coils. |
| Stroke | 78mm | | |
| Displacement | 992cc, 'Nigusil' cylinder lining. | Gearbox | 5-speed |
| Max power | 75kW (102 CV) at 8400rpm (CE) | Brakes | Front, hydraulic with adjustable lever position, dual 320mm, drilled, floating Brembo (racing type) discs and four-piston calipers with differentiated diameters. |
| Max torque | 88nm (9km) at 6600rpm (CE) | | |
| Compression ratio | 10.5:1 | | |
| Valves and operation | four valves per cylinder with single overhead camshaft driven by aluminium gears and two toothed belts. | | |
| | | Wheels | light alloy cast, three hollow spokes (rear with cush drive incorporated). |
| Exhaust system | two separate stainless steel pipes connected to a central collector and two silencers. | Tyres | Front, 120/70 ZR 17 tubeless radial. rear, 160/60 ZR 17 Tubeless radial. |
| Lubrication | high volume geared pressure pump, pressure regulator, thermostatic valve and cooling radiator. | Frame | Chrome molybdenum single steel beam, rectangular section with engine as stressed member. |
| Final drive | by shaft with two separate cardan joints and system of floating ring and pinion housing with a rubber damper block. Parallel arm to counter torque reaction at the wheel. | Suspension | Front, hydraulic telescopic fork WP inverted tubes. Rear, steel swinging arm, oval section, hydraulic WP monoshock adjustable for pre-load compression and rebound. |
| Clutch | double disc, dry type. | | |
| Fuel system | Weber-Marelli electronic injection with dual injector, 'Alfa-N' system, electric fuel pump with pressure regulator, optimized digital control of the injection times and high efficiency air filter with two dynamic intakes. | Instrument panel | speedometer, rev-counter and warning lights. |
| | | Fuel tank capacity | 19ltr (4gal) |
| | | Fuel consumption | 4.5ltr × 100km (62.7mpg) (CUNA) |
| | | Max speed | 149mph (240kph) |
| | | Length | 1,475mm (4ft 10in) |
| Electrical system | 12V, 14V 25A alternator, 12Ah sealed battery. | Dry weight | 223kg (491lb) (with battery) |

*Dr John Daytona Replica and racer at Brooklands in the summer of 1995.*

old gearbox with ten-spring clutch (the 1996-onwards machines feature a new much-improved gearbox and lighter eight-spring clutch). But, as with most small production-run machines, the Daytona Racing 1000 will probably become a collector's item in years to come; even though in truth it is a generation behind the still current Daytona RS.

# 12 Today and Tomorrow

In 1996 Moto Guzzi celebrated its seventy-fifth anniversary, making it the oldest surviving motorcycle manufacturer in Italy. But unknown to many of Guzzi's faithful band of enthusiasts around the world, 1996 was a vital year in the marque's history for a very different reason. It saw the completion of a final stage in a recovery programme and its much awaited new development stage. In 1995, after several years of stagnation and losses, the Mandello del Lario factory made a profit. Then in 1996, with an output of 6,500 motorcycles and a sales volume of 85 billion lira, the company once again was in the black – and looking to the future with more enthusiasm than for many a long year, with an exciting programme of development and a projected target output for the early years of the twenty-first century of 20,000 motorcycles and an expected sales volume of over 250 billion lira. So how and why has all this regeneration come about?

For a start, Alejandro de Tomaso, the man who had saved Moto Guzzi some two decades earlier in the early 1970s had by the early 1990s lost much of his drive and with it power. And finally, on 22 August 1996, following a number of changes within De Tomaso Industries Inc. (DTI), an American group quoted on NASDAQ (basically the stock exchange of the worldwide web), and the withdrawal of Alejandro de Tomaso himself, the group changed its business name to Trident Rowan Group Inc. (TGRI). The operation was conducted in line with changes which were taking place at DTI. The acquisition of TIM (Temporary Integrated Management), a leader in the field and the first firm to introduce the American concept of tempo-

rary management to Italy, had the effect of changing the mission of the whole organisation: it now concentrates its efforts on turning around companies with a strong potential for recovery, but which require (as Guzzi did!) the right managerial approach to win through.

The man given this task at Guzzi was Arnoldo Sacchi. Although having the title of managing director, his true task was that of 'crisis management'. This meant first to save Moto Guzzi, the second to formulate a plan for the future. When interviewed for this book recently, Keith Davies, boss of British Guzzi importers Three Cross, said of Sacchi, 'I was very sorry to see him go. He was a hard, but fair man who got things done!' And getting things done at Guzzi was vital. Bluntly put, Moto Guzzi had been a sleeping giant since the end of the 1970s and by the time Sacchi took the reigns of power it was

*As the 1990s progressed so Moto Guzzi finally began to change. Typical was the new entrance to the Mandello del Lario headquarters, seen here in 1995.*

at an all-time low. Looking at hard business facts in detail shows that in 1995 the company had a sales volume of 42 million dollars (American) as opposed to only 23 million in 1993 and was, as already noted, able to balance its books with a net profit of 33,000 dollars. Output had risen sharply: 5,314 bikes in 1995, a 70 per cent increase in two years. The share capital had been raised from 1.3 to 3.3 million dollars and new jobs were being created (in April 1996 the Mandello plant had a staff of 336).

Backing up Sacchi during this critical period was Gianluca Lanaro (marketing and sales manager), Guido Ranalli (Italian sales and public administration manager), Angelo Ferrari (technical manager) and Daniele Bartorelli (works manager). Sacchi's plan set out a development programme for the company until the year 2000. It envisaged a sales volume in 1996 of at least 56 million dollars, 80 million for 1997 and around 166–186 million by the year 2000 with total sales of 20,000 bikes. Perhaps most significantly of all, investment had been set aside for R&D and two main objectives announced: to become the market leader for high-power bikes and a return to the racing circuit by taking part in the World Super Bike (WSB) championship. In the author's opinion both these objectives, fine as they are, may not be achievable. Meanwhile, work had already begun on a series of new motorcycles, the first of which was destined to be the V10 Centauro and 1100 Sport Injection. These, together with other current and future developments, are discussed later in this chapter. At the end of 1997, Moto Guzzi announced that Oscar Cecchinato was to succeed Arnoldo Sacchi as its new managing director, the latter having completed the three-year restructuring phase. In his new post Cecchinato would oversee all aspects of Guzzi's operations, including production, marketing and sales. Oscar Cecchinato came to Moto Guzzi with a wide commercial background, no doubt benefiting greatly from his previous motorcycle industry experience (over five years) as chief executive officer of Aprilia. In that period Cecchinato headed a financial restructuring of Aprilia, which resulted in dramatic increases in revenues and profits. Previously, his management experience included working for such leading companies as Biemack SpA, Philips Electronics and Esso Standard Italia. Oscar Cecchinato had graduated from the University of Vienna with a degree in economics and had also done graduate work at both Harvard and Columbia Universities in the USA. As with Arnoldo Sacchi, Cecchinato was flanked by Mario Tozzi-Condivi as president and the combination of Gianlucca Lanaro, Sales and Marketing (formally at Laverda), and chief engineer Angelo Ferrari, the latter having been a designer at both the Bugatti and Lamborghini car companies, and also Laverda.

## 1100 SPORT

First announced at the end of 1993, the 1100 Sport did not actually begin production until almost another year had passed. Once it was available, however, it proved well worth the wait, being probably the best Guzzi sports bike since the Le Mans I of the mid 1970s, the Daytona included. Actually, the 1100 Sport was a clever move, using as it did the Daytona-based chassis and one of the new big-bore two-valve 1064cc engines. It featured the backbone frame and full-floating shaft drive of the Daytona powered by an engine that used all the company's vast experience with the two-valve 90-degree V-twin garnered over some three decades since the original V7.

Many of the best features from the Daytona were present including the 320mm front discs with their four-piston gold Brembo calipers, a single rear 282mm disc

*An 1100 Sport (carb), Autumn 1994.*

incorporated, a more compact rear shock adjustable for compression and rebound, and a choice of red (a different shade than the Daytona's silver) or black paint job. As for the engine, although clearly based on that found with the then current 1100 California, there were some notable differences: higher-compression 10.5:1 pistons forged in special non-deforming alloy; special light-weight clutch, flywheel, and pressure plate; and a stronger and lighter crankshaft assembly. Even though the 1100 Sport had been generally well received, Guzzi's new management did not rest on their laurels and in June 1996 an updated version was put in production.

Known as the 1100 Sport Injection, it benefited greatly, as had the California before it, by switching from carbs to the highly successful Weber-Marelli fuel injection system, also found on not just the California, but also the Daytona and the brand new V10 Centauro. Instantly noticeable was the change from conventional to new upside-down (inverted) front forks (as per the new Daytona RS), three-spoke Marchesini-made wheels. In fact, except for semi-floating front discs and Pirelli Dragon GT tyres, everything was the same as the Daytona RS.

with two-piston floating caliper, braided hoses, stainless steel exhaust system, 17in front and 18in rear wheels shod with tube-less radial tyres, 41mm Marzocchi MIR front forks, and a compact instrument panel incorporating a white-face Veglia speedo and tacho, plus warning lights for the machine's main functions. New features included a redesigned fuel tank (capacity decreased from 23 to 20 litres, seat, fairing (with 'ram' air intake vents), light alloy foot-rest mounts, 40mm Dell'Ortos (replacing the Daytona's fuel injection system), electronic inductive Marelli Digiplex 2S ignition, a new lightened frame (still of chrome-moly steel construction) with front sub-frame

*1100 Sports awaiting crating up in the factory, Spring 1995.*

## Déjà Vu
### By Rod Woolnough

I began riding back in 1969 and by 1977 had owned half a dozen motorcycles of various types. Then, in late 1977, I purchased a brand new Triumph T160 Trident. Unfortunately, although fast, it was to prove less than reliable – with the clutch as the main culprit. Heading home up the M1 motorway one day after yet another clutch rebuild, I took the A508 exit near Northampton and promptly ran out of petrol. There was a garage less than a mile away, so I set out to push the bike in that direction. I didn't know it at the time but I was about to begin a love affair that has been with me ever since.

The sound of thunder approached, and with it a bright red Moto Guzzi Le Mans, which proceeded to pull up beside me. 'Having trouble?' asked its rider. Soon I was climbing onto the pillion and we set off towards the filling station. Nothing had prepared me for the experience – the Guzzi accelerated down the road like a rocket. The glorious V-twin exhaust note coupled with the seemingly never-ending accelerative force was a revelation. Then the rider changed up and it all happened again and again. He shut off and changed back down the 'box. We had arrived at the garage. I thanked him and he was gone. The love affair had begun. If that rider recognizes himself, thanks again. You changed my life.

The Trident was refuelled and took me home. Three days later, in August 1978 *en route* to Italy for a motorcycling holiday, it broke down again. I was then stuck in a tent for a week whilst awaiting parts, and took the decision to buy – you've guessed it – a new red Le Mans as soon as possible, I took a friend with me – he bought a blue one! Twenty years later the two machines, ATO 296T and ATO 297T, have each covered in excess of 140,000 miles and are still going strong. In that time we have ridden them hard, we have ridden them far – they look after us, we look after them.

The early Le Mans – now universally known as the Mark 1 – is something special, a thing of great beauty, something never captured in the various later variations which followed. The years went by and during the 1980s Moto Guzzis were obsessed with restyling old bikes in much the same way as the British industry had done in the 1960s – with largely the same results.

Then came the Daytona. Brilliant, at last another drop-dead gorgeous Guzzi. Then the 1100 Sport. Then finally the 1100 Sport Injection – the modern-day Le Mans 1 – a perfect motorcycle. I'm falling in love again. And although we will never part with the two Le Mans, Alex Boyesen and I wanted new ones, so on the 21 May 1997, history repeated itself and two brand new, consecutively numbered, bright red, 1100 Sport Injections were ridden away from a Midland-based Guzzi dealership by their new owners.

Improvements over the standard 1100 Sport Injection have made a brilliant motorcycle even better. These have seen the rear tyre changed from a 160/70 to a 160/60 (same width, but lower profile). This has the effect of reducing the height at the rear of the machine. To counteract this the front fork legs were brought up through the yokes by 18mm. This not only means a lower bike, but also quickens the steering. The standard rear shock spring is too heavy, so this has been reduced to a 450lb spring, making the suspension more compliant. The performance has been improved by fitting a new chip and exhaust. This gets rid of any form of flat spot in the mid range (which with standard set-up is noticeable around 5000rpm). The replacement chip and exhaust (supplied by Raceco and fitted by Market Motorcycles of Tring, Hertfordshire) allows the engine to breathe more easily, providing a flat, chunky torque curve from as little as 2000rpm right up to the red-line. Finally a K&N type air filter replaced the original paper Guzzi item. And if this is fitted in the centrally located airbox no-one is the wiser.

P744 OVV and P745 OVV have reaffirmed that Moto Guzzi is again building very special bikes, and the future is again looking bright. Long live the Moto Guzzi V-twin!

*Rod Woolnough (left) and Alex Boyesen with their Le Mans 1 first purchased 17 August 1978.*

*Two decades on Alex (left) and Rod with their 1100 Sport Injections, 29 June 1998.*

The press responded by giving the newcomer a positive thumbs up, typified by the *Motor Cycle News* headline in their 14 August 1996 test, 'Guzzi outguns Duke in Battle of the Twins'. The test went on to say, 'At last, a Moto Guzzi you don't have to make apologies for! The 1100 Sport Injection has finally fulfilled the promise so many of the Mandello-built V-twins have shown but so often failed to live up to, usually because of some irritating minor problem. And in doing so, it's become a better bike than the long-running, top-selling Ducati 900SS. Its looks give it a head start. It attracts plenty of admiration from passers-by with its chunky, solid motor in full view beneath the curvaceous, well-balanced bodywork draped along the top of the bike. The colour of our test machine was simply described as black, but that does no justice to the way it turns metallic bronze in the sunlight! Also new was a bright yellow, which with the existing red proved the most popular with buyers.' The *MCN* tester, Kevin Ash, was impressed with the way the big Guzzi handled the corners saying, 'the bike is superbly stable and encourages you to really lay it far over, when the tyres dig in and hold it accurately on line.' He also greatly appreciated the fuel injection,

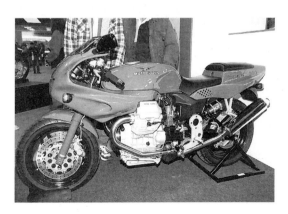

The much acclaimed 1100 Sport was in fact a successful marriage of Daytona cycle parts with an uprated two-valve engine.

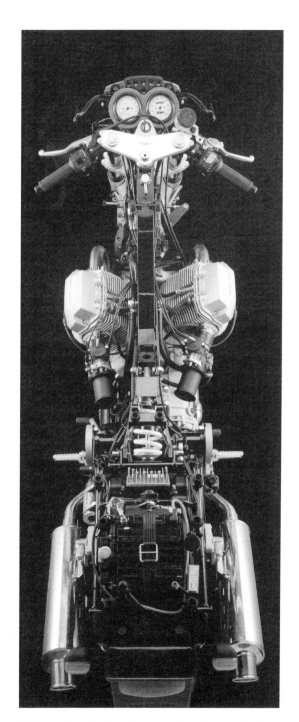

This overhead view gives an idea of not only the layout, but the length of the 1100 Sport (carb version shown).

*The 1100 Sport Injection debuted in 1996; improvements included not only the excellent Weber-Marelli fuel injection in place of carbs, but inverted front forks and other, more minor, changes.*

*Besides the original Italian racing red, the 1100 Sport Injection heralded a bright new yellow paint scheme as an alternative.*

*Francis Williamson winning the prestigious Mallory Park Post TT Sound of Thunder race in June 1996 with Jim Blomley's very special 1100 Sport-based racer.*

For 1998 Guzzi built a limited run (200) of the special 1100 Sport Corsa models. Here is the first UK machine being uncrated at importers Three Cross.

The 1998 1100 Sport Corsa. Available in either yellow/black or red/black. Termignoni carbon fibre silencers are just one of several performance extras.

'The first clue comes with lighter, smoother throttle action, which no longer demands two fistfuls of twistgrip to get fully open. But more importantly, throttle response had also been upgraded. The old bike misfired and gasped at lower revs and made itself difficult unless you were nailing it. The injected machine runs smoothly from tickover right up to the red line at 8000rpm. But no motorcycle is perfect and the 1100 Sport Injection's seat was on the hard side and the sidestand that's almost impossible to use while sitting on the bike and the idiot lights that are hidden from taller riders by the top of the screen.' Also, in the author's opinion, shorter riders will find life difficult due to the stretched out riding position. The final model of the 1100 Sport (still injection) arrived in February 1998 in the shape of the limited edition (200 only) Corsa models. Available in either red or yellow, the Corsa had an all-black engine assembly (except for polished rocker covers) which had an almost overbearing effect on the machine's appearance. Unique features of the model include a silver 'Limited Edition' plate on the fork top yoke; Termignoni carbon fibre silencers and Dutch White Power suspension. In the UK (July 1998) it cost £8,495 – a £500 premium over the standard model.

## V10 CENTAURO

The first true 'all-new' model of the new era began production in July 1996. Effectively it uses a 90bhp version of the 992cc Daytona RS four-valves-per-cylinder engine including toothed belt ohc and M16 Weber-Marelli fuel injector with 54mm injection body. The Centauro sports different (lower) rear bevel box drive gearing of 7/33 (against 8/33 on the Daytona S). It also features the new generation gearbox (shared by other post-1996 big Guzzis) which has a redesigned tooth profile – this also does away with half dogs – gives

*A group of British dealers at the factory and about to return to the UK with their new V10 Centauro machines, 21 April 1997.*

increased full dogs and reprofiling. Gearchange is now virtually up to Japanese standards. New generation machines (including the California Evolution from June 1997) have a different sump and oil pick-up assembly, plus oil coolers. It was also the first time on a production Guzzi that you do not have to remove the sump to change the oil. (This feature can now be retro-fitted to earlier bikes.) Other improvements included gel-filled, maintenance free batteries and a lighter eight-spring clutch. As for

*The V10 Centauro employs one of the 992cc (90 × 78mm) four-valves-per-cylinder Daytona type engines.*

cycle parts, the 1996 V10 Centauro employed the frame, wheels, suspension and brakes from the post-1996 1100 Sport Injection. But there was a different rear sub-frame and airbox. The styling, the work of Luciano Marabisi (also responsible for the 1100 Sport), and associated components were entirely new. All-in-all it is a bike which you will either love or hate. Sometimes, as with the author, it is a bike which you can even hate and then love! But whichever view you have, you simply cannot ignore the Centauro, it is a bike like no other, not even another Guzzi. For 1998 the Centauro was redesigned – not in its overall style, but to make it a better motorcycle. At the same time it was offered in two other versions, the GT and Sport. The GT featured adjustable handlebars, a dual seat and luggage rack/grab rails, together with a small Perspex screen, whereas the Sport (available in bright red or dark metallic green) was more aggressively styled with the new seat (rear section covered for solo use), adjustable handlebars and a mini handlebar fairing and belly pan. There is also a wide range of optional extras, including dual seat (as per GT), the luggage rack/backrest and Termignoni carbon fibre silencers. Improvements over the previous (original) naked version include the handlebars which

*For 1998 the standard Centauro was joined with the GT (shown) and Sport models. All cost the same price.*

provide a far more comfortable riding stance, the redesigned (and far more comfortable!) seat – both of which combine to give a more natural riding position. It has a side stand that can be left down like a Japanese machine, instead of the previous awful Guzzi mousetrap type, improved rear disc giving a bigger braking area, a new improved EP ROM for the combined fuel injection and ignition system, and White Power suspension. A comprehensive test of a 1998 Centauro Sport by the author revealed a transformation in riding pleasure from the original 1996 naked version; riding position and comfort being transformed. The Daytona RS-based engine with its lower gearing provides vast amounts of torque over the whole rev range. Stationary the Centauro looks heavy, almost to the point of excess. But get those wheels rolling and the weight 224kg (494lb) dry simply melts away. And together with the other latest models the fit and finish are a million miles away from the majority of earlier Guzzi V-twins. To be absolutely honest I was not really looking forward to testing the Centauro Sport, thinking instead that other models such as the 1100 Sport Injection/Corsa or California EV would be my favourites. But how wrong I was, of all the 1998 V-twin range it was the Centauro

*Centauro uses the excellent Weber-Marelli fuel injection system.*

*Centauro Sport. Available in either metallic red or metallic green, it is an excellent roadster. Much improved over the original, the 1998 machines have a better riding position, a more comfortable saddle and revised instrumentation.*

*1998 V10 Centauro Sport cockpit. Handlebar fairing is standard on this version.*

*A 1998 V10 Centauro with the author at the controls. He rates it as one of his all-time favourite motorcycles.*

Sport that I just kept on wanting to ride and I placed it top in the sheer pleasure it gave me. It just proves you should never consider buying a bike without riding it.

## OTHER DEVELOPMENTS

The 'new' models which have appeared recently are only the tip of the Guzzi iceberg in relation to the host of developments taking place. A couple which will not be making an appearance are a V-four which began life at the end of the 1980s (still in the de Tomaso era) and the V7 Ippogrifo which was displayed at a number of shows around Europe in 1996/1997. (For information on this latter project see separate box within this chapter.) As for the V-four, this came at a time when the company was struggling financially and there was simply no money to carry it through the development stage to production – all available funds going into the Dr John Wittner inspired Daytona – but a prototype engine and chassis were built. Of much more relevance to the future are the ongoing projects of today (this book was written in summer 1998).

*750 Drona (unmanned target aircraft) engine, coded V75Hie. A modified version was intended for use in the stillborn Ippogrifo motorcycle project.*

---

### 1996/1997 V7 Ippogrifo (prototype only)

The Hippogryph is a mythical winged beast, half horse, half eagle. But for Moto Guzzi it was to read a project stillborn by circumstances.

The Ippogrifo project was closely linked to the world of flight. Its engine, although still a 90-degree V-twin, was derived from aeronautical technology. Its direct descendent, with suitable modifications, is that built by Guzzi and used by the Israeli Air Force in unmanned reconnaissance aircraft (and by NATO forces in Bosnia). Able to stay in the air for over twelve hours at speeds up to 125mph, this engine passed stringent tests in both Israel and the USA involving 150 hours' continual full speed operation, and 2,000 hours' normal operaton, with no problem.

Besides the engine, much of the V7 Ippogrifo was new, at least for Guzzi, such as the six-speed gearbox (but now scheduled to appear on other models); the single WP rear monoshock visibly mounted almost horizontal on the offside of the machine; and tubeless cross-spoke wheels in anti corodal (and except for BMW the only motorcycle spoked wheels which were able to dispense with inner tubes).

Visually, the Ippogriffio came nearest to an 883 Harley-Davidson – and it is probably becasue of this more than any other reason that the project was ultimately terminated. After all, Guzzi is attempting to raise its profile and to be seen copying the concept, if not the technical details, of such a high-profile competitor as Harley-Davidson might not have been such a good idea. Also, unlike its other upcoming models, would there have been a market for this bike? With its cancellation, no-one will know.

---

During mid-1998 there was yet another version of the California, coded LR, which was marketed under the California Special name. It featured several new items including revised footpegs instead of boards, wider bars and round rocker covers. Next will come the eagerly awaited V11 Sport. This is very much a retro-styled sportster playing heavily on the original V7 Sport of the early 1970s but with modern running gear and technology including the two-valves-per-cylinder 1064cc 1100 Sport Injection motor, but with improvements, notably a new six-speed gearbox. The V11 Sport will be offered in both single and dual seat versions, and will feature a comprehensive option list. This will mean a competitive selling price and the ability of the owner to add extras either upon original purchase or later, making each bike that bit different to others of the same type. The solo seat model has already been seen in the stunning V7 Sport-inspired red frame with metallic lime green

tank, seat, panels and front mudguard! There will also be the V11 GT. This is a fully-faired sport/tourer development of the V11 Sport; besides the six-speed engine, it will boast integral panniers and other touring dedicated accessories.

Also soon to be released is a new range of Guzzi singles. These will use a development of the now defunct, but certainly not forgotten, Gilera Nuovo Saturno dohc engine. They are likely to appear in both roadster and enduro styles, the Guzzi management having concluded a deal with Piaggio over the use of the engine. The rest of the machine will be entirely of Guzzi's own creation.

Further into the future (probably for a launch date at the Milan Show in 1999) is an exciting brand new 1000cc category liquid-cooled transverse V-twin with either 65 or 70 degree instead of the long running 90-degree vee of the cylinders. Notably it is likely to be built with chain final drive and a

## Three-Year Warranty and Recovery Package

At the beginning of 1998 Moto Guzzi announced that it was to become the first motorcycle manufacturer in the world to offer a free three-year, unlimited mileage warranty and recovery package on it's entire range. The combined 36-month warranty and Moto Guzzi Assistance came into effect on all machines sold after the 1 March 1998. In Britain the warranty element was also back-dated to include those machines already sold new in the UK from 1 January 1998.

This move was inspired by the Moto Guzzi management team in Italy and is applicable to machines sold new throughout Europe. Its also proof that Guzzi themselves have increased confidence in their product. Richard Davies, sales director of Moto Guzzi's UK importer Three Cross Motorcycles said at the launch, 'Improving quality has been a major priority of the factory for some time and the new warranty and recovery package highlights the mechanical integrity of Moto Guzzi motorcycles'.

The full extract from the factory's leaflet covering the new 3-year warranty reads as follows:

*Three Cross Service Managers Mike Russell de Clifford (right) and Daryl Vyse.*

Moto Guzzi offers anyone purchasing one of its motorcycles exceptional reliability: a 3-year warranty ensuring totally carefree riding.

A warranty like this signifies much more than safeguarding your investment. It means the manufacturer has complete confidence in the quality of its products.

And for bikers, this is a really new deal.

The 'Moto Guzzi Warranty' runs the whole of 36 months covering spare parts and labour costs with no limit on the number of repairs.

But clients actually get much more: a personalized relationship with the manufacturer, the certainty of obtaining Moto Guzzi original spare parts and most importantly, a good trade-in price, thanks to the service programme.

Enjoying the benefits of the warranty couldn't be simpler: just fill in the form at the time of purchase, have it stamped by the dealer, and sent it by registered post to the Moto Guzzi Warranty Service.

The warranty will be valid as long as the routine service programme is observed by using all the appropriate coupons.

Your local Moto Guzzi dealer will be glad to provide any further information.

*The 1999-model year V11 Sport. Retro style available in solo or dual seat form. Very much a case of nostalgia with 1990s technology, not only offering much smoother running, but also improved warm up from cold start and mid-range power.*

shaft drive option. The new vee engine has been developed with input from the British Cosworth company, but the actual design is being carried out entirely 'in-house'. It is likely to be produced in sports/racing form at around 140bhp, and if successful, it will be the basis of the company's official debut in WSB (World Super Bike) in the year 2000.

Finally, and perhaps most controversial of all, the Mandello del Lario site – Guzzi's home ever since its original motorcycles were built at the beginning of the 1920s – is scheduled to be ditched in favour of an all-new plant near the Monza race circuit and thus its lakeside home will be exchanged for the Milanese suburban sprawl. With all these changes the next decade at Moto Guzzi promises to be the most exciting in the company's history since the glory days of the 1950s. The sleeping giant has awoken!

## The British Moto Guzzi Importers, Three Cross

Keith Davies's love affair with Italian motorcycles began during the 1970s when he was employed as sales manager by the then British Guzzi and Ducati importers Coburn & Hughes. One of his best dealers was Graham Miles, proprietor of the original Three Cross Motorcycles. 'I heard that he wanted out and the dealership was for sale at the beginning of 1980' recalls Keith, 'So I left C&H, sold my house, bought the business and moved to Dorset. We were selling Guzzis, Ducatis and Harley-Davidsons, as well as Laverdas imported by the Slater brothers.' Six months later, he relocated the operation from its main road site at a former filling station to a much more extensive industrial estate complex half a mile down the road in the village of Three Legged Cross, a few miles north of Bournemouth.

At the end of 1981 it became clear that the Laverda import concession might shortly become available. This proved correct and after a meeting with Richard Slater in January 1982 Three Cross became the new importer.

During 1984 Coburn & Hughes lost interest in Moto Guzzi (and Ducati) and ceased being importers at the end of that year. Keith Davies immediately telephoned Italy and made an appointment at the Guzzi factory.

A new company, Three Cross Imports, absorbed the existing Laverda business and became Moto Guzzi importers during 1985.

By the early 1990s Three Cross Imports had grown to also handle Ducati (shared at that time with two other companies), Cagiva and Moto Morini. Laverda meanwhile had long since fallen by the wayside. Strangely though, a reversal of marques was about to take place, as first Laverda re-emerged during 1994, whereas Three Cross severed (import) links with Ducati the following year.

As for Guzzi this has been, and continues to be, the foundation of Three Cross Imports activities on the Italian front. The Guzzi dealer network remaining around the same – thirty in 1991 and thirty-two in 1998. Three Cross are also the UK importers for Peugeot scooters, currently the most popular scooter range in Britain.

Keith Davies's son Richard is currently the Import Sales Director, whilst his daughter Lisa is in charge of the Press and Public Relations side of the company.

Keith sees the changes occurring within the Moto Guzzi company as ongoing and positive and is excited about the marque's possibilities as it prepares to enter the twenty-first century.

**British importers' details:**

Three Cross Motorcycles Limited
Woolsbridge Industrial Estate,
6 Old Barn Farm Road,
Three Legged Cross,
Nr Wimborne, Dorset
BH21 6SP

Tel. 01202 823344
Fax. 01202 820102.

# Index